Guide to the NextGen Bar Exam

EDITORIAL ADVISORS

Guide to the NextGen Bar Exam

Alex Ruskell

Director of Academic Success and Bar Preparation,
University of South Carolina, Joseph F. Rice School of Law

ASPEN PUBLISHING

To contact Customer Service, e-mail customer.service@aspenpublishing.com, call 1-800-950-5259, or mail correspondence to:

Aspen Publishing
Attn: Order Department
1 Wall Street
Burlington, MA 01803

Printed in the United States of America.

1 2 3 4 5 6 7 8 9 0

ISBN 979-8-8941-0162-0

Library of Congress Cataloging-in-Publication Data

Names: Ruskell, Alex author
Title: Guide to the NextGen Bar Exam / Alex Ruskell, Director of Academic Success and Bar Preparation, University of South Carolina, Joseph F. Rice School of Law.
Description: Burlington, MA : Aspen Publishing, 2026. | Series: Bar review series | Summary: "Study guide and practice for the NextGen Bar Exam, intended for law students"— Provided by publisher.
Identifiers: LCCN 2025043308 (print) | LCCN 2025043309 (ebook) | ISBN 9798894101620 paperback | ISBN 9798894101644 epub | ISBN 9798894101637 epub
Subjects: LCSH: Bar examinations—United States—Study guides | Law—United States—Examinations, questions, etc. | LCGFT: Study guides
Classification: LCC KF303 .R87 2026 (print) | LCC KF303 (ebook)
LC record available at https://lccn.loc.gov/2025043308
LC ebook record available at https://lccn.loc.gov/2025043309

SUSTAINABLE FORESTRY INITIATIVE Certified Sourcing
www.forests.org
SFI-01051

ABOUT ASPEN PUBLISHING

Aspen Publishing is a leading provider of legal education content and digital learning solutions in the United States and globally. Our innovative products and platforms—designed based on best practices in learning science—engage students and enhance outcomes. From textbooks and audiobooks authored by renowned experts to digital platforms and products like LEAF, Connected eBooks, Connected Quizzing, PracticePerfect, and JD-Next, we empower the next generation of legal professionals with innovative, trusted, and accessible resources.

The Aspen Casebook Series, affectionately known as the "red and black" casebooks among law faculty and students, includes hundreds of highly regarded textbooks across more than 80 disciplines. These range from foundational courses like Torts and Contracts to emerging electives such as Sustainability and the Law of Policing. Our study aids, including the popular *Examples & Explanations* series, help law students master complex topics with clarity and confidence.

Aspen's expertise extends to undergraduate education with our Paralegal, Criminal Justice, and Business Law series, offering the same hallmark quality to a broader audience. JD-Next, our groundbreaking online law school prep course and admissions test, provides a realistic preview of law school, equips students with essential skills for academic success, and evaluates their readiness for legal studies.

Aspen Publishing Is Proud to Be a UWorld Company

Since 2003, UWorld has been a global leader in developing high-quality learning tools for students preparing for high-stakes exams. With a commitment to excellence, UWorld has helped millions of students in undergraduate, graduate, and professional programs in fields such as medicine, nursing, finance, and law achieve their academic and career goals.

Founded by Chandra S. Pemmasani, M.D., during his medical residency, UWorld began focusing on medical education and has since expanded into various academic fields, including law. In 2020, UWorld launched its Legal vertical, starting with its comprehensive Multistate Bar Exam (MBE®) Question Bank, followed by the acquisition of Themis Bar Review, which integrated resources to provide a complete bar exam preparation experience. In 2024, UWorld expanded its offerings by acquiring Aspen Publishing, enhancing its suite of legal education products.

Today, UWorld offers an unparalleled range of study materials that blend active learning methods with expert content, ensuring students and educators can access the most effective resources. From bar preparation to law school success, UWorld is committed to supporting the next generation of legal professionals. Learn more at uworld.com.

For the Love of Lumpy.

Summary of Contents

Contents xi
Introduction xiii
Professional Responsibility xxv

PART I SUBJECT AREAS 1

Chapter 1. Civil Procedure 3
Chapter 2. Constitutional Law 21
Chapter 3. Contracts 43
Chapter 4. Criminal Law and Constitutional Protections of Accused Persons 67
Chapter 5. Evidence 91
Chapter 6. Real Property 109
Chapter 7. Torts 137
Chapter 8. Business Associations and Relationships 155

PART II PRACTICE TESTS 171

Integrated Question Set 1 173
Integrated Question Set 2 179
Performance Task 1 183
Performance Task 1 Answers 189
Performance Task 2 191
Performance Task 2 Sample Answer Outline 197

Contents

Introduction xiii
Professional Responsibility xxv

PART I SUBJECT AREAS 1

Chapter 1. Civil Procedure 3
Outline 3
Practice Multiple-Choice Questions 11

Chapter 2. Constitutional Law 21
Outline 21
Practice Multiple-Choice Questions 30

Chapter 3. Contracts 43
Outline 43
Practice Multiple-Choice Questions 55

Chapter 4. Criminal Law and Constitutional Protections of Accused Persons 67
Outline 67
Practice Multiple-Choice Questions 77

Chapter 5. Evidence 91
Outline 91
Practice Multiple-Choice Questions 98

Chapter 6. Real Property 109
Outline 109
Practice Multiple-Choice Questions 126

Chapter 7. Torts 137
Outline 137
Practice Multiple-Choice Questions 144

Chapter 8. Business Associations and Relationships 155
Outline 155
Practice Multiple-Choice Questions 159

PART II PRACTICE TESTS 171

Integrated Question Set 1 173

Police Report 173
State Criminal Statutes 174

Integrated Question Set 2 179

Memorandum 179
Integrated Question Set 2, Question 1 of 1 181
Suggested Answer 181

Performance Task 1 183

Performance Task Assignment—Memorandum from Supervising Attorney 183
Legal Research Question 1 187
Legal Research Question 2 187
Legal Research Question 3 187
Legal Research Question 4 188
Legal Research Question 5 188
Writing Assignment 188

Performance Task 1 Answers 189

Writing Assignment Sample Answer Outline 189

Performance Task 2 191

Memorandum 191
Excerpt of Interview Transcript 191
Excerpt of Interview Transcript 192
Excerpt of Copyright Law of The United States (Title 17) 193
Excerpt of the U.S. Constitution 193
Example Trivia Cards from the *Quazy Questions with Queso and Fromage* Game 194
Writing Assignment 196

Performance Task 2 Sample Answer Outline 197

Introduction

To succeed on the NextGen bar exam, you should study so much that the only feeling you have on exam day is pure anger that anyone makes you do this. In over 20 years of teaching about bar exams, I have noticed that the difference between those who pass and those who do not is the amount of preparation the student does. Avoid making yourself sick, but you want to feel that you have done everything you possibly could to prepare, which is the best way to deal with exam stress. You will not lie in bed the night before telling yourself, "If only I had done more work on hearsay, I'd be fine." Instead, you will think, "Just give me the exam, and let's get this over with." This book will help ensure you are in the angry column on bar exam day.

A WHY STUDENTS FAIL THE BAR EXAM

Most students who do not pass tend to have done very little to prepare for the bar exam, either because they are not motivated, have unexpected life problems, study incorrectly, procrastinate out of fear, or fail to take the exam seriously. Granted, sometimes a student does work very hard and still fails, but consider the analogy between taking the bar exam and being a pro football player. Clearly, you can work hard and still lose a game, but the more work that you put in before the game, the more likely you are to have the size, strength, and speed to win.

It is not the end of the world or your legal career if you do not pass the bar exam, but it is expensive, time-consuming, demoralizing, and frustrating to retake the bar exam, so you want to limit the chances that you will have to do so. Try to excel on the bar exam the first time and get it out of your life, so you can start suing the people who made you do this.

B ANXIETY

It is normal to fear the bar exam. Studying for the bar exam is a lot of work, and the stakes are high. In my experience, you will probably flip out at least once while you are studying. So, flip out, get past it, and go back to studying. Flip out several times if you want—as long as you go back to studying.

Two things about the NextGen bar exam will make you less nervous. First, the exam is designed to "test a broad range of foundational lawyering skills"—basically logical thinking, writing, and communication skills. You have spent a lot of time learning those things in law school, so all you need to do now is practice how the NextGen will test those skills. Second, the black letter law that you need to memorize for the exam is not an impossible amount to learn and might be easier to understand

and more straightforward on the NextGen than it ever was in your law school classes. In case "black letter law" is an unfamiliar term, it stands for the basic legal rules and exceptions that you need to know for a particular legal subject. Examples of black letter law are "Only defendants can remove to federal court" in civil procedure, or "Hearsay is an out-of-court statement used for the truth of the matter asserted" in evidence.

If you have the black letter law nailed down and use the testing strategies in this book, you will be set for the multiple-choice questions, which tend to be the questions students have the most difficulty with. The important thing is that there can only be one correct answer out of four or two correct answers out of six. Consequently, questions must be black and white to be valid, not a confusing amount of gray like your law school exams might have been. If you know the black letter law, you will do well.

For the integrated question sets and practice tests, you need to focus on reading, writing, and logic. You have spent several years of law school honing these skills. You can absolutely do this.

C RABBIT HOLES OF NONSENSE TO AVOID

Avoid going to the Internet and getting roped into sites that "predict" what will be on the bar exam. They are consistently wrong, which is super aggravating to someone who teaches in this area. Some sites even sell this information, which is straight-up crazy. Avoid Reddit and similar platforms. There is always someone looking for a shortcut or pretending to know something they do not. Going to the Internet for bar advice is like going to it for medical advice, but instead of becoming convinced that you have contracted the Black Plague, you will have someone telling you that there will not be any questions on contract formation. In everyday life, would you listen to someone who introduces themselves as "LawButtSCLover2000"? Maybe you would, but surely nothing good will come of it.

D BASICS OF THE NEXTGEN BAR EXAM

The NextGen exam is administered over one and a half days—two three-hour sessions on day one, and one three-hour session on day two. Examinees use their own laptops for the exam, and scores are transferable between participating jurisdictions.

The NextGen's exam time is divided into approximately 40 percent stand-alone multiple-choice questions with either four or six answer options, 25 percent integrated question sets based around a single scenario, and the remainder legal-writing performance tasks.

The multiple-choice questions will cover business associations, civil procedure, constitutional law, contract law, criminal law, evidence, real property, and torts. For these, you need to memorize the black letter law according to the outlines and practice questions in this book.

As stated above, integrated question sets are based on a common-fact scenario. Each integrated question set should take 24 minutes to complete. Usually, they will begin with some document and then ask six questions that require you to spot issues, note areas of investigation and evaluation, advise clients, and resolve disputes. The questions relating to the scenario will be a mix of multiple-choice and short-answer questions. Examples of scenarios might be a rental lease, a draft legislative bill, or a murder beginning with a witness's testimony.

Performance tasks should take 60 minutes to complete. These tasks will test your ability to draft and complete the work that a beginning lawyer might be required to do. The tasks may include multiple-choice questions, short questions based on research skills, and longer writing assignments. The performance tasks could include other areas of doctrinal law, such as trusts and estates, intellectual property, or administrative law. However, all the legal information that you need will be included in the question itself, so you will not need to memorize the black letter law in these areas.

For each three-hour session, you will get multiple-choice questions, integrated question sets, and performance tasks.

E TIPS ON STUDYING

For the performance tasks and at least half of the integrated question set answers, you need to do as many practice questions as you can to get the mechanics down and learn the question's expectations. The big issue for these parts of the exam is speed. Think of studying for them as practicing a basketball free throw until you can make the shot quickly and easily. You probably know the basic idea behind shooting a basketball; however, to improve, you need to tighten up your shot.

For the multiple-choice questions, you need to memorize the black letter law from the outlines included in this book. Still, you should also do as many practice questions as possible to learn how the questions are set up, how to anticipate question answers, and how to use the answer strategies included in this book.

Generally, you will get most of your learning from practice questions. Not that studying is "fun" or "easy," but doing practice questions is a lot more "fun" than just reading or memorizing something. Doing practice questions is also a lot easier to focus on than simply reading outlines. Think of it like reading a newspaper—if distractions are happening around you, it is a lot easier to pay attention if you are doing the crossword than reading an article on tax reform.

1. "BIG LIST OF THINGS I DO NOT KNOW"

As you go through your practice questions, keep a "Big List of Things I Do Not Know." When you miss a question, write the reason you missed that answer on a list. Every night before you go to bed, read that list. That list will grow as you study, but you will know it well by the time you get to the exam. The list is good for two reasons: (1) you did not know that answer for some reason, and (2) if you did not know the answer, it probably makes a pretty good question, so it will likely come back on the exam in some form. Keep your "Big List of Things I Do Not Know" short. For example, "In an assignment, both the original signer of the rental contract and the holder of the assignment are liable for rent," or "Excited utterance is completely dependent on how soon in time the statement was from the startling event, which does not have to be super exciting." After completing a set of questions and reviewing the answers, it is a great idea to try again to answer them all perfectly the second time around. If you can, you will have all those black letter laws nailed down.

2. STUDY ALONE

It is probably a bad idea to study in a group or with someone else unless you can sit in your study space together and concentrate on your own work. With all the work you need to do, it is easy to be distracted by talking, gossip, and other things. Every bone in your body will feel like procrastinating, so avoid temptation. A better idea is to have your group spread out in your law school and then come back together for lunch or coffee breaks.

3. MEMORIZING THINGS

There are a few proven ways to memorize things. The key to effective memorization is making a connection between the material you are memorizing and something else. For instance, I suspect you might sing the alphabet to yourself when trying to remember it. You learned it as a song because the letters connect to the music. As unique as we are individually, all our minds work in similar ways. (The alphabet song goes across cultures and alphabets. I also learned the Russian alphabet by singing it, which I do with great beauty and feeling.) This book provides a lot of possible connections in the outlines to help you memorize the law, and you can make a lot of connections for yourself. Over the years, I have had many students tell me, "I remembered . . . because of that weird example you said." Make your own connections. I am a huge fan of anagrams tied to popular songs, which is no surprise since I am a music nerd. Try to connect ideas in the law to things you like, whether it be anime characters or sports hall of famers.

F THINGS TO THINK ABOUT BEFORE THE BAR EXAM

1. WORKING

You should not work while studying for the bar exam. There is too much material to digest. If you must work or have small children (who are a different kind of boss), consider using this book to study and start your bar exam preparation during the semester before you plan to take the exam. It is too challenging to balance a full day of work or childcare with the energy needed to study for an extended period.

I realize I am repeating myself, but remember that if you study as hard as you can, you will likely pass. Consequently, you should treat bar study like a job. Start at the same time every morning, take regular breaks, and finish your studies at the same time every night. Plan for weddings or other events you need to attend during your break period. Have days off. But be as effective as you can be with all of this by keeping to a consistent schedule.

2. SIGNIFICANT OTHERS

Significant others can be a great help, but they can be a distraction. This counts for friends, family, pets, and anyone else. When I was studying for the bar exam in Texas, I lived with my girlfriend. The downside to her was that she was incredibly fun and would often suggest going hiking, dancing, or out to dinner, which made me feel guilty for being consumed by my bar studies. Eventually, she moved back to New York for the rest of the summer, allowing me to focus. It all worked out, and we got married, had kids, etc., but her moving out for that time was a good decision for both of us. You should tell your friends, "Don't call me; I'll call you," because even if they are going out to see a movie you have seen ten times, you will totally want to go when you would be better off studying and saving your free time for something more fun.

The best way to deal with significant others without hurting anyone's feelings is to have a set, job-like schedule. When you are studying, that is what you are doing. When you are done for the day, you can spend time with your friends and family and actually have fun. If your significant others are not lawyers, they probably do not know how hard you need to study to pass. But everyone understands that you need to focus on your job when you are at work.

If your significant others are also studying for the bar, try not to get on each other's nerves. If you do, realize why you are and that it is temporary.

3. HEALTH

Plan some time to exercise every day so you can focus and get some rest. You will be sitting in a chair a lot. There are dozens of studies linking mental health and good analytical thinking with physical health. When I was studying for the bar, I swam laps at the local pool every day. When I moved to a new state and had to take that state's bar, I started boxing again—which was good because I could hit people. Also, it is hard to be worried about the bar exam when someone is trying to punch you in the head.

Eat well. Years ago, a student of mine who was a very good home cook decided to eat only ramen during the exam period to save time. Her sodium levels skyrocketed, and she fell seriously ill a month into the study period. Avoid this.

During bar prep, avoid quitting or acquiring any bad habits. If you smoke, keep puffing that sweet, sweet nicotine until the exam is over. Keep your morning donut. Drink caffeine like there is no tomorrow if that is your regular habit.

Ultimately, all this is covered by the idea that you should try to get rid of as many hindrances to your bar study as you can.

G BAR EXAM DAY

Relax the day before the bar exam. If it makes you feel better, do a set of questions, but at this point, if you have been studying hard, you should have everything ready to go. There will be people at the bar exam studying in the parking lot 30 minutes before the exam. Again, if this makes you feel better, go ahead and do it, but you need to ask yourself, "What could you possibly learn that you don't already know at this point?" You are better off letting your brain and body relax. If you have studied enough to be angry, you are done.

Suppose you do not have a hotel near the bar exam and live in a big city, or you are going to a test site you have never been to before. In that case, it is a good idea to drive to the test site a few days before the exam, so you know where it is and if there is any construction, traffic, parking problems, or other things you will have to navigate on exam day. You want to be angry at the exam, not road-raging because there is no parking.

Plan for something to go wrong on exam day. Set at least two alarms, ensuring at least one is not dependent on electricity. Have your breakfast set and your lunch planned. Bring a credit card and some cash. Assume the test site will be extraordinarily cold, someone will get sick, your computer will explode, or the exam will have a weird question you were not expecting. When I took the bar exam, a woman next to me cried the entire time. Luckily, when I took the exam with the crying woman, I had studied so much that, although I felt awful for the woman, her crying did not distract me. If you do not feel like you have studied as much as you could, things going wrong during the exam will become much bigger problems because you will not be confident enough to take whatever comes at you in stride, put it aside, and pass the exam. If you have studied enough, such problems will be stories that you tell your friends later. Or maybe write a moody song about. You do you.

H GENERAL ADVICE FOR FOUR-CHOICE MULTIPLE-CHOICE QUESTIONS

The law is not really designed for multiple-choice questions. Consequently, you can use the way multiple-choice questions are written to guide you. When a test writer writes a multiple-choice question, the writer usually starts with a piece of black letter law they want to test, like "Hearsay is an out-of-court statement used for the truth of the matter asserted." The question writer then makes up a story to test that piece of black letter law, like:

> Alex was very egotistical and thought of himself as an incredibly handsome futurist, visionary, and law professor. As a prank, a female student told Alex after class that a male student was so jealous of Alex's extreme handsomeness that the male student was coming to kill Alex that day. Alex was so egotistical that he believed her. That afternoon, during office hours, the male student showed up to ask Alex a question about the Equal Protection Clause. The male student had no idea about the prank. Before the male student could say a word, Alex clubbed him with a very large constitutional law casebook. The male student sued Alex for battery. Alex wants to use the female student's statement at trial to explain why he hit the

student, namely, because Alex thought he was going to be killed. Alex has hired you as his attorney. Is the female student's statement admissible at trial? **Select one.**

After writing the story, the writer needs to write the answer choices. Usually, this will be two "yes" and two "no," followed by "because" with an explanation. Questions usually have two answer choices you can dismiss quickly, and two that hang you up.

To hide the correct answer, the question writer uses "foils" and "distractors." Foils are answer choices that make the correct answer look wrong, while distractors are shiny gems that look like they could be the correct answer. The question writer builds the foils and distractors by imagining what a student who half-knows the black letter law might think. For the above question, your choices might be:

(A) Yes, the statement is admissible because it is not hearsay.
(B) Yes, the statement is admissible because it is relevant.
(C) No, the statement is inadmissible hearsay.
(D) No, the statement is inadmissible because it was not a present sense impression.

Here, the correct answer is (A) because Alex does not want to use the statement for the truth of the matter asserted (that the student is coming to kill him). Alex wants to use the statement to explain why he threw the book at the student. It does not matter whether the student was actually coming to kill Alex; what matters is that Alex had heard that the student was coming to kill him, was scared, and had an excuse for throwing the book in apparent self-defense. (C) is meant to get those students who read the question and think it matters whether the student was actually coming to kill Alex. (B) and (D) are for students who half-know the black letter law and might be drawn to picking either of these answer choices because they see the evidentiary terms "relevant" and "present sense impression." Many students have an unclear understanding of present sense impression, making it a great distractor since it can sound like a plausible answer if you are unfamiliar with the concept. In fact, it is well-known that students who do not feel confident in their bar exam studying will often go for an answer that they do not know the law for because of that very fact. Basically, the student lacks confidence in themselves and fears that they will not know the answers to any of the questions, which becomes a self-fulfilling prophecy.

Realize that you have just spent several years of law school learning to be a terrible multiple-choice test taker. You have been trained to think of all the possibilities of a situation, and, as I stated above, the bar exam question writers will use that training against you. This is not a trick in the sense of trying to "fool" you—the writer has to make a valid test, so there cannot be questions like: "Who can remove to federal court? (A) Dogs, (B) Ducks, (C) Donuts, (D) Defendants." The correct answer is sitting right there, and the writer has to hide it to make the test valid.

1. FOUR-CHOICE MULTIPLE-CHOICE STRATEGY ONE—KNOW THE LAW

A common student complaint about commercial bar prep programs is that they focus on learning the law rather than on how to take the test. But knowing the law backward and forward is the best way to crush the bar exam. Consequently, strategy one requires that you learn the law (which you can absolutely do).

For the NextGen bar, some of the potential question topics are starred, and some are not. (This is included in the content outlines in this book.) According to NextGen, you only need to know the starred topics without additional materials. However, as of the writing of this book, the NextGen has released multiple-choice questions covering unstarred topics. Consequently, it is a good idea to know all the outline topics well. One, you will be more confident about the exam. Two, you might get a question on one of these topics. And three, there is not that much law to memorize for the NextGen. Consequently, some of the practice questions in this book cover unstarred topics.

I would not put too much thought into starred versus unstarred. A potential problem with starred/unstarred topics is similar to the issue caused by open-book exams. Sometimes students say, "That one's open book—I don't have to study as hard or really learn the material for the exam because I have my book." This is usually the kiss of death for that exam. Starred or unstarred, I would try to memorize all of it.

To answer multiple-choice questions using strategy one, you should read the call of the question first. Do not let the question writer get into your head with possible answer choices unless you have to do so. The call is the sentence that asks a specific question, such as "What's your best argument to admit the evidence?" or "What's your best argument in support of the man getting the property?" Then read the story. If you read the story and immediately get the answer in your head, look at the possible answer choices and see if the answer is there. If it is, pick it. Done and done, move on to the next one.

2. FOUR-CHOICE MULTIPLE-CHOICE STRATEGY TWO—PROCESS OF ELIMINATION

If your initial answer choice is not there, you need to move to strategy two, or the process of elimination. Eliminate any answer choice that could not be true because of a misstatement of the rule, a misstatement of the facts, or a lack of relevance to the situation. Hopefully, you will be left with one possible answer.

As an example, look at this question:

> Without seeking a warrant, the police attached a wireless tracker to the bumper of an alleged drug trafficker's car. The police went to the alleged drug trafficker's house, which was on a large piece of property bounded by woodland. As the police were looking for a place in the woods to surveil the drug trafficker's house, they stumbled across a tumbled-down shed in a remote area of the woodland. Two children were playing near the shed. The police asked the children what was in the shed. The children responded that there was a car. The police asked the children how they got inside the shed. The children opened a hard-to-see garage door and showed the officers that a car was in there. The police turned on the wireless tracker and realized that the car in the shed was the one they had been tracking. The police went into the shed, looked in the windows of the car, and saw hundreds of pounds of pills in clear plastic bags on the back seat. Based on this evidence, the drug trafficker was arrested. In court, the drug trafficker claimed that the pills should be suppressed as a result of an unlawful search. You are an attorney working for the prosecution.

Which of the following is your best argument to support admitting the pills into evidence? **Select one.**

- **(A)** The drug trafficker had no expectation of privacy in the shed.
- **(B)** The drug trafficker had no expectation of privacy in his car.
- **(C)** A wireless tracker can never result in an unlawful search.
- **(D)** The children were not acting on behalf of the police when they showed the police the car.

Imagine that you looked at this question and did not know the answer right away. At that point, you want to start eliminating answers that cannot possibly be correct.

Starting from the bottom, (D) cannot possibly be correct because it is a misstatement of the facts. The children were absolutely acting on the directions of the police, so (D) misstates what happened in the question. You can X that one out.

(C) cannot be correct because that is a misstatement of the law. A wireless tracker can result in an unlawful search. Additionally, avoid answer choices that say "always" or "never" or something similar. You attended law school. You know that there is always an exception or unique situation that will render an unqualified statement untrue.

(B) cannot possibly be correct because it is another misstatement of the law. People reasonably expect that the government cannot search their car at will. In addition, the police did not "search" the car; they looked through a window, so it is also a misstatement of the facts.

That leaves you with (A), the correct answer. Here, the shed is out in a "remote area of the woodland." As such, it is covered by the open fields doctrine. Upon examining the question, you realize that all the details about trackers, children, and cars are merely attempts to obscure the fact that this is a question about open fields.

If you can only eliminate two and are left with two choices that might be right, pick the one that your gut believes is right. If you have studied enough, trust your gut. Use your "Big List of Things I Did Not Know." You want to train your gut to be on the lookout in case you find yourself in this situation.

3. FOUR-CHOICE MULTIPLE-CHOICE STRATEGY THREE—BASIC GOAL OF THE TOPIC

Hopefully, you will not be left to guess. If you feel like you are, calm down, and go with whatever seems to further the basic goal of the topic. As examples, the Uniform Commercial Code (UCC) is designed to facilitate smoother commercial sales; evidence is intended to ensure a defendant is convicted of the charged crime, not merely because they are generally disliked; civil procedure aims to streamline cases and expedite the resolution of all issues.

As an example, look at this question:

> You represent a movie director. A man sued the director for damages, claiming that he had suffered emotional distress because the director chose to have a young woman play a superhero who was usually portrayed as an older man. How should you respond to the man's complaint? **Select one.**
>
> **(A)** Make a motion for a more definite statement.
> **(B)** Make a motion for declaratory judgment.
> **(C)** Make a motion for summary judgment.
> **(D)** Make a motion to dismiss for failure to state a claim.

If you do not have any idea about this question, you can look at each answer choice and consider the basic goal of the topic. Here, the topic is civil procedure, and its basic goal is to streamline litigation and make the court system efficient. The man's claim seems unconvincing, so it is likely not a case we want the court system to spend a lot of time on. Looking at our answer choices, (D) eliminates the claim with the least amount of work on the part of the court. The court reviews the claim and dismisses it. (A) requires the complaint to be returned to the man for editing and then returned to the court. This will not streamline anything. (B) is incorrect because it requires the court to determine the rights of the parties. This also takes more time than the man's claim deserves. (C) is incorrect because summary judgment requires the court to look at all the evidence. Again, there is no reason to do this since the claim is so silly. Choice (D) supports civil procedure's goal of efficiency.

4. FOUR-CHOICE MULTIPLE-CHOICE STRATEGY FOUR—THE CLASSIC "C"

According to legend, "C" on any exam is statistically more likely to be correct than any other answer choice. If you have still got nothing after the first three strategies, go for "C" and move on. You do not need to get 100 percent correct on the bar exam. No one does. Just do not leave it blank and think you will come back to answer it later. If you leave it blank, you might get off track on filling in bubbles, which is an absolute disaster.

The biggest mistake students make on multiple-choice questions is overthinking the question and talking themselves out of the correct answer. Ninety percent of the time, this is the reason why a student does not do well on them. Generally, revising answers will lead to incorrect choices, but test this theory with practice questions. If you choose the correct answers when you go back, go ahead and go back. However, I have had tons more students talk themselves out of the correct answers than into the wrong ones.

GENERAL ADVICE FOR SIX-CHOICE MULTIPLE-CHOICE QUESTIONS

1. SIX-CHOICE MULTIPLE-CHOICE QUESTIONS—LOGICAL STARTS

The general advice for six-choice multiple-choice questions is the same as for four-choice. The only difference is that the question will likely have to be more general because two of the six answers are correct.

Specifically, a six-choice question will likely ask a question regarding the start of litigation. For example, what sources of law might you research, or what questions do you need to have answered for a successful suit? Most of these types of questions are really asking you what the most relevant issues are and where a logical place would be to start research for a claim or a motion. Consequently, answer these questions by first noting what legal topic you are in. Then see where the question is narrowing your focus within that topic, and pick the two answer choices that fit that narrower area. Partial credit is available if you only get one right, but if you keep in mind that both answer choices are in the same narrow area (think of the correct answers as being at the bottom of a funnel made up of the larger topic), you should be able to get both correct if you can get one.

For example:

> You are working as a prosecutor in a murder case. While investigating the defendant, the police went to the defendant's father's home to conduct a search because the defendant had recently been living there. The father, who was very angry with the defendant, told the police that they could search his entire home. When the police went up to the defendant's bedroom, they discovered that the defendant had put a padlock on the door. The father said the padlock had been on the door since the defendant moved in because the defendant "wanted his privacy." The father said he owned the house himself and told the police to cut the lock off. The police broke the lock, entered the defendant's room, and found the murder weapon.

Which of the following legal issues should you research concerning the search of the defendant's room? **Select two.**

- **(A)** Consent
- **(B)** Standing
- **(C)** Exigent circumstances
- **(D)** Warrant
- **(E)** Protective sweep
- **(F)** Probable cause

If you look at the question, you should immediately see that this is a question about searches. Note that you are in the criminal procedure topic area. After that, you should quickly notice that the father owned the house and gave consent to the search. So (A) is a definite issue, because the entire question seems built around that consent, especially when paired with the lock on the door, which seems like a rejection of consent or possibly a rejection of the father's authority over the room. Once you have (A), imagine the other possible answer choices as being stuck in a "funnel" of criminal procedure. What is likely to be closest to consent? Going backward, (F) is far away from consent because consent takes away any issues of probable cause. (E) seems far away because consent would generally eliminate the need for a protective sweep. (D) would be far away because you do not need a warrant if you have consent. (C) would be far away because consent would mean you do not need exigent circumstances to conduct a search. Finally, you are left with (B), the other correct answer. Standing and consent are entwined together—if you are asking about consent, you also need to ask if the person had standing to give valid consent. Thus, (A) and (B) are correct.

J GENERAL ADVICE FOR INTEGRATED PRACTICE SET MULTIPLE-CHOICE QUESTIONS

As with multiple-choice questions in the multiple-choice section, identify the black letter law being tested and answer accordingly. If you are unsure, consider the other three suggested answering strategies.

K GENERAL ADVICE FOR INTEGRATED PRACTICE SET QUESTIONS

For the integrated practice set questions, you will not be reading all the materials at once. You will read a small part, answer a question, and then the set will continue building upon itself. The narrative evolves as the NextGen adds more facts and documents that apply to the question immediately following.

The integrated practice set questions are meant to test your abilities as a beginning lawyer. For these, you want to remember that another term for "lawyer" is "counselor." Consequently, many of the questions are completely dependent upon logic. Along the same lines, many of the questions seek sensible advice and a rationale for it. For example, suppose your client is a family vacation company facing a wrongful death lawsuit, and someone gets the idea to force the plaintiff into arbitration based on a click-through agreement for the client's streaming video trial. In that case, you might advise your client not to do it due to potentially negative publicity, decreased streaming trials, and other negative consequences. You want to show the examiners you have a solid head on your shoulders.

Along with these considerations, review the short chapter in this book regarding professional responsibility and ethics. The NextGen notes explicitly that it will test students on the rules listed in that chapter, so know their basic contours. The integrated question sets are perfect opportunities to test this knowledge on the exam.

For the short-answer questions, stay within the lanes of logic and practicality. Also, pay close attention to how many sentences the question asks for (usually something along the lines of two to three sentences). Write the short answers that appear most obvious to you—avoid coming up with the most creative thing you can think of. For example, there is a long-running game show where contestants try to pick the answer that was most popular among the studio audience watching the contest. Part of the comedy of the show is when contestants pick some crazy, idiosyncratic answer—for example, "What are most people's favorite foods?" And the contestant answers "opossum." Imagine the bar examiners as your audience and try to pick the answers that would be most popular with them. Practice will help you with this. Here is an example:

> Your client (a supermarket) is concerned about the potential damages it could face if a customer sues for injuries she received after slipping on a puddle in the store. List two factual issues you could investigate to determine the client's potential damages.

Here, the question is about torts, specifically about available damages. A customer has injured herself. Think about the big damages topics in torts. A "bar examiner audience member" would most likely think of big things like "customer's lost wages," "seriousness of the customer's injuries," and "seriousness of the supermarket's negligence." They would not think of "whether the customer has children" or "size of puddle." Keep your answers simple.

L GENERAL ADVICE FOR PERFORMANCE TASKS

For the longer drafting assignments, imagine yourself as the boss writing the task memo. What would you want from your associate lawyer, and how would you want it? You would want an answer to your exact question, and you would want that answer in the first sentence. If you want a memo, you want it to clearly and simply lay out all the parts of a claim. If you asked your associate to write a brief, you want it to be argumentative. If you asked for a letter, you want something a client can understand and that you can drop in the mail immediately. Create something that does not require further work for your boss. They are very busy. Also, keep in mind the responsibility and ethics rules listed in the short chapter in this book. The performance tasks are another perfect place to test students on these rules.

While some performance tasks will have one big writing assignment (basically, a brief, a memo, or a client letter), some performance tasks focus on legal research and contain multiple-choice and short-answer questions as well as a writing task. For legal research questions, remember the basics you learned about legal research. What is primary authority? What is the holding of a case? What authority controls another authority? At the time of this writing, the released questions for the legal research performance task concern the basic concepts of legal research, which you should know from law school. The legal research performance task at the end of this book should help you remember these concepts.

For the task assignments, keep your boss in mind. Here is an example of what the beginning part of a memo would typically look like for a memo assignment. Notice how your "boss" could use this to talk to a client without looking at anything else.

To: Supervising Attorney
From: Examinee
Date: July 27, 2025
Re: DeWitt Copyright Claim

You have asked me to draft an objective memorandum analyzing Jim DeWitt's (DeWitt) possible claim for copyright infringement against our client, Rocking Alex Productions, Inc. (RAP). According to DeWitt, RAP violated the Copyright Act by taking DeWitt's song, "I Love You Like a Rose," and turning it into a parody song called "I Picked You Like My Nose." Specifically, you have asked me to research how RAP may defend itself by claiming protection under the fair use doctrine.

1. Fair Use Under the Copyright Act

Under Section 107 of the Copyright Act, a person may use a copyrighted work if it falls under "fair use." In determining fair use, the act looks at "(1) the purpose and character of the use, including whether such use is of a commercial nature or is for nonprofit educational purposes; (2) the nature of the copyrighted work; (3) the amount and substantiality of the portion used in relation to the copyrighted work as a whole; and (4) the effect of the use upon the potential market for or value of the copyrighted work."

a. The Purpose and Character of the Use

The critical inquiry under the first factor is generally whether the allegedly infringing work merely supersedes the original work or "is transformative by adding something new, with a further or different character, that alters the first with new meaning or messages." *Froman v. Berg* (Franklin S. Ct. 2019). For example, in *Parker v. Loeschman Johnson Publishing* (Franklin Ct. App. 2006), one book specifically made fun of another book by changing the name of the main character from "Henry" to "Hunky." It also changed the description of that character from "eyes that fall into the universe, deep sad pools, that burst with blue around the edges like a burgeoning sunrise" to "eyes that fall backward into his skull sockets and make you want to eat cheese—blue cheese." The court found that the second book's use of the original copyrighted book was transformative and entitled to fair use protection as satire or parody.

Here, RAP's "I Picked You Like My Nose" takes the lyrics of "I Love You Like a Rose" and makes them ridiculous. "I Love You Like a Rose" is a popular and grand romantic statement song where the singer compares his lover to a beautiful flower. The music, performed by a 100-piece orchestra, bears a strong resemblance to renowned classical works, and the singer delivers an operatic tenor. In contrast, "I Picked You Like My Nose" has lyrics like "I dig for you so merrily, and what I find is scare-i-lee." The music itself is played on a single kazoo, and the singer sings with a voice altered into a high squeak by sucking on helium balloons. The relationship between the two songs is very similar to the relationship between the books in *Parker*. As such, this factor likely lies in favor of fair use.

. . .

. . . and the memo would continue down the elements of fair use to the conclusion. As you can see, you do not need to read anything else to understand the laws, cases, and story of the memo assignment, which should be your goal in writing your performance tasks. The boss asked you to do the work because they do not want to.

OVERALL—REMEMBER—THE GOAL IS TO STUDY ENOUGH TO BE SIMPLY ANGRY BY EXAM DAY!

Professional Responsibility

The NextGen specifically states that test takers should keep in mind the following American Bar Association Model Rules of Professional Conduct. These rules will not be assessed in stand-alone questions but may be evaluated in the context of answering questions that involve client counseling and advising, negotiation and dispute resolution, and client relationship and management.

I. MPRC RULE 1.1: COMPETENCE

A. A lawyer must provide competent representation.

1. Competence includes legal knowledge, skill, thoroughness, and the preparation reasonably necessary for representation—generally, the required competence is of a general practitioner unless it is a special matter. A lawyer can accept representation after studying to reach the required level of competence.
2. The relevant factors in determining if a lawyer is competent include the complexity and specialized nature of the matter, the lawyer's general experience, the lawyer's training and experience in the field in question, the preparation and study the lawyer can give to the matter, and whether it is feasible to consult with a lawyer of established competence in the field.
3. In an emergency matter, the lawyer may advise on a matter in which the lawyer does not have the skill ordinarily required if referral would be impractical. However, the advice should be limited to what's reasonably necessary under the circumstances.
4. A lawyer can contract with another lawyer for assistance, but they should obtain informed consent to the arrangement from the client.
5. To maintain competence, lawyers should keep up with changes in the law and engage in continuing legal education and study.

II. MPRC RULE 1.2(A) AND (D): SCOPE OF REPRESENTATION AND ALLOCATION OF AUTHORITY BETWEEN CLIENT AND LAWYER

A. A lawyer should follow the decisions of their client and accept the client's decision to settle or enter a plea. If the lawyer and client disagree, the lawyer may withdraw from representation, or the client may discharge the lawyer.

B. A lawyer may discuss the legal consequences of a client's proposed conduct, but a lawyer cannot help a client engage in crimes or fraud. If the client uses the lawyer's services in the commission of a crime or fraud, the lawyer should withdraw.

III. MPRC RULE 1.3: DILIGENCE

A. A lawyer shall act with reasonable diligence and promptness in the representation of clients.

1. Maintaining a reasonable workload and avoiding procrastination are crucial in this regard.

IV. MPRC RULE 1.4: COMMUNICATIONS

A. A lawyer should keep the client reasonably informed of all matters.

V. MPRC RULE 1.6(A) AND (C): CONFIDENTIALITY OF INFORMATION

A. A lawyer shall not reveal information relating to the representation of a client without the client's informed consent. A lawyer should also make reasonable efforts to avoid the accidental disclosure of client information.

VI. MPRC RULE 1.7: CONFLICT OF INTEREST: CURRENT CLIENTS

A. A lawyer should not provide representation if that representation is directly adverse to another client or there is a significant risk that the representation will be materially limited by responsibilities to another client, a former client, a third person, or by the lawyer's personal interest.

B. However, a lawyer may still represent a client in the above situation if: (1) the lawyer reasonably believes they will be able to provide competent representation; (2) the representation is not prohibited by law; (3) the representation does not involve assertions between the lawyer's clients; and (4) each client gives informed consent, confirmed in writing.

VII. MPRC RULE 3.1: MERITORIOUS CLAIMS AND CONTENTIONS

A. A lawyer may not assert a frivolous claim that has no basis in law or fact.

VIII. MPRC RULE 3.3(A)(1)-(2): CANDOR TOWARD THE TRIBUNAL

A. A lawyer may not make a false statement or fail to correct a false statement made to a tribunal.

B. A lawyer may not fail to disclose legal authority in the controlling jurisdiction known by the lawyer to be directly adverse to the client's position but which was not disclosed by opposing counsel. The idea is that a legal argument is a discussion to determine the laws properly applicable to a situation, so a party should not suffer just because their attorney is not skilled in legal research.

IX. MPRC RULE 4.1: TRUTHFULNESS IN STATEMENTS TO OTHERS

A. While representing a client, a lawyer shall not knowingly make a false statement to a third person or fail to disclose a material fact to a third person when necessary to avoid assisting a client in committing a criminal or fraudulent act.

X. MPRC RULE 4.2: COMMUNICATION WITH PERSON REPRESENTED BY COUNSEL

A. In representing a client, a lawyer shall not communicate about the subject of the representation with a person known to be represented by another lawyer in the matter. If that person initiated the conversation, the lawyer must terminate it immediately.

XI. MPRC RULE 4.3: DEALING WITH UNREPRESENTED PERSONS

A. In dealing on behalf of a client with a person not represented by counsel, the lawyer should not act uninterested and should not give legal advice if the lawyer reasonably knows that the interests of that person have a reasonable possibility of conflicting with the client's interests.

Subject Areas

I

Civil Procedure

1

Topics with asterisks (*) require you to know the black letter law cold; topics without an * require you to recognize the topic as part of the fact scenario or require you to analyze and apply legal resources provided for the topic efficiently.

MAIN POINT OF CIVIL PROCEDURE—MAKING THE COURT SYSTEM RUN AS EFFICIENTLY AS POSSIBLE

OUTLINE

I. JURISDICTION AND VENUE

A. Federal Subject-Matter Jurisdiction

1. **Federal Question Jurisdiction***

   a. **Well-Pleaded Complaint Rule**—The federal issue must be presented in the plaintiff's complaint; the defendant's response is irrelevant.

   b. **General Requirement**—The case must involve the interpretation of the Constitution or laws of the United States or "arise under" the federal law that creates the cause of action.

2. **Diversity Jurisdiction***

   a. If the complaint does not present a federal question, diversity jurisdiction allows a claim to be brought in federal court if the parties are citizens of different states and the amount in controversy is over $75,000. However, there is no diversity jurisdiction available for claims involving child custody, alimony, or divorce, which are matters of state law. (A helpful mnemonic is CAD (child custody, alimony, or divorce). A "cad" is a man who acts with deliberate disregard for one's feelings, which you can link with the idea of family claims.)

b. **Citizenship of Individuals**—An individual is a citizen of where they are domiciled, which is the state where they live and intend to stay.

c. **Complete Diversity Rule**—All parties on each side of the "versus" line must be diverse from each other. So, none of the plaintiffs may share a state with a defendant, and none of the defendants may share a state with a plaintiff. Diversity is determined at the time the case is filed, not when the claim occurred.

d. **Citizenship of Entities**
   i. **Corporation**—A corporation is a citizen of both the state where it has its principal place of business and the state in which it is incorporated. The principal place of business is where the corporate nerve center and decision making are done. For example, if all the executives of a company live in South Carolina, and all the factories are in Texas, the principal place of business is South Carolina. The way to remember this is to think about the complaint—to serve the business, the most obvious place to get the business's attention is to serve the executives (who could then call the lawyers). If you serve someone running one of the factories, what will they do with the complaint?
   ii. Partnerships and unincorporated associations are considered citizens of each state in which one of their members is domiciled. For example, be on the lookout for unions.

e. Amount in Controversy Requirement needs a good faith allegation that the amount in controversy exceeds $75,000. If it is an injunction, just one of the parties needs to believe it will cost more than $75,000.

f. **Aggregation of Claims**—A single plaintiff can add all their claims against a single defendant to reach the amount in controversy. If multiple plaintiffs have claims, they can aggregate all their claims if they are enforcing a shared right or interest.

3. **Concurrent and Removal Jurisdiction***

   a. Only defendants can remove cases from the state court to the federal court if the claim could have been filed in federal court (because the plaintiff made the initial choice where to file their claim, so why should they get to move it around willy-nilly?).

   b. If the claim is in federal court based on federal question jurisdiction, the action is removable without regard to the citizenship of the parties. This makes sense because the federal court is deciding federal law, and what does any state advantage have to do with it? However, all the defendants must consent for removal to be proper.

   c. If the claim can get into federal court because of diversity jurisdiction, it cannot be removed from state court if one of the defendants is a citizen of that state. The idea of removal to federal court in diversity cases is that no plaintiff gets an in-state advantage over a defendant, so if the defendant is already a citizen of the state where the claim is filed, the defendant should not be at any disadvantage.

   d. A notice of removal must be filed within 30 days of the time when the grounds for removal become apparent. Usually, this would be when the process is served, but an amendment to the pleadings could set the clock back (like if a defendant is dropped, and now there is complete diversity between the plaintiffs and defendants).

If a party misses 30 days, that party can join a removal if it is initiated by a codefendant served later. Basically, everybody gets 30 days, which is fair.

e. Concurrent jurisdiction refers to the fact that both a federal court and a state court may have jurisdiction over the same claim. In that case, removal is essentially a forum-shopping tactic where the defendant tries to determine which court would be most favorable.

f. If removal was incorrect, the claim can be remanded back to the state court.

4. Supplemental Jurisdiction

a. "Same Case or Controversy" Requirement—A federal court with jurisdiction over the suit will also have jurisdiction over other claims if they arise from the same case or controversy. The idea is to enhance judicial efficiency by settling the whole claim at once, preventing people from repeatedly suing on the same issue.

b. Discretionary factors permitting court to decline jurisdiction—The federal court can refuse supplemental jurisdiction if the supplemental claim raises a novel or complex issue of state law, if the supplemental claim substantially predominates over the claim within original federal jurisdiction, all of the claims within the court's original jurisdiction have been dismissed, or if there are other compelling reasons to refuse jurisdiction. Basically, if it seems the feds are intruding on state decision making, that is a concern.

B. Personal Jurisdiction*

1. Specific In Personam Jurisdiction refers to a federal court's ability to hear a complaint concerning a particular matter (i.e., the foreseeability of being "haled into court" in that state). Forum state should also have a legitimate interest in the claim. For example, a state would absolutely have a legitimate interest in a claim involving a company that sells insurance in the state, considering how much insurance affects people's lives and well-being.

a. Minimum Contacts—A nonresident defendant must have sufficient minimum contacts with the forum state to make suing the defendant fair in that state. For example, if the defendant personally avails themselves of doing business in the state, this is a sufficient contact (like calling into a state to sell crypto).

b. Arising out of—If the claim arises out of the defendant's contact with the forum state, jurisdiction is fair. If the claim does not arise from contact with the state, there needs to be systemic and continuous activity to make it foreseeable to be "haled into court." For example, if the suit arises from a defendant's car wreck in that state.

c. Reasonableness—The forum state's jurisdiction over the defendant in this claim must be reasonable and fulfill the requirements of Due Process.

d. Intentional Torts—A forum state has personal jurisdiction over a defendant who is being sued for committing an intentional tort in that state.

e. Contracts—Some contracts contain choice of forum provisions, while others might be evidence of minimum contacts with the forum state.

f. "Stream of Commerce"—It is unclear whether a manufacturer is subject to personal jurisdiction in any state just because the manufacturer sells a product and may know that the product might enter a particular state.

g. **E-Commerce Claims**—Whether a website creates personal jurisdiction in a forum state depends on how closely that website is connected with a forum. A website that is merely accessible to anyone on the internet does not create jurisdiction, but a website that is integral to a business in the forum state could create jurisdiction. For example, a website that has commercial contacts with hundreds of state citizens and offers them services in the state would likely create personal jurisdiction in the state.

h. **Long-Arm Statutes**—Many states have long-arm statutes creating personal jurisdiction over out-of-state defendants. For example, a long-arm statute might create personal jurisdiction for defendants who enter into contracts to supply goods in the state.

i. **Consent**—A defendant may consent to being sued in a forum state. This can either be express (e.g., agreed to in a contract) or implied by the defendant's actions (e.g., driving a car through the state and getting into a wreck).

j. **Service**—If a defendant is served with process in a forum state, that state has jurisdiction so long as the defendant was not lured into the state by fraud or the defendant is merely passing through to attend other judicial proceedings. But, if a process server tricks a defendant's assistant into telling them that the defendant is passing through the state on the way to somewhere else (like changing flights in Illinois), the process server can still serve the defendant in Illinois and create Illinois jurisdiction.

k. **Waiver**—The defendant can waive personal jurisdiction issues by failing to bring the issue up with the court. For example, if the defendant appears in court in the forum state after receiving the complaint.

2. **General In Personam Jurisdiction**—Foreseeability of being "haled into court" in that state also applies here—seems pretty foreseeable if you live there.

   a. **"At Home"**—If a claim does not arise out of a defendant's contacts with the state, jurisdiction is proper over the claim only if the defendant is essentially "at home" there.
      - **i.** Individuals are "at home" where they are domiciled.
      - **ii.** Corporations are "at home" in their state of incorporation and primary place of business.

C. Service of Process and Notice

1. **Constitutional Requirement of Notice**—Due Process requires that parties have notice and an opportunity to be heard. Neither party may personally serve the other party. The only requirement for those providing service is that they be over 18 years old.

2. **Serving Individuals**—Service may be made by personally giving the summons and complaint to the defendant, leaving the summons and complaint at the defendant's home with a person of suitable age and discretion who lives there, or by delivery to an appointed agent.

3. **Serving Corporations**—Service may be made by delivering the summons and complaint to an officer or agent of the corporation.

4. **Waiver of Service of Process**—A plaintiff may give notice of the complaint to the defendant and request that the defendant waive service. If the defendant agrees, they get more time to answer.

D. Venue, Forum Non Conveniens, and Transfer

1. **Where Venue Is Proper**—The idea is to make it easy enough for defendants to attend court and defend themselves, while also ensuring the state has a vested interest in the action. The district may be where:

   a. any defendant (individual or corporation) resides, so long as all defendants reside in the same state;

   b. a "substantial part of" the events occurred; or

   c. any defendant can be found if either 1 or 2 does not work.

2. **Remedies When Venue is Improper**—If the case is filed in an improper venue, the court can either dismiss the case or transfer it to the proper venue. It depends on whether the court wants to make the plaintiff go through filing the case again.

3. **Rules Governing Transfer of Venue Based on Forum Non Conveniens**—If a venue is incredibly inconvenient, a defendant may request a transfer to another venue. In determining whether to transfer, the court will look at whether another venue is available; what law will apply; and the location of the parties, evidence, and witnesses.

II. STATE LAW IN FEDERAL COURT

A. Erie Doctrine—Courts apply federal procedural law and the substantive law of the state in which the court sits. This is easy to remember if you think that a court generally follows its own procedures (for example, how many pages are allowed in the complaint, whether an issue is legal or equitable, etc.), while the parties are generally trying to follow the law of the state they are in (for example, what counts as a battery, how contracts are interpreted, etc.).

B. When State Law, Including State Choice-of-Law Rules, Displaces Federal Rules—If federal and state law conflict, the federal law applies. If a state civil procedure rule and a federal civil procedure rule conflict, the court must decide whether the federal rule abridges, enlarges, or modifies a substantive right. If it does not, the federal rule applies.

III. PRETRIAL PROCEDURES

A. Preliminary Injunctions and Temporary Restraining Orders

1. **Purpose of Temporary Restraining Orders**—To preserve the status quo until a hearing can be held. Generally, these can only last 14 days.

2. **Preliminary Injunctions as Tools to Maintain Status Quo Pending Adjudication of a Case**—Before a full hearing can be held, a plaintiff can get a hearing on whether to grant a preliminary injunction to preserve the status quo before the full hearing. To get a preliminary injunction, the plaintiff must show likely success on the merits, irreparable harm without the injunction, that the equities are in the plaintiff's favor, and that the injunction serves the public interest.

3. **When Preliminary Injunctions Can Become Permanent Injunctions**—After a full hearing, the plaintiff can get a permanent injunction to force the defendant to do or not do something.

B. Notice Pleadings and Amended Pleadings*

1. **Notice Pleadings—**A complaint must give a short and plain statement of the claim showing that the pleader is entitled to relief and give the defendant fair notice of what the claim is and what the grounds of the claim are. A pleading can be inconsistent. For example, a defendant could respond, "My dog didn't bite the plaintiff, but if he did, the plaintiff totally provoked the attack." However, complaints involving fraud, mistake, or special damages must be pled with particularity.
2. **Amended Pleadings—**A party may amend a pleading once as of right within 21 days if no responsive pleading is required. If a responsive pleading is required, a party may amend within 21 days of service of the responsive pleading or within 21 days of being served with a motion to dismiss the claim, whichever is earlier.
3. **Relation-Back Doctrine—**For statute of limitations purposes, a pleading amendment will relate back to the date of the original pleading when the amendment asserts a claim or defense that arose out of the same conduct at issue in the original pleading.
4. **Responsive Pleading—**An answer or pre-answer motion to a complaint must be made within 21 days after service of process (which may be why a defendant waives service to get more time).

C. Rule 11*

1. **Reasonable Inquiry—**The plaintiff's attorney must make a reasonable inquiry into the validity of the plaintiff's complaint.
2. **Good-Faith Arguments for Changes in the Law—**If the complaint contains arguments that require a change in the law, such arguments must be made in good faith.
3. **Proper Purpose—**The attorney must certify that the claim or pleading is not being made to harass the other party, cause unnecessary delay, or needlessly increase the cost of litigation. However, Rule 11 does not apply to discovery requests, so those can be intentionally burdensome, at least as far as Rule 11 goes. (However, avoid being a jerk when you pass the bar and enter practice; it will hurt you much worse later when no one in town refers any business to you.)
4. **Timing and Procedures for Rule 11 Sanctions—**Sanctions can either be initiated by the court or the other party. If a party moves for sanctions, the party must serve the opposing party with the motion and give the other party 21 days to fix the problem before presenting the motion to the court.

D. Joinder of Parties and Claims

1. **Joinder of Multiple Claims*—**A plaintiff may join as many claims against the defendant as they would like, and the claims do not need to be related.
2. **Joinder of Parties*—**A party is required to be added to the claim through joinder if that party does not deprive the court of subject matter jurisdiction, and the court cannot accord complete relief without that party or that party claims an interest that cannot be protected without the party's presence or may leave an existing party at risk for incurring inconsistent obligations. If a required party cannot be joined, the court must determine if the action should continue.

3. **Counterclaims***—A counterclaim is a claim brought back against the other party. A compulsory counterclaim is a claim that arises out of the same transaction or occurrence—again, think of judicial efficiency and getting all this stuff settled.
4. **Crossclaims***—A claim filed against a coparty that arises out of the same transaction or occurrence—like a plaintiff sues two defendants for a car wreck, and the two defendants sue each other.
5. **Third-Party Practice***—A defendant may sue another party as a third-party plaintiff if that other party may be liable for all or part of the claim against the defendant. For example, in the case of an employer's vicarious liability. Also known as *impleader*.
6. **Court's Overriding Power to Sever***—A court can also sever a misjoindered party or claim.
7. **Intervention Under Rule 24**—A court must permit a party to intervene who has the right to do so according to federal statute or claims an interest in the action that the current parties cannot adequately represent.

E. **Disclosures and Discovery**

1. **Scope and Limits of Discovery***—Discovery is generally allowed for nonprivileged matter relevant to a party's claim or defense. However, it can be limited to the proportional needs of the case, considering the size and importance of matters at issue. Rule 26(a) covers mandatory disclosures, which could show up on the exam as part of a question that deals with discovery.
2. **Rule 26(f) Conference and Planning for Discovery***—At least 21 days before a scheduling conference is held, the parties must meet to:
   a. discuss the claims and defenses and the possibility of settlement,
   b. make or arrange for any automatic disclosures,
   c. discuss any issues about preserving evidence, and
   d. develop a discovery plan.
      i. **Parties' obligation to confer to develop a proposed discovery plan**—If a party does not participate in good faith in a discovery plan, the court may require that party to pay any expenses incurred as a result.
3. **Discovery Tools and Mechanisms, Including E-Discovery***
   a. **Depositions**—Without leave of the court, the parties may take up to ten oral or written depositions.
      i. **Corporate Representative Discovery**—A corporation must designate a representative to take depositions on its behalf—the deposition request must describe with reasonable particularity the areas sought to be covered with the deposition, so the corporation can assign a representative who knows something.
   b. **Interrogatories**—Any party may serve up to 25 written interrogatories asking questions regarding anything relevant that is not protected by privilege.
   c. **Requests for Production and Inspection**—A party may request that another party allow inspection of evidence, including records, tangible things, or land.

d. **Physical and Mental Examination**—If the mental or physical condition of a party is at issue, a court may order that party to submit to physical or psychological examination.

e. **How to Handle Electronically Stored Information**
   i. **Metadata**—The metadata that identifies electronic data (for example, the creation date of a computer file) may be used to authenticate records, reconstruct records, or prove timelines.
   ii. **Large Volumes of E-Discovery Material**—As part of the discovery conference, the parties should decide how to organize large volumes of relevant electronic data and how to make discovery requests that exclude unnecessary data.

4. **Discovery Motions**

a. **Protective Orders**—A party may request a protective order from the court to prevent the disclosure of information that may be privileged or otherwise harass, prejudice, or embarrass a party.

b. **Process for Claiming Privilege**—To request a protective order based on privilege, the party should describe the materials and identify the specific privilege being invoked.

c. **Motions to Compel Disclosure or Response**—A party may request that a court order another party to disclose information or respond to a discovery request if that party refuses to do so.

d. **Possibility of Sanctions**—Courts may impose sanctions if a party refuses to comply with valid discovery requests.

IV. PRESERVING THE RIGHT TO A JURY TRIAL

A. **Need to Preserve the Right to a Jury Trial in the Complaint**—Under the Seventh Amendment, parties are provided a right to a jury trial. Either party may make a demand for a jury trial by serving the demand 14 days after service of the last pleading directed at the issue involved.

B. **Consequences of Failing to Do So (Waiver)**—A party waives the right to a jury trial unless a demand is properly served and filed.

V. DISPOSITIVE MOTIONS

A. **Motion to Dismiss for Failure to State a Claim***—A defense where the defendant moves to dismiss the case by arguing that even if the court takes everything in the complaint in the light most favorable to the plaintiff, the complaint still fails to contain sufficient facts to state a plausible legal claim. A goofy example would be a complaint stating, "The defendant owes me $100 in damages because he's a jerk." Even if everything were true, "being a jerk" is not legally actionable, although it should be.

B. **Summary Judgment Motion***—A motion that asks for judgment without a trial. The movant must show that no genuine issue of material fact exists, and the opposing party would lose even if all the party's allegations are accepted as accurate.
A motion for summary judgment may be filed within 30 days after the close of discovery.

C. **Motion for Judgment as a Matter of Law (Directed Verdict and Judgment Notwithstanding the Verdict)**—Once a party has been fully heard on an issue, the court may grant a motion resolving that issue if it finds there is insufficient evidence for a reasonable jury to find for that party.

VI. JUDGMENTS

A. **Default Judgment*—**A judgment in favor of the plaintiff when the defendant fails to respond to a summons or does not appear in court.

B. **Effect of Judgment***

1. **Claim Preclusion (also known as res judicata)—**A final judgment on the merits of an action precludes the parties from litigating the same claim against each other in another action. Basically, the same people cannot keep suing each other until they get their way.
2. Issue Preclusion does not allow relitigating an issue that was already decided in an earlier claim. This does not require the same parties as in claim preclusion, but it does require the party against whom issue preclusion is going to be used to have been the party in the original action.

VII. APPEALABILITY AND REVIEW

A. **Final Judgment Rule—**A judgment may only be appealed if it is a final judgment.

B. **Availability of Interlocutory Review—**Appeals are available for certain types of non-final orders, which pause the trial while the ruling is being considered—for example, the appeal of an order denying arbitration.

C. **Standard of Review on Appeal**

1. **De Novo—**A reviewing court makes its decision without considering the previous court's decision.
2. **Clearly Erroneous—**The review standard for questions of fact. The reviewing court looks at the evidence and decides whether an apparent mistake was made in the earlier decision.
3. **Abuse of Discretion—**The reviewing court will decide whether the earlier court made a plain error in a decision left to its discretion.
4. **Plain Error—**An error that is clear from looking at the prior decision's record. For example, a math error in the calculation of a prison sentence.
5. **Harmless Error—**A reviewing court finds that an error in the earlier decision was not sufficient to affect the rights of a party.

PRACTICE MULTIPLE-CHOICE QUESTIONS

1. An attorney represented a builder from State A who claimed a developer from State B had refused to pay him according to the terms of a written contract. The builder gave the attorney a contract signed by the developer that stated that half of the agreed payment was due when the builder had completed half of the agreed-upon work. The attorney sued in federal court on behalf of the builder to enforce the agreement. At a preliminary hearing, the developer denied signing the alleged contract and provided conclusive evidence that the builder had forged the developer's signature.

You are a clerk working for the judge. The judge asks you whether the court can impose a $500 fine on the attorney for filing a false claim. **Select one.**

(A) Yes, because the attorney did not verify the developer's signature.
(B) Yes, because the attorney aided the builder in providing false evidence to the court.
(C) No, because the forged contract would likely satisfy an objectively reasonable attorney.
(D) No, because a court may impose only nonmonetary sanctions.

2. You represent a truck driver domiciled in State A. The truck driver was involved in a car accident with a doctor domiciled in State B. The accident occurred in State C. The doctor chose to file his lawsuit in federal court in State B, and the truck driver was personally served with process in State D while he was attending church within 50 miles of the State B federal courthouse. The truck driver travels to State B once per year for a three-day fishing tournament that he has been competing in for 30 years. You are unsure whether the State B federal court is a proper forum.

Which of the following legal subjects would be most useful to research in determining whether the truck driver can be sued in State B? **Select two.**

(A) State D long-arm statute
(B) Service of process
(C) Erie Doctrine
(D) Minimum contacts
(E) Waiver
(F) Personal jurisdiction

3. A woman was injured when she slipped and fell while she was waiting tables at a restaurant. The woman told the restaurant that she was going to sue for her injuries, and the restaurant hired you as its defense attorney. The next day, the woman showed up at the restaurant and gave the summons and complaint to the restaurant's manager, who was also a president of the restaurant corporation. The day after that, the restaurant corporation fired the manager. In anger, the manager threw the summons and complaint into the trash without telling anyone. A default judgment was later entered against the restaurant. The applicable state rules of civil procedure mirrored the federal rules.

Should you move for the court to quash service? **Select one.**

(A) Yes, because the woman brought the summons and complaint to the restaurant.
(B) Yes, because the restaurant never received notice of the summons and complaint.
(C) No, because the manager was also a president of the restaurant corporation.
(D) No, because the restaurant no longer employed the woman.

4. A woman, a citizen of State A, was injured in a car accident with a man, a citizen of State B. The woman sued the man for $100,000 in personal injuries. The man represented himself in defense. After a trial in a State A federal court, the woman was awarded $76,000 in damages. The man then came to you, claiming that he had also suffered over $100,000 in damages in the same accident. The man told you that he would like to file suit against the woman in federal court, but that he was planning on moving to State A soon.

May the man file his claim against the woman in federal court? **Select one.**

(A) Yes, because the man represented himself.
(B) Yes, because the man's claim was for over $100,000 in personal injuries.
(C) No, because the claim was in federal court based on diversity jurisdiction.
(D) No, because the man's claim is barred.

5. You represent a man who worked for 35 years for a corporation. The man was domiciled in State A for most of those 35 years, although he lived in State B for a few years. The corporation was incorporated in State B, had most of its factories in State A, and was run from an executive suite located in State C. The man sought to sue the corporation in a state court, alleging that his termination violated his rights under the Americans with Disabilities Act. The man sought $50,000 in damages. The corporation filed a notice of removal to a federal court in State A. You are considering filing a motion for remand back to the state court.

Is your motion likely to be successful? **Select one.**

(A) Yes, because there is a lack of diversity.
(B) Yes, because the man is seeking less than $75,000 in damages.
(C) No, because the corporation's executive suite is in State C.
(D) No, because the man's claim is a federal claim.

6. You represent a woman suing a corporation for breach of contract. Which of the following does the woman not need to disclose without a formal discovery request from the corporation? **Select two.**

(A) The email address of individuals likely to have discoverable information.
(B) The telephone number of individuals likely to have discoverable information.
(C) A copy of the contract in the woman's possession.
(D) The names of all witnesses to the contract.
(E) The woman's litigation plan.
(F) A description of the damages claimed by the woman.

7. You represent a plastic surgeon who is a citizen of State A. A man, a citizen of State B, sued the plastic surgeon in federal court in State B for medical malpractice. The man claimed that the surgeon committed malpractice, leaving him looking like a cat instead of a human. After researching the claim, you discover that the State B statute of limitations for medical malpractice has expired.

Should you move for summary judgment based on the expiration of the State B statute of limitations? **Select one.**

(A) Yes, because statutes of limitations are substantive law.
(B) Yes, because the federal court must follow the law of the state in which it sits.
(C) No, because the man brought his suit in federal court.
(D) No, because medical malpractice is not a federal claim.

8. You represent a comic book author. The author has been sued by a middle-aged man who claims damages for negligent infliction of emotional distress because the author changed the sex and ethnicity of his comic's main character. The man also brings a claim for damages done to his part-time business, where he dresses up as the character and goes to children's birthday parties.

How should you respond to the man's complaint? **Select one.**

(A) Make a motion to dismiss for failure to state a claim.
(B) Make a motion for summary judgment.
(C) Make a motion for declaratory judgment.
(D) Make a motion for a more definite statement.

9. A potential client comes to your office and tells you that he wants to sue his neighbor for battery. According to the client, the neighbor was tossing a football with his son when they accidentally threw the football over the fence and hit the neighbor in the neck. The client suffered a slipped disc, which required surgery costing over $10,000. The client seeks to recover the cost of the surgery, as well as damages for pain and suffering, and lost pay for the three weeks he was required to stay home from work. The state rules of civil procedure mirror those of the Federal Rules of Civil Procedure.

Would it be proper for you to file a complaint for battery based on the potential client's assertions? **Select one.**

(A) Yes, because the alleged facts support a possible claim.
(B) Yes, because the complaint puts the neighbor on notice of a potential claim.
(C) No, because the complaint requires more detailed assertions regarding the nature of the alleged damages.
(D) No, because the alleged facts do not support a plausible claim.

10. While attending court on another matter, you saw a woman injured when she fell down the state courthouse steps. Although there was a security camera filming the steps, you were the only physical witness to the fall. The woman sued the state for her injuries and served you with 10 interrogatories regarding what you saw when she fell. The state rules of civil procedure mirror those of the Federal Rules of Civil Procedure.

Are you required to answer the woman's interrogatories? **Select one.**

(A) Yes, because you are the only physical witness to the woman's fall.
(B) Yes, because you are an officer of the court.
(C) No, because you are not a party to the woman's claim.
(D) No, because the woman could get the necessary evidence from the security camera.

11. Another attorney came to your office and asked you for your thoughts on whether she should file a motion for Rule 11 sanctions against the opposing party in the case she was currently litigating. She was working as an attorney for the city. The plaintiff was suing the city for unlawful religious discrimination in the city's failure to hire him as an independent building contractor.

Which of the following facts, if true, could expose the opposing party to Rule 11 sanctions? **Select two.**

(A) At the time of filing the complaint, the plaintiff could not prove part of his claim.
(B) After discovery, the plaintiff discovered that one of his factual allegations was false, but he still presented those factual allegations in his case-in-chief.
(C) When the plaintiff discovered that one of his factual allegations was false, he failed to file an amended complaint to remove the false allegations.
(D) Because the plaintiff's attorney learned of the client's claim three days before the relevant statute of limitations expired, he did minimal investigation into the claim before filing the complaint.
(E) None of the controlling cases in the jurisdiction recognized the plaintiff's claim.
(F) The plaintiff's claim was only supported by circumstantial evidence.

12. You were hired by a client who wanted you to represent him in a lawsuit against his former employer for age discrimination. According to your client, he worked at the corporation for 35 years before a younger man was hired as his immediate supervisor. The supervisor repeatedly made jokes about the client's age. According to your client, the supervisor also "seemed weird," and the client once saw a prescription bottle on the supervisor's desk. After six months of working for the supervisor, the supervisor gave your client his first unsatisfactory job evaluation, and your client was demoted to a lesser position. You filed a complaint against the corporation and were informed that the corporation had hired defense counsel.

Which of the following would be LEAST useful for you to do at this stage of the litigation? **Select two.**

- **(A)** Contact the corporation's attorney to set up a discovery plan.
- **(B)** Contact the corporation's attorney to set up a mental examination of the supervisor.
- **(C)** Contact the corporation's attorney to set up a scheduling conference.
- **(D)** Contact the corporation's attorney to discuss the possibility of settlement.
- **(E)** Contact the corporation's attorney about preserving evidence.
- **(F)** Contact the corporation's attorney to arrange for automatic disclosures.

13. A man came to you for advice regarding a lawsuit he and his sister were considering. He told you that he and his sister were driving in his car when they collided with a large commercial truck. You thought that the man and his sister might be more successful filing their action in federal court than if they filed in state court. You decided it would be best for them to sue both the truck driver and truck company, but you believed it was likely that the truck company would implead its insurance company to defend and pay the claim.

Which of the following would be LEAST likely to affect whether the claim could be brought in federal court? **Select two.**

- **(A)** The truck driver's domicile
- **(B)** The amount of damages sustained by the man
- **(C)** The insurance company's place of incorporation
- **(D)** A possible defense based on federal trucking law
- **(E)** The sister's domicile
- **(F)** The domicile of the trucking company's chief executive officer

14. A woman hired you to defend her from claims arising from a car accident. She told you that the plaintiff was suing both her and another man for the accident, and that she believed that the man was primarily responsible for both her and the plaintiff's injuries. She also believed that a truck was involved in the accident that was not part of the plaintiff's suit.

Which of the following legal concepts are most relevant to the woman's claims? **Select two.**

- **(A)** Impleader
- **(B)** Crossclaim
- **(C)** Joinder
- **(D)** Counterclaim
- **(E)** Third-party practice
- **(F)** Severance

15. Your client wanted to sue a large corporation in federal court for negligence and defamation. According to your client, he had worked for the corporation for several years in its Maryland office. During that time, he had lived in Maryland since he was in college. While working in that office, he hurt his back several times while installing the corporation's products. He also said he injured himself several times while he was temporarily based in New Jersey. All his physical injuries amounted to $70,000 in damages. After receiving a bad employment review from his immediate supervisor, your client was fired from the corporation. Because he was out of work, your client moved back home with his mother, who lived in Illinois, before contacting you about the lawsuit. Your office was in New York.

Which of the following facts, if true, would be most detrimental to your client's ability to sue the corporation in federal court? **Select two.**

(A) The corporation's largest concentration of employees was in Maryland.
(B) The corporation's chief financial officer worked in the corporation's Illinois office.
(C) All of the corporation's factories were in Maryland.
(D) The client only wanted to file claims for negligence and defamation.
(E) The client claimed only $70,000 in defamation damages.
(F) The corporation was incorporated in Illinois.

16. A woman owned a catering company in State A near the border with State B. She came to your office and said a consumer called and threatened to sue the catering company in federal court in State B for a botched catering order and the resulting destruction of the consumer's wedding.
Which of the following facts, if true, are most likely to subject the woman's company to State B federal court jurisdiction? **Select two.**

(A) The catering company headquarters are within 100 miles of the State B federal court.
(B) The catering company had a single billboard in State B.
(C) The consumer was a citizen of State B.
(D) The catering company's website can be accessed by State B citizens.
(E) The catering company phoned event spaces in State B looking for business.
(F) The woman was a citizen of State B.

17. You filed suit in State A court on behalf of your client, a State A woman who was injured when a bicycle she was riding in State C lost a tire. The woman sued the bicycle company under a state-law products liability claim, claiming $80,000 in damages. The company was incorporated in State B, had all its bicycle factories in State C, and was run by a group of executives in State A. A week after you served the bicycle company, the company successfully removed the case to federal court in State A. You believe the state court in State A would be more favorable to your client's case.
Which of the following two arguments would be most useful in convincing the court to remand the woman's claim back to state court? **Select two.**

(A) The woman and the company are not completely diverse.
(B) Removal is an issue of substantive law.
(C) Removal is an issue of procedural law.
(D) The company's executives were in State A.
(E) A federal products liability claim must exceed $150,000 in damages.
(F) The plaintiff's complaint, whether initial or amended, controls the location of the suit.

18. You represent a group of homeowners who believed that their water supply was poisoned due to the negligent actions of a local pesticide company. After discovery was completed, the pesticide company moved for summary judgment. In support of its motion, the pesticide company attached a report from its expert scientist that claimed to show that the poisoning was caused by chemicals that the pesticide company did not use.
What should you do in response? **Select one.**

(A) Submit an affidavit from an expert contradicting the scientist's report.
(B) Move for summary judgment in the homeowners' favor.
(C) Submit an affidavit from the homeowners stating that they saw spilled barrels of chemicals at the pesticide company.
(D) Submit your own affidavit stating that you believe there are still questions of material fact.

19. You represent a man who wants to sue a truck driver, alleging that the truck driver was negligent and caused an accident that resulted in the man's injuries. While you are researching the case, you discover that a woman was involved in the same accident and that she had already sued the truck driver. In that case, the jury ruled in favor of the truck driver and found that the truck driver was not negligent in the accident. You are concerned that the earlier verdict might cause a problem for your case.

Which of the following legal concepts should you research to determine whether the woman's case will adversely affect the man's claim? **Select two.**

(A) Judgment as a matter of law
(B) Issue preclusion
(C) Res judicata
(D) Jury nullification
(E) Interlocutory review
(F) Final judgment rule

20. An independent contractor from State A asks you to represent him after he received the following complaint from a State B businessman: "The independent contractor has breached his contract with me, causing me damages in excess of $100,000." The complaint from the businessman was filed in State B state court.

Which of the following motions would be most useful to file on your client's behalf? **Select one.**

(A) Motion for a more definite statement
(B) Motion for summary judgment
(C) Motion for removal
(D) Motion to dismiss for failure to state a claim

ANSWERS

1. The correct answer is (C). Under Federal Rule of Civil Procedure Rule 11(b), an attorney must have evidentiary support for a client's claim. Generally, an attorney can rely on documents supplied by their client, and there was nothing to indicate that the attorney should have known that the document was forged. (A) is incorrect because an attorney is not generally required to verify the signature on a document provided to them by their client unless the attorney has a reason to believe the document is false. (B) is incorrect because the attorney did not knowingly aid the builder in trying to fool the court. (D) is incorrect because the court may impose both monetary and nonmonetary sanctions.

2. The correct answers are (D) and (F). The most important issue here is whether the State B court has personal jurisdiction over the truck driver. Because the truck driver is not a citizen of State B, was not served in State B, and the accident did not occur in State B, the only way State B could have personal jurisdiction over the truck driver is if the truck driver had sufficient minimum contacts with State B. Under the facts here, it is unlikely the truck driver has sufficient minimum contacts. (A) is incorrect because the State D long-arm statute would be irrelevant to the situation. (B) is incorrect because personal service in State D would not give State B jurisdiction over the truck driver no matter how close the service was to the State B federal courthouse. Importantly, the "bulge" rule concerning service of process would not apply in this situation. (C) is incorrect because the Erie Doctrine concerns what law will be used by the federal court in a particular case, not whether the court has jurisdiction over the parties. (E) is incorrect because nothing indicates that any waiver occurred.

3. The correct answer is (A). Under Federal Rule of Civil Procedure 4, service of process cannot be done by someone who is a party to the lawsuit. Consequently, the woman could not serve process on the restaurant. (B) is incorrect because service upon the manager, as a president of the restaurant corporation, likely gave notice to the restaurant. (C) is incorrect because the woman was a party to the action and delivered service herself. (D) is incorrect because the fact that the restaurant no longer employs the woman is irrelevant.

4. The correct answer is (D). Because the man's claim arises from the same transaction or occurrence (the accident), the claim is a compulsory counterclaim. It should have been asserted by the man in the original action. Since he did not do so, the claim is now barred. (A) is incorrect because the fact that the man represented himself is irrelevant. (B) is incorrect because the amount the man is claiming is also irrelevant. (C) is incorrect because the fact that the claim was in federal court based on diversity jurisdiction is irrelevant.

5. The correct answer is (D). Since the man's claim is based upon a federal claim, he can have his claim heard in federal court despite any lack of diversity or amount in controversy. Thus, any remand to state court is likely to be unsuccessful. (A) is incorrect because the man is bringing a federal claim, so diversity issues don't matter. (B) is incorrect because "amount in controversy" is not an issue for a federal claim. (C) is incorrect because whether remand is appropriate does not depend on the citizenship of the parties.

6. The correct answers are (A) and (E). Federal Rule of Civil Procedure 26(a) does not require mandatory disclosure of the email addresses of individuals likely to have discoverable information, nor does it require mandatory disclosure of a party's litigation plan. All the other choices provided contain information subject to mandatory disclosure.

7. The correct answer is (A). Under the Erie Doctrine, a federal court in a diversity case must apply the substantive law of the state in which it is sitting. Statutes of limitations are substantive law, so you should move for summary judgment based on the expiration of the statute of limitations. (B) is incorrect because federal courts follow their own federal procedural law, not state procedural law, making (A) the better answer. (C) is incorrect because of the rule of the Erie Doctrine. (D) is incorrect because the court should apply the State B statute of limitations in this case.

8. The correct answer is (A). Under Federal Rule of Civil Procedure 12(b), a defendant can move to dismiss the plaintiff's claim if there is no claim for which the court could grant relief. Here, the man is basing his claim on the fact that the author changed his character, which the author had every right in the world to do. Even if all the man's facts are accurate, there is nothing actionable that the man could bring against the author. If you are granted this motion, you will not need to file any answer to the man's complaint. (B) is incorrect because a summary judgment motion requires the court to consider all the evidence, whereas this complaint can be resolved much more quickly. (C) is incorrect because declaratory judgments are merely used to determine the rights and status of the parties involved. (D) is incorrect because the issue is not that the complaint is too vague.

9. The correct answer is (D). A complaint must state a plausible claim. Battery is an intentional tort, so claiming that the football accidentally hit the client could not support a plausible claim for battery. (A) is incorrect because a complaint must state a plausible claim, not just a possible one. (B) is incorrect because a complaint must do more than merely put the defendant on notice. (C) is incorrect because the issue here is not the lack of detail in the complaint.

10. The correct answer is (C). Under Federal Rule of Civil Procedure 33(a), only parties to a claim must answer interrogatories. Here, you are not a party to the woman's claim. (A) and (B) are incorrect because you are not a party to the woman's claim. (D) is incorrect because it is irrelevant that the woman could obtain the necessary evidence from the security camera.

11. The correct answers are (B) and (E). Under Rule 11, the plaintiff's attorney must make a reasonable inquiry into the validity of the plaintiff's complaint. In addition, if the complaint contains arguments that require a change in the law, such arguments must be made in good faith. (B) is correct because if the plaintiff discovered one of his factual allegations was false, he could not continue to present his case to the court as if that fact were true. (E) is correct because if none of the controlling cases in the jurisdiction recognized the plaintiff's claim, the claim would be frivolous because there would be no support for it under the controlling law. (A) is incorrect because a plaintiff can file a complaint and then prove all the necessary facts for the complaint during discovery. (C) is incorrect because the plaintiff would not need to amend the complaint; he would only not have to try his case as if the false allegation were true. (D) is incorrect because it would be reasonable for the attorney to file the complaint with minimal research if the statute of limitations was about to expire. (F) is incorrect because a claim can be proven with only circumstantial evidence.

12. The correct answers are (B) and (C). Under Rule 26(f), at least 21 days before a scheduling conference is held, the parties must meet to: (1) discuss the claims and defenses and possibility of settlement; (2) make or arrange for any automatic disclosures; (3) discuss any issues about preserving evidence; and (4) develop a discovery plan. (B) is correct because this is not part of an initial Rule 26(f) meeting. (C) is correct because a scheduling conference should not occur before (A), (D), (E), or (F).

13. The correct answers are (C) and (D). (C) is correct because diversity jurisdiction would not be affected if the trucking company decided to implead its insurance company. So long as the plaintiff is not suing the insurance company directly, the citizenship of the insurance company does not matter. (D) is correct because federal jurisdiction is based on the plaintiff's complaint, not on any possible federal defenses brought up by the defendant. Since this is a car accident, the claim can only get into federal court based on diversity jurisdiction. Diversity jurisdiction depends on the domiciles of the parties, as well as the amount in controversy. Consequently, (A), (B), (E), and (F) are incorrect.

14. The correct answers are (B) and (C). (B) is correct because the woman appears to have a claim against the man, her co-defendant, and that would be a crossclaim. (C) is correct because the woman appears to want to join another party, which would be joinder. (A) and (E) are incorrect because both refer to the fact that a defendant may sue another party as a third-party plaintiff if that other party may be liable for all or part of the claim against the defendant. (D) is incorrect because a counterclaim would be a claim brought by the woman against the plaintiff. (F) is incorrect because severance refers to severing parties from a lawsuit.

15. The correct answers are (B) and (F). Because the client wanted to bring a suit for defamation and negligence, the only way he could bring suit in federal court was to meet the requirements for diversity jurisdiction. Because the client is filing the suit while living in Illinois, with no apparent intention to leave, he is considered a citizen of Illinois. A corporation is a citizen of its state of incorporation and its corporate nerve center. (B) is correct because if the corporation's chief financial officer worked in Illinois, it would mean that the corporation's nerve center is likely in Illinois, making the corporation a citizen of Illinois. (F) is correct because if the corporation were incorporated in Illinois, its other state of citizenship would be Illinois. Importantly, if the corporation were a citizen of Illinois, there would be no diversity between the client and the corporation. (A) and (C) are incorrect because the corporation could be a citizen of Maryland without destroying diversity. (D) is incorrect because the client's intention to sue only for negligence and defamation would not affect diversity. (E) is incorrect because the client's two claims could be joined together to meet the required $75,000 amount in controversy.

16. The correct answers are (B) and (E). To determine whether personal jurisdiction over a company is appropriate, courts look closely at whether a company has availed itself of a particular state's market. Here, both (B) and (E) show an intentional act by the company to reach into State B, so these two facts would be most likely to give the State B federal court personal jurisdiction over the company. (A) is incorrect because the 100-mile bulge rule would not apply to this situation. (C) is incorrect because the consumer's citizenship would not affect the company's personal jurisdiction. (D) is incorrect because simply allowing another state's citizens to access a company website would not be enough for personal jurisdiction. (F) is incorrect because even if the woman were a citizen of State B, that fact alone would not affect the company's citizenship depending on the company's corporate structure.

17. The correct answers are (A) and (D). First, because the woman is not bringing a federal claim, the woman and the company must be diverse from each other. The woman is a citizen of State A, while the company is likely also a citizen of State A because its corporate nerve center, the group of executives running the company, is in State A. Consequently, there is no complete diversity, and (A) is correct. Secondly, even if the parties were diverse, the company could not remove to a State A federal court because it is a citizen of State A. Thus, (D) is correct. (B) and (C) are irrelevant concepts dealing with the Erie Doctrine. (E) is incorrect because there is no such law, and this is not a federal claim. (F) is incorrect because the plaintiff's complaint does not necessarily control the location of the suit—if the plaintiff files in the incorrect court, it can obviously be removed.

18. The correct answer is (A). To defeat a motion for summary judgment, you need to show that there is a genuine issue of material fact. Your best way to do this is to call the scientist's report into question, which makes (A) the correct answer. (B) is incorrect because a motion for summary judgment does not do anything in this situation. (C) is incorrect because whether the homeowners saw spilled barrels does not address the problem regarding the exact chemicals used by the company. (D) is incorrect because your own affidavit would not create an issue of material fact.

19. The correct answers are (B) and (C). Res judicata and claim preclusion both refer to the fact that a party is barred from asserting the same claim in a subsequent lawsuit. Issue preclusion does not allow relitigating an issue that was already decided in an earlier claim. Issue preclusion does not require the same parties as claim preclusion, but it does require the party against whom issue preclusion is going to be used to have been the party in the original action. Here, only (B) and (C) would have any relevance to the issue of whether the woman's prior claim would affect the man's claim. Consequently, (A), (D), (E), and (F) are incorrect.

20. The correct answer is (D). A motion to dismiss for failure to state a claim is a defense where the defendant moves to dismiss the case by arguing that even if the court takes everything in the complaint in the light most favorable to the plaintiff, the complaint still fails to contain sufficient facts to state a plausible legal claim. (D) is correct because the complaint does not specify which contract is at issue, or what the contract was for, or for how much. Consequently, a motion to dismiss for failure to state a claim would be a good move to get rid of the claim at this time. (A) is incorrect because a more definite statement will help the businessman clarify his claim. (B) and (C) are incorrect because you could get rid of the claim now.

Constitutional Law

2

Topics with asterisks (*) require you to know the black letter law cold; topics without an * require you to recognize the topic as part of the fact scenario or require you to analyze and apply legal resources provided for the topic efficiently.

MAIN POINTS OF CONSTITUTIONAL LAW—KEEPING A BALANCE OF POWER BETWEEN THE BRANCHES OF THE FEDERAL GOVERNMENT, A STATE AND THE FEDERAL GOVERNMENT, AND AN INDIVIDUAL AND THE FEDERAL GOVERNMENT

OUTLINE

Generally, the bar exam takes three years before they will test a change in Constitutional Law. The idea is that the exam is testing you on something you took in your first year of law school. If a Constitutional Law change is less than three years old, use the old law if the topic is tested.

I. FEDERAL JUDICIAL POWER

A. Justiciability Requirements: Case or Controversy and Standing*

1. Standing

a. Personal—I Can **R**emedy!

i. **Injury**—Actual and imminent concrete injury caused by the law.
ii. **Causation**—The law is the cause in fact of the injury alleged.
iii. **Redressability**—The plaintiff's injury will be solved by a ruling in their favor regarding the law.

b. **Associational**—The members of the organization must have standing in their own right, the claim asserted must be related to the organization's purpose, and the case does not require the individual members' participation in the lawsuit.

c. **Third Party**—Requires individual standing and either a special relationship between the plaintiff and the third party, or it must be difficult for the third party to assert their own rights. For example, doctors providing abortions have standing to raise the rights of patients who were unlikely to be able to assert their own rights (because pregnancy is less than nine months) and because a doctor clearly needs a patient to perform an abortion.

2. **Taxpayer Standing**—There is no general federal taxpayer standing. The only situation that will provide standing based on being a taxpayer is when the law was enacted under the power to tax and spend, and it violates the Establishment Clause.

3. **Case or Controversy in Enforcing Statutes**—There must be an actual case or controversy in dispute. A person cannot bring a suit just because a law has been passed.

B. Other Justiciability Doctrines

1. **Ripeness**—There must be a live case or controversy or immediate threat of harm. For example, if the law is unlikely to be enforced against a person, they cannot sue simply because the law is on the books.

2. **Mootness**—If events have occurred that have taken away the plaintiff's stake in the litigation. For example, an abortion case after the plaintiff is no longer pregnant.

   a. **Exceptions:**

      i. A situation capable of repetition, but evading review. Abortion is also an example here because the plaintiff could get pregnant again.

      ii. The defendant's voluntary stopping of the activity causing the litigation because the defendant could just start up again.

      iii. Collateral consequences that keep the parties adverse. For example, a felon who has been let out of prison but still cannot carry a gun or vote.

3. **Advisory Opinions**—Because there must be a case or controversy, a judge cannot give a formal opinion with no legal effect. For example, if the affected party has the discretion whether to follow the judge's opinion or not, that is an advisory opinion.

C. The Eleventh Amendment and State Sovereign Immunity

1. **Suits Against States**—A private person cannot bring a federal suit against a state.

2. **Suits Against Local Governments**—A private person can bring a suit against a city or county.

3. **Litigation Between State and Federal Governments**—The federal government and states can sue each other.

4. **Claims Against Government Officials**—Injunctions can be brought against state officials.

5. **Suits for Damages and Injunctive Relief**—Claims for damages and injunctions may be awarded against government officials.

6. **State Law Claims and Federal Law Claims**—A private person's federal claims may be decided in state court, but a federal court may not decide state law claims. However, federal claims may be appealed to a federal court.
7. **Consent to Be Sued**—A state may consent to be sued.
8. **Congressional Power to Abrogate State Immunity**—Congress can take away state immunity if Congress is acting to enforce rights created by the Thirteenth (abolishing slavery), Fourteenth (equal protection), or Fifteenth (right to vote) Amendments.

D. Judicial Authority to Interpret the Constitution and Laws

1. The judicial branch has the power to determine the constitutionality of any law passed by Congress.

II. LEGISLATIVE POWERS

A. Congress's Commerce, Taxing, and Spending Powers*

1. **Commerce Clause**—Congress may regulate the channels of interstate commerce (roads, planes, etc.), the instrumentalities of interstate commerce (cars, trucks, the Internet), persons and things moving through interstate commerce (televisions, kidnap victims), and activities that substantially affect interstate commerce.
   a. **Substantial Effect**—Purely local activities that affect interstate commerce in the aggregate (growing your own wheat, growing your own loco weed, renting out private homes), private conduct that affects commerce (a private restaurant that does not serve people based on color), and noncommercial activity if it has a direct and substantial economic effect on interstate commerce—but this really never passes muster. For example, guns near schools or violence against women affecting commerce—you can argue that they do, but the connection between the two is far too attenuated.
2. **Regulation of Economic and Noneconomic Activity**—Noneconomic activity, even if it arguably affects the economy (like guns near schools adversely affecting education), is rarely able to be regulated through the Commerce Clause.
3. **Regulation Through Spending**—Congress has the power to tax and spend for the general welfare. Funding allocations may be made if they are clear, relate to a specific area, and are not excessively coercive. For example, Congress withholding federal highway funds unless states raise the drinking age to 21—federal highway funds are not necessary for states to have roads, and the entire point of raising the drinking age is to cut down on drunk driving on highways.

B. Congress's Power to Enforce the Thirteenth, Fourteenth, and Fifteenth Amendments

1. Congress can take away state immunity if Congress is acting to enforce rights created by the Thirteenth (abolishing slavery), Fourteenth (equal protection), or Fifteenth (right to vote) Amendments.

III. EXECUTIVE POWERS

A. The President's Power as Commander in Chief

1. Congress has the authority to declare war, but the president serves as the commander-in-chief of the military when it is called into service.

B. The President's Power to Appoint and Remove Officials

1. **Executive Branch Officials**—The president can appoint high-level officers with the approval of 50 percent of the Senate (examples are federal judges and cabinet members). Congress cannot appoint inferior federal officers, but it can determine who has the power to make those appointments. The president can remove high-level officers unless Congress puts limitations on removal.
2. **Congress's Authority to Limit the President's Appointment and Removal Powers**—The Senate may provide advice and consent and also determine who appoints inferior federal officers.

C. The Powers of Federal Administrative Agencies

1. **Executive Enforcers**—Under the Take Care Clause, the president has the duty to enforce the laws passed by Congress. As an example, Congress could not pass a law, and the president choose not to enforce it because it goes against his personal beliefs.
2. **Legislators with Rule-Making Authority**—Congress can grant agencies the authority to issue rules through statutes.
3. **Judges Conducting Hearings and Issuing Decisions**—Administrative Law judges may conduct hearings where they serve as both judge and trier-of-fact in cases involving the enforcement of federal regulations.

IV. THE RELATION OF NATION AND STATES IN A FEDERAL SYSTEM

A. Intergovernmental Immunities

1. **Prohibition on State Taxation of Federal Entities**—A state cannot tax a federal entity—for example, a state could not tax a federal bank. Remember, "The power to tax is the power to destroy."
2. **Prohibition on Federal Commandeering of State Legislation and Enforcement**—The federal government may not command a state government to pass a law, nor may it order a state to use its own personnel to enforce a federal law. For example, the federal government may not pass a rule requiring background checks for guns and force the states to use their own people to make those background checks.

B. Federalism-Based Limits on State Authority

1. **Supremacy Clause and Preemption***
   a. Express Preemption – occurs when the federal government explicitly states that its laws or regulations will take precedence over state laws or regulations, or when a federal law directly conflicts with state law. If the federal government does not intend to occupy a field completely, states may enact similar legislation. States may also create greater protections than a federal law, provided those greater protections do not conflict with it.

   b. Implied Preemption describes when the federal law does not explicitly state that it preempts state laws, but following both the federal law and a state law is either impossible or the state law frustrates the objectives of a federal law.
2. **Dormant Commerce Clause prohibits states from passing laws that discriminate against interstate commerce or unduly burden interstate commerce**—a state law that does so must pass strict scrutiny analysis to be

lawful—the government must show that the law is narrowly tailored and is necessary to further a compelling state interest. For example, one state bans the importation of cows from another state because the other state's cows all have mad cow disease.

a. **Congressional Authorization of Otherwise Invalid State Action**—Congress can consent and authorize a state regulation—the big example is state laws imposing taxes on out-of-state insurance companies.

b. **Market Participant Doctrine**—When the state owns or operates a business, it can favor local interests over out-of-state interests. For example, a state-owned concrete plant can sell concrete to in-state builders at a discount.

V. INDIVIDUAL RIGHTS

A. **State Action Requirement**—For a constitutional violation to occur, the government must be involved in the alleged violation.

1. **Exception for Exclusive Government Functions**—There is an exception in the case of a private actor performing a traditional and exclusive public function—for example, running a park, running a prison, owning a town, or running elections.

B. **Substantive Due Process allows the Constitution to protect certain fundamental rights, even if those rights are not enumerated in the Constitution.**

1. **The Right to Privacy**

a. **Right to Reject Unwanted Medical Care**—A person may reject unwanted medical care, such as life support; however, there must be sufficient evidence of that person's wishes to reject care.

b. **Right to Educate One's Children**—Parents have the right to direct the education of their children, for example, by sending them to private school.

c. **The Right to Live with Whomever One Chooses**—A fundamental right exists for related people to live together, including extended family members.

d. **The Right to Marriage**—A person may marry whomever they want, regardless of race or sexual orientation.

e. **The Right to Contraception**—Married, unmarried, and minor people all have the right to use contraception.

f. **Standards of Review**—Government interference with a fundamental right must meet the requirements of strict scrutiny—specifically, the government must show that the law is narrowly tailored and is necessary to further a compelling state interest.

2. **The Right to Vote**

a. **Voting Restrictions**—U.S. citizens over the age of 18 have a fundamental right to vote in all federal, state, and local elections.

b. **Dilution of the Right to Vote**—Voting districts should generally follow the rule of "one person, one vote"—for example, it is unlawful for gerrymandering to reduce the voting power of a particular group intentionally.

c. **Racial Gerrymandering**—States may not make up voting districts based on race.

d. **Standards of Review**—Government interference with the right to vote must meet the requirements of strict scrutiny—specifically, the government must show that the law is narrowly tailored and necessary to further a compelling state interest. However, a restriction on the right to vote that is just a matter of practicality, such as making people line up by party or making a new state resident wait 30 days before they can vote, is only subject to rational basis review, which means a plaintiff must show that there is no rational basis for the law.

3. **The Right to Travel**—The Privileges and Immunities Clause protects the rights of every citizen to travel freely between the states. Durational residency requirements for government benefits are subject to strict scrutiny analysis, although reasonable residency requirements are allowed for divorce and reduced tuition at state universities.

4. **The Right to Bear Arms**—A state may not pass a law infringing on a person's right to keep and carry a gun unless that law has a historical basis in the nation's traditions.

C. Procedural Due Process, Including Administrative Hearings*

1. **Entitlement to Due Process**—The Due Process Clause protects against the deprivation of life, liberty, or property without the due process of the law. If a question has a plaintiff asking that the government follow a particular "process" before taking away property, the correct answer will likely be something regarding procedural due process.

2. **Notice and the Right to Be Heard**—In general, due process requires notice, an opportunity to be heard, and a neutral decision-maker.

3. **Waiver of Procedural Due Process Rights**—A person can waive procedural due process rights, but that waiver must be knowing and voluntary.

4. **Access to Courts**—Procedural due process guarantees people access to the courts to protect their property interests.

5. **Welfare and Disability Benefits**—A statutory entitlement to welfare and disability benefits is a protectable property interest.

6. **Creditors' Remedies**—A creditor cannot receive a prejudgment attachment or garnish a person's wages without notice and a hearing.

7. **Civil Forfeiture**—In civil forfeiture cases, no preliminary hearing is required. Due process only requires a timely forfeiture hearing.

D. Equal Protection* prohibits the government from treating similarly situated persons differently. For multiple-choice questions, it is crucial to memorize the definitions of the three levels of scrutiny, as incorrect answers often misplace the burden of proof or misinterpret the definitions.

1. **Classifications Subject to Strict Scrutiny**—The government must show that the law is narrowly tailored and is necessary to further a compelling state interest. If a law has a discriminatory impact, it will not violate the Equal Protection Clause unless it also had discriminatory intent based on:

   a. Race

   b. Ethnicity

   c. National Origin

   d. Alienage

For example, a police officer test that only happens to have a greater negative impact on minorities will not be struck down.

i. **Special rule**—Rational basis scrutiny is applied to restrictions that involve functions important to the government, such as voting, executing public policy, running for office, or teaching in schools. For example, a law requiring police officers to be citizens would only be subject to rational basis review.

e. **Fundamental Rights (See above)**

2. **Classifications Subject to Intermediate Scrutiny**—The government must show that the law is substantially related to achieving an important government interest.

   a. **Gender**—Most gender classifications that are based on gender stereotypes will be struck down.

   b. **Nonmarital Children**—This is a classification that is unlikely to appear on the exam. This classification is given intermediate scrutiny due to historical reasons and a state's interest in property transfers through wills and intestacy.

3. **Classifications Subject to Rational Basis Review**—This covers basically any other classification you can think of. The plaintiff must show that the law is not rationally related to a legitimate government interest.

E. **Takings**

1. **Taking**—Private property cannot be taken for a public use without just compensation.

   a. A permanent physical invasion or confiscation of property is a taking, no matter how small it is.

   b. A use restriction that denies all economically beneficial use of a piece of property is also a taking.

2. Just Compensation is measured by the market value at the time of the taking. Courts assess the fairness of the compensation.

3. **Public Use**—The use only has to be rationally related to a conceivable public purpose. A notable example is the acquisition of land for a public highway. Still, a less obvious one is taking property to foster economic development, such as acquiring private riverfront homes and transferring them to a developer to create jobs and increase the area's tax revenues.

4. **Regulatory Taking**—In determining whether there is a taking, courts will balance the value of the social goal behind the regulation, the loss in value to the landowner, and the investment-backed expectations of the owner.

5. **Regulation That Is Not a Taking**—A regulation will not result in a taking if there is still an economically viable use for the property. Zoning, landmark preservation, and environmental protections are not usually considered takings.

F. **Ex Post Facto Laws**

1. **Article I and Section 9**—The government may not pass a law that criminalizes conduct that was legal when the defendant originally engaged in the conduct or that increases punishment for a crime already committed.

2. **Due Process Requirements**—A defendant may not be convicted for conduct that was not criminal at the time of the conduct.

G. First Amendment Freedoms: The Religion Clauses

1. The Establishment Clause* prohibits laws that endorse or favor a particular religious group.
   a. **Applicability to States**—Through the Fourteenth Amendment, the Establishment Clause applies to the states.
   b. **Religious Displays on Public Property**
      i. A religious display violates the Establishment Clause if it has a predominantly religious purpose. However, if it also communicates a secular moral message or a historical and social meaning, it might not violate the Clause.
      ii. Holiday displays do not violate the Establishment Clause if they acknowledge rather than endorse religion.
   c. **Discrimination Among Religions**—The government may not discriminate between religions.
   d. **Financial Benefits to Religious Entities**—Government aid to religious entities is allowed if the aid is secular, used for secular purposes, distributed between both secular and religious institutions, and the distribution criteria are religiously neutral. For example, school lunches and school textbooks are provided to all schools in the area, regardless of their religious affiliation.
   e. **Tax Exemptions**—Property-tax exemptions for religious institutions are valid, so long as those exemptions are not available only to religious institutions.
   f. **Curriculum Controls**—Posting the Ten Commandments on public classroom walls and prohibiting the teaching of Darwinism have been found to violate the Clause.
   g. **Accommodations for Religious Students**—Accommodations are generally required under the Free Exercise Clause.
   h. **Religious Activities in Public Schools**—Students may pray, read religious material, or engage in religious activities during student activity times so long as they do not interfere with the school's educational mission. However, school officials should not lead such activities.
   i. **Religious Activities Off School Property**—The same rules apply to school activities that take place off school property, such as football games or field trips.
2. The Free Exercise Clause* gives people the freedom to believe or not believe in a religion and sometimes provides protection to religious conduct. Strict scrutiny applies when the government purposefully targets religious conduct, whereas neutral state laws of general applicability that have only an incidental effect of interfering with religious conduct come under rational basis scrutiny. For example, Native American religious observers may be held subject to a law criminalizing peyote for everyone.
   a. **Applicability to the States**—The Free Exercise Clause applies to the states.
   b. **Meaning of "Religious Belief"**—A court cannot judge the reasonableness of a religious belief, although it may judge the sincerity of a person's religious belief.
   c. **Right Not to Work on the Sabbath**—There is no absolute right not to work on the Sabbath. Still, employers are required to make reasonable accommodations for employees' religious beliefs.

d. **Exemptions from Antidiscrimination and Other Laws**—Under the ministerial exception, a religious institution is not subject to federal and state employment discrimination laws when hiring or firing a minister.

e. **Punishment of Religious Conduct Because It Is Religious**—A state law that is designed to suppress religious activity must pass strict scrutiny analysis. The government must show that the law is narrowly tailored and is necessary to further a compelling state interest.

H. First Amendment Freedoms: The Free Speech Clause

1. **Content-Based Regulation of Protected Expression***—Laws that limit speech based on the substance of what the speech communicates, such as its subject matter, topic, or viewpoint, are subject to strict scrutiny. The government must show that the law is narrowly tailored and is necessary to further a compelling state interest.

2. **Content-Neutral Regulation of Protected Expression and Forum Designations***—In a public forum, the government may generally impose reasonable restrictions on the time, place, or manner of the protected speech, so long as the restriction is narrowly tailored and leaves open ample alternative channels for communication—for example, regulations on the size of signs.

3. **Regulation of Expressive Conduct***—Expressive conduct or symbolic speech is also protected as speech, but it has less protection than actual words. The regulation of expressive conduct will only be upheld if the:

   a. regulation is within the government's power,

   b. regulation furthers an important governmental interest,

   c. interest is unrelated to the suppression of ideas, and

   d. burden on speech is no greater than necessary. For example, the government could stop the burning of draft cards during the Vietnam War because the government needed a smooth-functioning draft system.

4. **Regulation of Unprotected Expression***—Free Speech rights protect neither obscenity nor child pornography.

   a. **Obscenity**
      i. appeals to the prurient interest (excites lustful thoughts);
      ii. depicts sexuality in a patently offensive way; and
      iii. lacks serious literary, artistic, or scientific value.

5. **Regulation of Commercial Speech***—Advertising and other economically related speech is subject to intermediate scrutiny:

   a. The commercial speech must concern lawful activity that is not false or misleading.

   b. The government's interest must be substantial.

   c. The regulation must directly advance the asserted interest.

   d. The regulation must be narrowly tailored to serve that interest. For example, a law prohibiting tobacco billboards within 1,000 feet of schools was struck down because it effectively banned any outdoor tobacco advertising in a city.

6. Regulation of Public School Students and Public Employees, Licenses, or Benefits

Based upon Exercise of Expressive or Associational Rights—School students have a right to free speech, and public employees have a right to free speech so long as they are speaking as citizens about a matter of public concern.

7. **Prior Restraint, Vagueness, and Overbreadth**

   a. **Prior Restraint**—Regulations of speech that occur before the speech is expressed. These regulations are generally unconstitutional, unless there is:
      i. a particular harm to be avoided, and
      ii. certain procedural safeguards protecting the speech (such as a reasonably drawn standard). An example of an activity that would not be unconstitutional would be the publication of troop movements during a war.

   b. **Vagueness**—A statute affecting speech is void for vagueness if it fails to provide a person of ordinary intelligence fair notice of what is prohibited. For example, a law could not prohibit signs that are "annoying." Because what would that mean?

   c. **Overbreadth**—A statute is void if it burdens a substantial amount of other speech or conduct protected by the Constitution. For example, a law that makes it illegal for three or more people to gather on a sidewalk and annoy others—such a law would harm a lot of protected speech so that it would be void for overbreadth.

I. Freedom of the Press

1. **Publication of Truthful Information**—The press has the right to publish truthful information about matters of public concern.

2. **Access to Court Proceedings**—The press may attend criminal trials, but that right may be outweighed by an overriding interest that cannot be accommodated by other means.

3. **Press Access to Prisons to Interview Prisoners**—The press does not have a constitutional right to interview prisoners.

J. Freedom of Association

1. **Electoral Process**—A state can require a primary system where only registered party members and independents can vote in the party's primary.

2. **Bar Membership**—Bar membership may not be denied based on political association, unless the bar candidate knowingly belongs to a subversive organization.

3. **Laws Prohibiting or Punishing Membership in Associations**—A person may generally form, join, or participate in any group or association.

PRACTICE MULTIPLE-CHOICE QUESTIONS

1. During a state election, numerous claims of voter fraud were made. Specifically, the losing party claimed that voters from a neighboring state had infiltrated the process and cast votes, even though they were not state residents and had no intention of residing in the state. In response, the state passed a new law stating that no person could vote in a state election until that person had resided in the state for a full year. A man who moved to the state was

prohibited from voting in the most recent election because he had only resided in the state for six months. Six months later, the man hired you to bring suit on his behalf, claiming his constitutional rights had been violated.

Is the man's suit likely to succeed? **Select one.**

- **(A)** Yes, because the state is unlikely to show that the law is substantially related to achieving an important government interest.
- **(B)** Yes, because the state is unlikely to show that the law is narrowly tailored to further a compelling state interest.
- **(C)** No, because the issue is moot since the man will be able to vote in the next state election.
- **(D)** No, because the state is likely to show that a one-year residency requirement is a rational way to combat the legitimate state interest of stopping voter fraud.

2. A state passed a law that required all lawyers to complete 20 hours per year of state-approved continuing legal education courses. A lawyer could take any class they wanted, whether those classes were directly related to their practice area. If a lawyer failed to complete 20 hours in any particular year, their license was suspended.

You are a third-year law student who plans on building a practice catering to low-income clients. You are considering suing in federal court and arguing that the courses are very expensive and would likely lead to a loss of access to justice for low-income clients, as few lawyers would be able to cater to them and also afford the class fees.

Is your claim likely to be successful? **Select one.**

- **(A)** Yes, because denying access to the courts violates the fundamental rights of low-income clients.
- **(B)** Yes, because there is likely no rational basis to require a lawyer to take classes that may or may not be relevant to their practice area.
- **(C)** No, because you lack standing to challenge the law.
- **(D)** No, because there is no indication that the highest state court has made any decision regarding the validity of the law.

3. A local theater group put on a play called *Eros*. The play was based on a recently discovered manuscript written by a Greek playwright in B.C. 524. In the play, all the performers were nude and acted out various sex acts. After receiving many complaints, the sheriff shut the play down and arrested the performers for violating state obscenity laws. The theater group hires you to challenge their arrest in federal court, arguing that the arrest violated their rights under the First Amendment.

Which of the following two facts, if true, would be most helpful to the group's claim? **Select two.**

- **(A)** Their performance of the play was nominated for a national award.
- **(B)** The performance of the play was sold out every night, whereas the former theater group's plays had little popularity.
- **(C)** Although the performers were nude, the simulated sex acts occurred behind a red curtain that obscured them from the audience.
- **(D)** The play had already been performed by several theater groups in other cities without complaint.
- **(E)** No person under 18 years old was admitted to see the performance.
- **(F)** The sheriff's arrests for violation of the obscenity laws far outpaced other sheriffs in the state.

4. A state study revealed an epidemic in the state of childhood obesity, which could cause a future drain on the state healthcare system as the children grew into adulthood. Many respected studies showed a strong link between candy and childhood obesity. In response, the state enacted a law prohibiting the advertising of candy in any media within the state. A candy company hires you to challenge the law.

Should you argue that the law violated the company's First Amendment rights? **Select one.**

(A) Yes, because there are less restrictive means to protect against childhood obesity.
(B) Yes, because the state is unlikely to show that the law is necessary to further a compelling government interest.
(C) No, because corporations do not have First Amendment rights.
(D) No, because commercial speech regulations only must pass rational basis scrutiny, and it is unlikely the company can show no rational basis for the law.

5. A city government's main building was located on a very busy street with limited public parking. After receiving several complaints from disabled individuals who had business in the building but had to park several blocks away due to public protests in the parking lot and on the sidewalk, the city passed a law stating that it was unlawful for three or more people to assemble for a protest or demonstration in the public parking lot or sidewalk unless that protest or demonstration directly related to matters under consideration by city officials. Violation of the statute was a misdemeanor. Your client, a woman, was arrested after taking part in a demonstration that protested foreign whaling and blocked access to the building.

At trial, should you defend the woman by arguing that the city law violated the First Amendment? **Select one.**

(A) Yes, because public areas such as public sidewalks and parking areas are traditional public forums.
(B) Yes, because the law unlawfully regulates the subject matter of public demonstrations.
(C) No, because the law was a valid "time, place, and manner" restriction.
(D) No, because the city has a compelling interest in providing access to government buildings.

6. A state statute required fire department employees to retire at age 55. The statute stated that retirement at that age was necessary due to the extreme physical demands of firefighting and the increase in workers' compensation claims among fire department employees aged 55 and older. A fire chief hired you to bring a lawsuit seeking an injunction against enforcing the retirement requirement.

Should you argue that the statute violated your client's Fourteenth Amendment rights? **Select one.**

(A) Yes, because the law is unlikely to be necessary for a compelling state interest.
(B) Yes, because the law is unlikely to be necessary for a substantial state interest.
(C) No, because the man is unlikely to show that the law is not rational.
(D) No, because the man is unlikely to show that the law is unnecessary for a compelling state interest.

7. A woman was fired from her job in state government after refusing to work on Tuesdays or Thursdays. She claimed that her religion required worshippers to spend those two days resting and doing "fun" things, such as watching television, going to the movies, or betting at the horse track. When the woman's supervisor asked her more about her religion, the woman said that only her immediate family members were members of the church and that a major tenet of the religion was worshipping her great-grandfather, who was destined to come back from the dead and rule for 2,000 years. The woman sued the state, arguing that her constitutional rights were violated. You are working as a court clerk, and the judge asks you what would be proper considerations for the court in this case?

Which of the following would be an unlawful consideration for the court? **Select one.**

(A) Whether the woman's religious beliefs were sincere.
(B) Whether the woman's religious beliefs were reasonable.
(C) Whether other religions shared the woman's religious beliefs.
(D) Whether many other people shared the woman's religious beliefs.

8. After a disease killed many millions of bees, Congress passed a law regulating the sales of all honey, combs, or other products produced by bees. An Amish beekeeper only sold honey from his backyard hives to his Amish friends and neighbors, and never in amounts that resulted in over $250 in sales. Additionally, all sales proceeds were donated to the Amish community church. The beekeeper hired you as his attorney.

Should you argue that the law is unconstitutional as applied to the beekeeper? **Select one.**

(A) Yes, because the law regulates all sales of bee products without considering whether they moved through interstate commerce.
(B) Yes, because the law violates the beekeeper's free exercise of religion.
(C) No, because there is no guarantee that the beekeeper's products will remain in the state.
(D) No, because individual beekeepers' sales could affect interstate commerce.

9. A woman was hired as a groundskeeper for the state's governor's mansion. Under state law, her position was listed as Employee Level One. Employee Level Ones were paid in weekly segments, resulting in an hourly rate of $5 per hour. After working for the state for a year, the woman hired you to sue the state in federal court, arguing that the $5-an-hour state wage for Employee Level Ones violated the federal minimum wage law, which was $2.25 higher. Before you filed the woman's lawsuit, the state raised the wages of Employee Level Ones, allowing the woman to move up to $8 per hour.

Should you continue with the woman's lawsuit? **Select one.**

(A) Yes, because the state law conflicts with federal law.
(B) Yes, because the state law resulted in an hourly wage lower than federal law.
(C) No, because the state was acting as a market participant.
(D) No, because the woman's lawsuit is now moot.

10. Congress enacted the Healthy Child Act, which authorized the expenditure of federal tax dollars to buy breakfast and lunch for all low-income students at all public and private schools, including private religious schools. Under the act, the food provided would be selected by government nutritionists without regard to any religious restrictions. An advocacy group, Taxpayers for Religious Freedom, asked you to challenge the act in federal court, arguing that the act violated the Constitution.

Is an action on behalf of the group likely to be successful? **Select one.**

(A) Yes, because the act violates the Establishment Clause by spending federal tax dollars to benefit religious schools.
(B) Yes, because the act violates the Free Exercise Clause by not taking religious food restrictions into account.
(C) No, because the act provides tax dollars to both religious and nonreligious schools.
(D) No, because there is no general taxpayer standing.

11. A state passes the Freedom to Work Act, which requires that citizens who receive state welfare benefits work at least 40 hours per week. A single mother recently gave birth to her third child under four years old. The woman has no reliable free childcare and cannot afford to pay a commercial childcare provider. However, she cannot afford to raise her children without her state welfare benefits. Under the act's terms, the state can terminate a state welfare recipient's child custody rights if they cannot either work to receive the benefits or not work and still have the financial capability to raise their children. Because the woman has been unable to work for six months, the state has initiated an action to terminate the woman's child custody rights. The woman has come to you for advice. You think a defense based on the woman's constitutional rights would be most effective.

There is no similar act under federal law. Which of the following constitutional terms should you research in crafting the woman's defense? **Select two.**

- **(A)** Freedom of Choice.
- **(B)** The Fourteenth Amendment
- **(C)** The Fifth Amendment
- **(D)** Fundamental rights
- **(E)** The Privileges and Immunities Clause
- **(F)** The Commerce Clause

12. You are working as an attorney for a U.S. representative. The representative is considering the constitutionality of several proposed laws and would like your input on the matter.

Which of the following laws are most likely to be found constitutional? **Select two.**

- **(A)** To aid food-processing workers injured on the job, Congress passes a law requiring food-processing companies to pay compensation to workers, even if those workers were terminated before the law took effect.
- **(B)** To curb gun violence, a state passes a law restricting the carrying of certain firearms outside the home to those who can show proper cause.
- **(C)** To combat fraud, a regulation requires charities soliciting funds in the state to disclose information about their donors.
- **(D)** To protect voting, a state law bans political insignia from being worn at polling places.
- **(E)** To streamline voting, a state plan redrew two congressional voting districts.
- **(F)** To encourage nuclear power, a state law limits the potential liability of any operator of a nuclear plant.

13. You are working as a state election attorney. The state government has decided to undertake a comprehensive overhaul of voting in the state due to concerns about voter fraud. To do so, state legislators have proposed several new laws. You have been tasked with determining which of the potential new voting laws would be most vulnerable to being deemed unconstitutional.

Which of the following new voting laws are most likely to be found unconstitutional? **Select two.**

- **(A)** All polling places may only be open from 9 A.M.-5 P.M.
- **(B)** A person cannot vote in a statewide election without having been a state citizen for one year.
- **(C)** A person cannot vote in a county election without living in that county for at least 30 days.
- **(D)** Voting can be done by mail for people who do not wish to go to the polls.
- **(E)** At polling places, people must line up to vote in lines of Republicans, Democrats, or others.
- **(F)** A redistricting plan for the state's seven seats in the U.S. House of Representatives places most Black voters in a single district.

14. A State A woman worked at a small grocery store in State B. The store had nine employees, five of whom were from State A and four from State B. State B passed a law that 50 percent of the employees of any business located in State B must be State B citizens. The following day, without warning, the store owner informed the woman that she had been fired because she was the newest State A employee, and the store had to reduce the number of State A employees to four. The woman came to your office to ask whether a constitutional complaint against the store would be successful.

Which of the following constitutional concepts would be most useful for you to research in crafting the woman's constitutional complaint? **Select two.**

- **(A)** Supremacy
- **(B)** Equal Protection
- **(C)** Procedural Due Process
- **(D)** Interstate Commerce
- **(E)** Privileges and Immunities
- **(F)** The Fifth Amendment

15. You are an attorney working for a new congressperson. The congressperson does not have a legal background, although he knows that the legislation he is about to vote on pertains to the Commerce Clause. He asks you what types of things are generally governed by the Commerce Clause.

Which of the following things are least likely to be governed by the Commerce Clause? **Select two.**

- **(A)** Violent crimes against women
- **(B)** A man who grows marijuana only for his own use
- **(C)** A county highway
- **(D)** The Internet
- **(E)** The rental of private vacation homes
- **(F)** Illegal drugs near churches

16. You are an attorney working for the city. For the past 25 years, the city has been hosting live music events in one of its parks. These events have hosted just about every type of music, including country and western bands, rap musicians, rock bands, orchestras, and opera singers. There has never been a sound limitation on the venue because warehouses once surrounded it. However, over the past several years, new residential neighborhoods have been developed near the park. Consequently, neighborhood residents have started complaining about the loud noise of the events, especially at night when they are trying to sleep. Events that have received complaints have included rock bands, rap musicians, and dance DJs, as these tend to be the loudest events held at the park. Additionally, many music events have become overtly political, doubling as political rallies for politicians who appear alongside the musical performances. In fact, these are the types of events that generate the vast majority of complaints because the performers and crowds are often the loudest. However, there is some indication that residents also complain based on party affiliation. The mayor asked you what the city could do to reduce complaints from local residents, but she is concerned about any potential constitutional challenges.

Which of the following things could the city do that would be least likely to violate the Constitution? **Select two.**

(A) Base event lineups on volume: for example, the band likely to be loudest plays at the earliest part of the day.
(B) Specifically inform bands that quieter bands have booking priority over louder bands.
(C) Require the events to end by 10 P.M.
(D) Exclude from the park events that are likely to be loud.
(E) Exclude political messages at music events.
(F) Require all musicians to perform with acoustic instruments.

17. The city wanted to build a new affordable housing complex for its poorest residents. The city's housing department announced a plan to choose a site within one of the city's residential neighborhoods. The department planned to inspect several potential neighborhoods in the city and determine where a new housing complex would have the least impact on the existing neighborhood, as well as where residents would have the easiest access to public transportation and downtown jobs.

Before any neighborhood inspections took place, a neighborhood close to the downtown area was widely considered the likely candidate for the new development. A group of residents from that neighborhood sued the city in federal court, arguing that placing the new development in the neighborhood would be unconstitutional.

You work as an attorney for the city. You have been asked to file a motion to dismiss the neighborhood group's claim.

Which of the following facts would be most useful to highlight in your motion to dismiss? **Select two.**

(A) Poverty is not a suspect classification.
(B) There is no indication of when the site will be selected.
(C) The site of the complex is a political question.
(D) The Eleventh Amendment bars citizen suits of this type.
(E) There is no guarantee that this neighborhood will be selected.
(F) There is no general taxpayer standing.

18. After a highly contested election where the city was covered in large signs supporting the differing candidates and parties, the city passed a beautification ordinance that limited all freestanding signs to 8" by 11" unless the sign was directly linked to a city business and was on that business's property.

A political party hired your firm to challenge the constitutionality of the ordinance.

Which of the following would be the most useful arguments to challenge the ordinance? **Select two.**

(A) The ordinance is a prior restraint on speech.
(B) The ordinance favors some speech over others.
(C) The ordinance is not the least restrictive means of promoting a compelling governmental interest.
(D) The ordinance is not narrowly tailored to further an important government interest.
(E) The ordinance does not leave open alternative channels of communication.
(F) The ordinance is not rationally related to a legitimate government interest.

19. To bring down the federal deficit, Congress passed a statute imposing a 7 percent sales tax on all retail sales of goods.

Several large commercial retailers have announced that they intend to challenge the new statute as unconstitutional. You are an attorney working for the federal government. You have been asked to write a memorandum in support of the new statute.

Which of the following would be the most useful arguments in defending the new statute? **Select two.**

- **(A)** The tax is generally applicable.
- **(B)** Retail sales involve goods shipped in interstate commerce.
- **(C)** The tax is narrowly tailored to further an important government interest.
- **(D)** The tax is rationally related to a legitimate government interest.
- **(E)** The tax is the least restrictive means of promoting a compelling governmental interest.
- **(F)** The tax provides revenue for federal activities.

20. The legislature of a state decided to start a new initiative to improve child health in the state, which was ranked dead last among states in several national studies. To do so, the legislature proposed a law prohibiting fruit-flavored soft drinks from containing words or images that implied they were "healthy" or "natural" unless they contained over 90 percent real fruit juice. A recent study had shown that many overweight children in the state drank primarily soft drinks, as opposed to milk, water, or actual fruit juice. The study noted that part of the problem might be parents' misunderstanding when a soft drink was marketed as "healthy" or "natural."

You are an attorney working for the state. The legislature expected a constitutional challenge to be brought against the new law, so you were given the task of finding arguments to defend it.

Which of the following would be the most useful arguments in defending the new law? **Select two.**

- **(A)** The law is a reasonable restriction on the manner of advertising soft drinks.
- **(B)** The state has the freedom to regulate misleading commercial speech.
- **(C)** The study shows that the law is rationally related to a legitimate government interest.
- **(D)** The law regulates only commercial speech.
- **(E)** The law is narrowly tailored to further an important government interest.
- **(F)** The state is using the least restrictive means of promoting a compelling governmental interest.

ANSWERS

1. The correct answer is (B). The right to vote is a fundamental right, and any restriction on this right (as opposed to administrative restrictions, such as requiring voters to vote at a particular location) is subject to strict scrutiny analysis. Strict scrutiny requires the state to show that the law is narrowly tailored and necessary to further a compelling state interest. (B) states the correct level of scrutiny, and one-year residency restrictions on voting have not passed this level of scrutiny. (A) is incorrect because that states the rule for intermediate level scrutiny. (C) is incorrect because, although the man will be able to vote in the next election, his rights have already been violated, and the new voting law creates a situation where the violation is capable of repetition yet evades review. (D) is incorrect because it incorrectly states the rule for rational basis review by putting the burden of persuasion on the state. Additionally, rational basis would not be the correct level of review.

2. The correct answer is (C). To have standing to challenge the constitutionality of a law, a plaintiff needs to show injury, causation, and redressability. Here, you would be unable to show any injury because you are only a law student and not yet a licensed attorney subject to the law.

(A) is incorrect because you would be unable to use the potential standing of potential clients to gain standing on your own. (B) is incorrect because your lack of standing would end this challenge before you could get to any argument regarding the new law. (D) is incorrect because a federal court does not have to wait until a state court decision before deciding the constitutional validity of a state law.

3. The correct answers are (A) and (C). Unprotected obscenity is an expression that (1) appeals to the prurient interest (excites lustful thoughts); (2) depicts sexuality in a patently offensive way; and (3) lacks serious literary, artistic, or scientific value. If (A) were true, the performers could show that the play had serious artistic value. If (C) were true, the performers could show that the sexuality in the play was not presented in a patently offensive way. The other answer choices would not help the performers. (B) would only show that the play was locally popular, which does not address any of the three elements. (D) is incorrect because the fact that the play had been performed in other cities without complaint shows nothing regarding its artistic value or patent offensiveness. (E) is incorrect because an age limit would not address whether the play was obscene in and of itself. (F) is incorrect because the sheriff's potential bias would not be particularly relevant to the offensiveness issue.

4. The correct answer is (A). Advertising and other economically related speech is subject to intermediate scrutiny: (1) the commercial speech must concern lawful activity that is not false or misleading, (2) the government's interest must be substantial, (3) the regulation must directly advance the asserted interest, and (4) the regulation must be narrowly tailored to serve that interest. Here, there are likely much less restrictive means of achieving the government's goal than banning absolutely all soft drink advertisements in any media whatsoever. (B) is incorrect because the correct level of scrutiny for commercial speech is intermediate scrutiny. "Necessary to further a compelling government interest" is strict scrutiny. (C) is incorrect because corporations do have First Amendment rights and can challenge laws violating those rights. (D) is incorrect because commercial speech regulations must pass intermediate scrutiny, not rational basis scrutiny.

5. The correct answer is (B). A city may impose "time, place, and manner" restrictions on public protests and demonstrations, but it may not base those restrictions on the message content of the protest or demonstration. Here, the law permits certain demonstrations but not others based on the message content, which is unlawful. (A) is incorrect because the law unlawfully regulates message content. (C) is incorrect because the law also unlawfully regulates message content. (D) is incorrect because even if the city has a compelling interest in providing access to government buildings, the law is impermissibly based on message content.

6. The correct answer is (C). In determining whether a law unlawfully discriminates against a person in violation of the Equal Protection Clause of the Fourteenth Amendment, courts examine the basis of discrimination to determine the level of scrutiny to apply. Discrimination based on age does not involve a suspect class or a group entitled to either strict or intermediate scrutiny, so rational basis review will apply. To fail a rational basis review, the plaintiff must show that the law is not rationally related to a legitimate government interest. This is a very difficult test to fail. Here, the law has provided rational reasons for the mandatory retirement rule. Thus, (C) is the correct answer. (A), (B), and (D) are incorrect because they refer to the incorrect levels of scrutiny.

7. The correct answer is (B). It is unlawful for a court to inquire into the reasonableness of any religious belief. (A), (C), and (D) are incorrect because courts may ask whether the woman's beliefs were sincere, shared by other religions, or shared by other people.

8. The correct answer is (D). Congress may regulate interstate commerce under the Commerce Clause. If individual in-state sales could affect interstate commerce in the aggregate, Congress may regulate even individual in-state sales. Here, it is likely that a court would find that intrastate bee product sales have an impact on interstate commerce when considered in the aggregate. (A) is incorrect because the intrastate sale of bee products could affect interstate commerce in the aggregate. (B) is incorrect because there is no indication any religious belief is at issue. (C) is incorrect because application of the Commerce Clause to a law does not require that a product will leave the state.

9. The correct answer is (B). A state law is invalid under the Supremacy Clause if it conflicts with a federal law covering the same subject matter. However, states may give people more protection than a federal floor. Here, the issue is that the state wage law conflicts with the federal minimum wage law, resulting in a minimum wage lower than the federal minimum wage. If the state wanted to implement a higher minimum wage for its residents, it could pass such a law because it would not conflict with the federal law, which guarantees a minimum wage. This makes (B) the best answer. (A) is incorrect because the issue is that the state law results in a wage less than the federal minimum. (C) is incorrect because the market participant rule applies to Commerce Clause issues, and this is an issue regarding the Supremacy Clause. (D) is incorrect because even if the woman now has a raise, she still had over a year of underpaid wages.

10. The correct answer is (C). Government aid to religious entities is allowed if the aid is secular, used for secular purposes, distributed between both secular and religious institutions, and the distribution criteria are religiously neutral. Here, food is provided to both secular and religious institutions, and eating is not considered a religious activity. (A) is incorrect because government aid to religious schools is allowed under the circumstances stated above. (B) is incorrect because there is no indication that the act restricts religious practice. (D) is incorrect because there is taxpayer standing when the law challenged was enacted under the power to tax and spend, and it might violate the Establishment Clause.

11. The correct answers are (B) and (D). (D) is correct because raising one's own children is a fundamental right under the U.S. Constitution. (B) is correct because the Fourteenth Amendment makes rights under the U.S. Constitution applicable to the states, and the question deals with a state act. (A) is incorrect because Freedom of Choice is not a constitutional right. (C) is incorrect because the Fifth Amendment only applies to the federal government. (E) is incorrect because the Privileges and Immunities Clause deals with states discriminating against out-of-state citizens. (F) is incorrect because there is no indication that this act is dependent upon any interstate commerce.

12. The correct answers are (A) and (F). Economic regulations are only subject to the rational basis test, which is a relatively easy test for a law to pass. As (A) and (F) are economic regulations, they are the most likely laws out of the six to be found constitutional. (B) is incorrect, because there is a likely violation of the Second Amendment. (C) is incorrect, as it likely violates Freedom of Association. (D) is incorrect because it likely violates Freedom of Speech. (E) is incorrect because it could violate the Equal Protection Clause.

13. The correct answers are (B) and (F). Voting is a fundamental right. (B) is correct because courts have found that a one-year prohibition on voting is unconstitutional. (F) is correct because courts have found unconstitutional districting plans that unfairly limit a racial group's power in government. (A) is incorrect because rules that involve how voters vote are usually subjected to rational basis analysis, which is very easy to pass. (C) is incorrect because courts have found 30-to-60-day voting prohibitions constitutional (any longer than that causes trouble). (D) is incorrect because there is no general issue with voting by mail. (E) is incorrect because it is also a rule stating how voters will vote, and there is no privacy interest in party affiliation.

14. The correct answers are (D) and (E). Here, by discriminating against out-of-state workers, the state is likely violating the Privileges and Immunities Clause of the Fourteenth Amendment. (A) is incorrect because there is no conflict between state and federal law present in the question. (B) is incorrect because there is no indication that the woman is being treated differently from others similarly situated based on a suspect classification. (C) is incorrect because procedural Due Process only applies to procedures, and there are no facts regarding the procedures in the question. (F) is incorrect because the Fifth Amendment only applies to the federal government.

15. The correct answers are (A) and (F). Congress may regulate the channels of interstate commerce (roads, planes, etc.), the instrumentalities of interstate commerce (cars, trucks, the Internet), persons and things moving through interstate commerce (televisions, kidnap victims), and activities that substantially affect interstate commerce. (A) and (F) are two things that do not necessarily involve commerce or crossing state lines. (B) is incorrect because even if the man grows marijuana only for his own use, that man's marijuana will affect interstate commerce (in that he might not buy out-of-state marijuana). In the aggregate, everyone growing their own marijuana would have a significant effect on interstate commerce. (C) is incorrect because a county highway could be a channel of interstate commerce. (D) is incorrect because the Internet is an instrumentality of interstate commerce. (E) is incorrect because renting out homes is a commercial transaction, and individual home rentals could have a large effect on interstate commerce in the aggregate.

16. The correct answers are (A) and (C). The acts playing at the park have free speech rights in their performances. In a public forum, the government may generally impose reasonable restrictions on the time, place, or manner of the protected speech so long as the restriction is narrowly tailored and leaves open ample alternative channels for communication, which makes (A) and (C) correct. Laws that limit speech based on the substance of what the speech communicates, such as its subject matter, topic, or viewpoint, are subject to strict scrutiny—the government must show that the law is narrowly tailored and is necessary to further a compelling state interest. The other potential restrictions seem based on the performer's message itself, specifically by focusing on what exactly the performer is saying and how they choose to say it. In that case, a restriction is likely to be struck down as unconstitutional. Thus, (B), (D), (E), and (F) are incorrect. While the acoustic instrument thing may seem like no big deal, there are some messages and musical styles that are not super conducive to acoustic instruments (for example, a rap song).

17. The correct answers are (B) and (E). Here, it is likely that the action is not ripe for adjudication because no decision has been made yet, so pointing out these facts would likely be your best move in a successful motion to dismiss. (A) is incorrect because the citing of the complex is not based on any constitutional classification. Who gets to live in the complex might be based on poverty, but that has nothing to do with where the complex is located. (C) is incorrect because the site of the complex would not be a political question. (D) is incorrect because the Eleventh Amendment puts restrictions on suits against a state, not against a city. (F) is incorrect because the neighborhood group is not suing because they are taxpayers. They are suing because they live in the potentially impacted neighborhood.

18. The correct answers are (D) and (E). Because the city ordinance only restricts the size of signs and not their content, it must satisfy intermediate scrutiny. To do so, the city must demonstrate that the ordinance is narrowly tailored to further an important government interest and that it has left open alternative communication channels. If the city cannot show this, the political party will win its challenge. (A) is incorrect because the ordinance does not require government approval of a sign's message before the sign can be displayed. (B) is incorrect because, although the ordinance might favor some speech, this would not be enough to overturn the ordinance. (C) is incorrect because this is the standard for strict scrutiny, and a time, place, or manner restriction does not trigger strict scrutiny. (F) is incorrect because the rational basis standard would not apply in this situation.

19. The correct answers are (A) and (F). Under the Tax Clause of Article I, Section 8, Congress has plenary power to raise revenue through a generally applicable test. Consequently, (A) and (F) would be the most useful arguments to make in defending the new tax. (B) is incorrect because the power to tax does not come from the Commerce Clause. (C), (D), and (E) are incorrect because congressional taxes are not subject to levels of scrutiny analysis.

20. The correct answers are (B) and (D). Under the First Amendment, the government may regulate commercial speech that is false or misleading. Consequently, (B) and (D) would be the best arguments for the constitutionality of the law. (A) is incorrect because the law is not a time, place, or manner restriction. (C), (E), and (F) are incorrect because the issue here is not one regarding the appropriate level of scrutiny.

Contracts

3

Topics with asterisks (*) require you to know the black letter law cold; topics without an * require you to recognize the topic as part of the fact scenario or require you to analyze and apply legal resources provided for the topic efficiently.

MAIN POINT OF CONTRACTS—MAKING AND ENFORCING FAIR AGREEMENTS AS EASILY AS POSSIBLE

OUTLINE

I. IDENTIFICATION OF GOVERNING LAW*

A. **Common Law**—applies to real estate contracts or contracts for services (like mowing a yard)

B. **Uniform Commercial Code, Article 2 (UCC)**—applies to the sale of goods, which are tangible things moveable at the time of sale (spoons, widgets, chocolate bars, etc.)

C. **Hybrid Transaction**—If a contract involves both selling goods and providing services, the predominant test applies—in that case, the applicable law is whatever the predominant purpose of the contract is. A classic example is a contract for new tires, where the garage installs the tires for you. The predominant purpose of the agreement (the thing the buyer wants most) is the tires, which are goods, so the UCC applies. The service of putting on the tires on your car is simply something the garage does for people who buy tires.

II. FORMATION OF CONTRACTS

A. **Mutual Assent**

1. **Offer***—An offer is a communication to the offeree that creates the power of acceptance in the offeree. Example: "Would you like to buy my car for $500?" A common-law offer must contain the parties, the subject matter of the agreement, the price, and the quantity. Look out for *firm offers* (see below). Students always want to find a firm offer when there is none.

2. **Acceptance***—An acceptance is a communication by the offeree to the offeror that the offeree agrees to be bound by the terms of the offer. Example: "Yes! I will buy your car for $500!" An offeree must know of the offer before accepting it.
3. **Manner of Acceptance**—The offeror may dictate the manner of acceptance. For example, the offeror could require that the offeree's acceptance be in writing.
4. **Manifestation of Assent***—For a bilateral contract, acceptance may be made by exchanging promises. For a unilateral contract, where the offeror specifically requests performance, acceptance may only be made by commencing the performance. For example, "I'll give you $500 to paint my fence by tomorrow." For unilateral contracts, look out for someone promising to do something (like mow a yard, paint a fence, etc.).
5. **Offer Terminates***
    a. **Revocation**—The offeror may revoke the offer at any time before acceptance by communicating with the offeree. In addition, if the offeree receives reliable information that the offer can no longer be accepted, the offer is revoked. For example, the offeror offers to sell the offeree their barbecue grill. The next day, the offeree sees his neighbor with the grill. At that point, the offeree knows that the grill has been sold to the neighbor instead, and the offeree can no longer accept. The bar exam loves barbecue grill hypos.
    b. **Lapse**—The offeror can set a time limit for acceptance. If there is not one, an offer lapses after a reasonable amount of time has passed.
    c. **Rejection**—If the offeree rejects the offer, the offer is dead.
    d. **Death**—If either the offeror or offeree dies, the offer terminates.
    e. **Counteroffer**—A counteroffer kills the original offer. Look out for the exact wording of the offeree's alleged acceptance. If the offeree asks, "Would you accept less money for that?" the offer is still alive. If the offeree says, "I'll only pay $50 for that," the offer is dead. The bar exam loves that question as much as it loves barbecue grills.
6. **Mirror Image Rule**—Under the common law, if the offeree's acceptance conflicts with the offer's terms or adds new terms, the acceptance acts as a counteroffer, so the original offer is dead. Under the UCC, an acceptance can include additional or different terms, provided that the acceptance is not expressly made conditional on agreeing to the additional or different terms. If there are additional terms, the agreement's terms are determined by the "battle of the forms." If one party is not a merchant, the additional term can only become part of the agreement if the other party assents to it. If both parties are merchants, the additional term becomes part of the contract unless it constitutes a material alteration, the offer expressly limits itself to its terms, or the offeror objects within a reasonable time.
7. **Limits on Power to Revoke**
    a. **Option Contracts**—An option contract happens when the offeree gives separate consideration to hold the offer open for a certain amount of time.
    b. **Firm Offers**—The UCC allows merchants to create "firm offers" that do not require consideration to be held open. To be a firm offer, the offer must be made (1) by a merchant, (2) signed and in writing, and (3) with an assurance that the offer will be held open for a certain amount of time. Firm offers cannot be held open for longer than three months. The basic idea is that without the firm offer

rule, merchants would have to send consideration back and forth, and that would absolutely slow down business. Additionally, three months is a reasonable timeframe for the offeree to organize their logistics, such as arranging for ships to transport the goods or warehouses to store them. Remember that if the parties give consideration to hold the offer open, it can remain open for longer than three months. That is another favorite question on the bar—a question set up to appear like a firm offer that is too long, but the offeree has given consideration, so it is acceptable.

c. **Reliance**—If the offeree has detrimentally relied on the offer, the offer may remain open as an option contract. For unilateral contracts, this means the offeree has begun performance (not mere preparation). Bilateral contracts require that the offeree has made preparations, and justice requires that the offer be held open (for example, when a general contractor uses a subcontractor's bid in trying to win a contract to build a new building).

8. **Unilateral***—A unilateral contract can only be accepted by performance, not a promise to perform or mere preparation. For example, if the offeror says, "I'll give you $500 to paint my portrait." Buying paints is mere preparation (the offeree can probably use them for something else). Starting the portrait is performance (what else is the offeree going to do with a partially done portrait of the offeror?).

9. **Bilateral***—Bilateral contract is a promise in exchange for a promise. For example, "I'll pay you $500 if you agree to paint my portrait by signing this letter."

10. **Implied-in-Fact Contract**—Intentional conduct by the parties that objectively appears to show that an agreement has been made.

11. **Advertisements**—An advertisement is generally not an offer, but an invitation to make offers. This is because advertisements are disseminated globally with no limit on the number of people who can accept them. However, an advertisement can be an offer if it states a particular price, quantity, and time for acceptance. For example, "Fur coats for $1. First three customers only."

12. **Rewards**—A reward is a unilateral contract that can be accepted like any other unilateral contract. So, if a person posts a reward sign for a missing golden retriever and another person goes into the woods looking for it and finds it, the reward constitutes an enforceable contract. That is the entire point of rewards—to get people to find your golden retriever.

B. Consideration*

1. **Bargained-For Exchange**—Consideration is a legal detriment. It can be a promise to do something or not to do something that a person is otherwise entitled to do.

2. **Adequacy of Consideration**—Courts do not consider the adequacy of consideration unless it is sham consideration, where consideration is recited in an agreement but not actually paid, or nominal consideration, where the consideration is so minor that the agreement was really just a gift.

3. **Past Consideration**—An agreement to pay for something already received will not count as consideration. However, a new promise to pay an old debt after the statute of limitations on collecting it has run out is enforceable without consideration.

4. **Moral Obligation**—A moral obligation, or a general belief that the right thing to do is to enforce the contract, does not count as consideration.

5. **Preexisting Duty Rule**—If a person already has a preexisting duty to do something, that person's doing of the thing does not count as consideration. A favorite example on the bar exam is police officers and rewards because police officers already have a duty to solve crime. After all, that is their job (although if they work on the case outside of their work hours, a reward is enforceable). Another example is an employee doing something exceptional in the course of their duties, and the boss promises them a bonus, only to retract it later. Although the employee did a great job, they were already supposed to do that job, so being great at it cannot be consideration .

6. **Forbearance to Sue as Consideration**—Promising not to sue someone on a claim can count as consideration.

C. Obligations Enforceable Without a Bargained-For Exchange*

1. **Promissory Estoppel**—If a promisor makes a promise that results in foreseeable reliance in the promisee, the promise is enforceable without consideration. For example, I promise to sell you my dog; you go and build a doghouse.

2. **Restitution**—An otherwise unenforceable agreement can be enforceable if it results in one party's unjust enrichment. Upon breach of the agreement, the non-breaching party is entitled to damages equal to what was expected under the contract.

D. Modification of Contracts*

1. **Requirements**—Under the common law, you need consideration to modify an existing contract.

2. **Distinctions Between Modification, Waiver, and Course of Performance**
   a. **Modification**—Changing the terms of the contract, like changing the price.
   b. **Waiver**—Giving up a right in the contract, like not enforcing the due date.
   c. **Course of Performance**—The actions between the parties to a contract, which are considered the best evidence in interpreting what the contract was supposed to mean.

3. **Effect of No-Oral-Modification Clauses**—No-oral-modification clauses in contracts are binding.

E. Contract Formation and Modification Under the UCC

1. **Formation**—A UCC contract can be formed in any way that shows agreement, including mere actions of the parties that appear to show a contract has been formed.

2. **Modification**—No consideration is required under the UCC. The only thing that needs to be shown is good faith.

3. **Gap-Fillers**—The UCC provides provisions to fill in missing terms in a UCC contract.

III. DEFENSES TO ENFORCEABILITY

A. Incapacity to Contract

1. **Minors**—Generally, minors do not have the capacity to contract, and any agreement they make is voidable by them. A "voidable" contract is a contract that can be enforced unless a party chooses to invalidate it. However, for minors, there is an exception for necessities, such as food and shelter. The idea is that in an emergency, a person should be encouraged to make a contract with a minor for necessities even though they are a minor.

2. **Impaired Individuals**—If a person is adjudicated mentally incompetent, then the contract is void. A "void" contract is inherently unenforceable, and neither party can enforce it even if they want to. Suppose the person has not been adjudicated mentally incompetent. In that case, the contract is voidable if the person demonstrates that they did not understand the transaction or were unable to act reasonably regarding it.
3. **Guardianship**—If a person is under a guardianship for mental issues or addiction, they cannot make a contract, and any attempted contract is void.
4. **Influence of Drugs or Alcohol**—A person who agrees to a contract while under the influence may void the contract.

B. Duress and Undue Influence

1. **Duress**—If a person makes a contract because of a physical threat, the contract is void.
2. **Undue Influence**—When determining whether a party made a contract under undue influence, courts look at whether one party sought to manipulate the other party by approaching the other party at an unusual time, using multiple people to persuade the other party, or by alleging that there was time pressure on the deal.

C. Mistake and Misunderstanding*

1. **Mutual Mistake**—If (1) both parties make a mistake regarding a basic assumption of the agreement at the time of contracting, (2) the mistake's effect on the agreement is material, and (3) neither party assumed the risk of the mistake, the contract is voidable. For example, the parties enter into an agreement involving the sale of a cow that both believe is infertile, and the cow unexpectedly gives birth.
2. **Unilateral Mistake**—If only one party makes a mistake regarding the contract, the contract can be enforced according to its terms. However, the mistaken party can void the contract if the mistake renders the contract unconscionable, or if the party that did not make the mistake caused the mistake or should have known the other party was acting in reliance on a mistake.
3. **When a Party Bears Risk of Mistake**—If a party bears the risk of a mistake, that party cannot void the contract based on a mistake.
4. **Misunderstanding in Meaning**—A misunderstanding between the parties regarding the meaning of a term in a contract can be a defense to contract formation. For example, a contract states "dollars," but it is unclear whether it refers to Canadian or U.S. dollars.
5. **Scrivener's Error**—A scrivener's error is a typo in the contract document. A court can use the basic rules of interpreting contracts to fix it.

D. Fraud, Misrepresentation, and Nondisclosure*

1. **Fraudulent Misrepresentation**—A contract can be voided if one party made a false factual assertion to the other that induced the other's justifiable assent to the contract.
2. **Material Misrepresentation**—A misrepresentation that would cause a party to act differently if they knew the truth can make the contract voidable.
3. **Concealment**—A contract is voidable if a party intentionally or unintentionally fails to disclose a material fact.
4. **Nondisclosure**—A contract is voidable if a party knows that nondisclosure of a material fact would be a violation of good faith and fair dealing.

E. Illegality and Public Policy

1. **Illegality**—A contract cannot be enforced if the consideration, purpose, or subject matter is unlawful. For example, a contract to buy illegal drugs.
2. **Public Policy**—A contract is also unenforceable if legislation provides that the contract is unenforceable.

F. Unconscionability Under the Common Law—A contract may be unenforceable if, at the time of the contract, a contract term was so unfair that no reasonable person would agree to it.

G. Unconscionability Under the UCC—If any clause of the contract was unconscionable at the time it was made, the court may refuse to enforce the contract, enforce the remainder of the contract without the unconscionable clause, or limit the application of any unconscionable clause as to avoid any unconscionable result.

H. Statute of Frauds—Certain types of contracts have to be in writing to be enforceable.

1. **Contracts Covered by the Statute of Frauds***—You can remember it with **MY LEGS**—**Marriage**; contracts that cannot be completed in one **Year**; **Land**; **Executory agreements** to pay the debt of another; sale of **Goods** over $500; or **Suretyship**. I remember this by thinking that you can misread "statute of frauds" as "statue of frauds," and I imagine the Statue of Liberty with her leg sticking out.
2. **Satisfaction of the Statute of Frauds***—A writing that contains the essential terms of the contract, basically the subject matter and the amount of goods. The writing must be signed by the party being charged.
3. **Exceptions to the Writing Requirement***—In some cases, a contract usually subject to the statute of frauds can be enforced without a writing.
   a. A confirming memo sent between two merchants and not objected to within ten days of receipt.
   b. An admission in pleading or testimony that there was an agreement.
   c. Detrimental reliance calling for the use of promissory estoppel.
4. **Statute of Frauds Under the UCC***—The UCC also follows the statute of frauds rules for the sale of goods over $500.
   a. **Requirements**—A writing that contains the essential terms of the contract, basically the subject matter and the amount of goods. The writing needs to be signed by the party to be charged.
   b. **Part Performance**—A party can enforce a contract that violates the statute of frauds if the party has already performed part of it.
   c. **Specially Manufactured Goods**—If the goods are specially manufactured for the buyer and are not suitable for sale to others in the ordinary course of the seller's business and the seller has made either a substantial beginning or commitments for procurement, a contract violating the statute of frauds can still be enforced.
5. **Electronic Transactions**
   a. **Uniform Electronic Transactions Act**—An act adopted by every state but New York covering electronic signatures and electronic retention of records.
   b. **Electronic Signature**—Signing something online or on a computer.
   c. **Electronic Record**—A record kept in an electronic database.

IV. CONTRACT CONTENT AND MEANING

A. **Parol Evidence Rule***—Parol evidence is evidence of writings or discussions that did not make it into the final contract.

1. **Partially Integrated Contract**—A contract that is intended to be a final agreement but not intended to include all the details of the agreement. In that case, parol evidence cannot be used to contradict a term of the contract; however, it can be used to supplement the contract. For example, you cannot present evidence that the contract was supposed to be for a blue bicycle if the contract said it was a red one, but you can present evidence that the bike was supposed to come with a horn.
2. **Completely Integrated Contract**—A contract that is intended to be a final agreement of all details. In that case, parol evidence cannot be presented at all.
3. **Exceptions to the Parol Evidence Rule**
   a. **Interpretation**—Parol evidence can always be used to interpret ambiguous contract terms.
   b. **Fraud**—Parol evidence can be used to prove fraud in the agreement.
   c. **Mistake**—Parol evidence can be used to show a mistake was made.
   d. **Conditions**—Parol evidence can be used to show there was a condition precedent to the formation of the contract. For example, two parties make a contract to repaint a house, and the parties orally agree that the contract will not go into effect until the party's spouse says the new house color is acceptable.

B. **Parole Evidence Under the UCC**—If there is no parole evidence available to interpret a contract, the UCC allows evidence of the course of performance, course of dealing, or normal trade usage to interpret an ambiguous contract term.

C. **Omitted and Implied Terms**

1. **Omitted**—Generally, a contract is unenforceable if it omits a material term.
2. **Implied**—A contract term that is not in the contract but is assumed to be in there because of common law, statute, custom, or the parties' apparent intent.

V. PERFORMANCE

A. **Conditions***

1. **Distinction Between Promises and Conditions**—A promise is a contract term that must be met, or there is a breach. A condition is something that must occur before the promise becomes enforceable. For example, a promise is "I will sell you my car for $50." A condition on that promise is, "I will sell you my car for $50 if my wife says it's OK."
2. **Nonoccurrence of Conditions**—If an agreed-upon condition does not occur, the other party is excused from performance.
3. **Excuse of Conditions**—The party that is receiving the benefit of the condition may waive the condition.
4. **Conditions of Satisfaction**—If the condition is that one of the parties must be satisfied with the other's performance, any dissatisfaction must be reasonable and in good faith. If it is, the agreement cannot be enforced.

B. **Obligation of Good Faith and Fair Dealing***—Every party to a contract has the obligation to perform the agreement as intended by the parties.

C. **Performance Under the UCC**

1. **Tender**—A seller must deliver goods that perfectly reflect the contract's terms.
2. **Risk of Loss**—The contract may allocate the risk of loss. If the risk of loss is not allocated, any loss incurred is borne by the buyer upon taking possession of the goods. If the seller is not a merchant, the risk of loss passes to the buyer when the seller declares the goods to be ready for pickup by the buyer.
3. **Title**—Title to the goods is passed from the seller to the buyer according to the terms of the contract.
4. **Rejection**—A buyer may reject goods tendered by the seller. However, the rejection must be made in a reasonable time and with notice to the seller.
5. **Cure**—A seller may cure any problem with the goods before the time for performance has expired.
6. **Acceptance**—If the offeror is not informed of the offeree's acceptance within a reasonable time, the offeror may treat the offer as lapsed.
7. **Revocation of Acceptance**—The buyer may revoke acceptance of goods if the goods' nonconformity substantially impairs the goods' value.

D. **Warranties and Disclaimers Under the UCC***

1. **Creating Express Warranties**—Any sample, description, or affirmation regarding the goods creates an express warranty that the goods shall conform to that sample, description, or affirmation.
2. **Breach of Express Warranties**—If an express warranty is breached, the contract is breached.
3. **Warranties of Title**—The seller warrants to transfer good title to the buyer and that the title is free of any encumbrances the buyer did not know about.
4. **Warranties Against Infringement**—The seller warrants that the goods do not infringe upon the rights of others. However, if the buyer furnishes specifications regarding the goods to the seller, the buyer agrees to hold the seller harmless from any liability arising from the specifications. For example, if the buyer specifies that a mouse doll looks a particular way, the buyer must hold the seller harmless if Disney claims a copyright violation.
5. **Implied Warranty of Merchantability**—Unless the parties agree otherwise, the seller guarantees that the goods will work for their intended purposes. For example, a dishwasher will actually wash dishes.
6. **Implied Warranty of Fitness for a Particular Purpose**—If the seller knows the buyer intends to use the product for a particular purpose, the seller guarantees the product will work for that particular purpose. For example, a phone charger will fit in your particular phone.
7. **Sellers' Defenses to Breach of Warranty**

   a. **Warranty Disclaimers**—The parties may agree to disclaim warranties. If the seller does so in a writing, that writing must be conspicuous. The seller may also exclude implied warranties by saying the good is sold "as is," "with all faults," or some similar language. Warranties may also be excluded if they are excluded in the course of dealing or if the buyer examines or refuses to examine the goods and does not express any concerns about any problems.

b. **Failure to Provide Notice**—The seller may defend themselves by arguing that the buyer failed to provide notice of a problem within a reasonable time.

VI. BREACH AND DISCHARGE

A. Breach*

1. **Material Breach**—If one party does not substantially perform the contract, the other party is excused from performance.
2. **Partial Breach**—If the breach is minor, the nonbreaching party still must perform the contract but may sue for damages. For example, if a delivery of wood were a few days late but did not significantly impede the construction of a house, it would not be considered a problem.
3. **Substantial Performance**—Courts consider whether the breaching party intended to breach, whether the nonbreaching party has received a substantial benefit, any hardship affecting the breaching party, and the extent of any partial performance.

B. Anticipatory Repudiation*

1. **Anticipatory Repudiation**—When one party unequivocally states before the time for performance is due that they will not perform the contract, or if that party commits an action that makes performance impossible. The nonbreaching party has a duty to mitigate damages.
2. **Retraction of Repudiation**—The repudiating party can take the repudiation back unless the other party has sued for breach, acted in reliance on the repudiation, or tells the repudiating party that the repudiation was final.
3. **Demand for Adequate Assurance**—If a party reasonably believes that the other party will not perform, that party may demand an assurance in writing that the other party will complete performance. The worried party may stop their own performance until the assurance is received.

C. Anticipatory Repudiation Under the UCC

1. **Under the UCC**—The nonrepudiating party may wait and see if the repudiating party actually performs or does what it needs to do to remedy the situation. In either case, the nonrepudiating party does not have to complete performance.

D. Impossibility, Impracticability, Frustration of Purpose, and Risk of Loss*

1. **Impossibility**—When an unforeseeable event makes performance of the contract impossible. In that case, neither party has to perform. For example, the parties enter into a contract to buy a car, but someone steals the car and sets it on fire.
2. **Impracticability**—When an event occurs that the parties assumed would not occur, and that event makes performance extremely difficult. For example, an opera singer gets a sore throat the night of the performance.

3. **Frustration of Purpose**—If both parties know the purpose of the contract and that contract may no longer be performed because of an unforeseeable event, the performance may be excused. For example, a landlord knows that the renter wants to use the property for gambling, and the state makes gambling illegal.
4. **Risk of Loss**—In all of the above, the parties may allocate the risk of loss so that only one party bears the responsibility of something going wrong.
5. **Partial Excuse**—The parties to a contract may agree to excuse only parts of the contract.
6. **Temporary Excuse**—The parties to a contract may agree to excuse performance of the contract temporarily.
7. **Force Majeure Provisions**—Contract provisions that free both parties from performance under a contract if something extraordinary happens. For example, a war breaks out or a workers' strike occurs.

E. Impossibility, Impracticability, Frustration of Purpose, and Risk of Loss Under the UCC—The UCC also recognizes impossibility, impracticability, frustration of purpose, and risk of loss.

F. Discharge of Duties: Accord and Satisfaction, Substituted Contract, Novation, Rescission, and Release*

1. **Accord and Satisfaction**—An agreement where the two parties to a contract agree to a substitute performance. Consideration is required, but it can be less than the payment required under the original contract.
2. **Substituted Contract**—A new contract that replaces all provisions of an old contract.
3. **Novation**—Another term for a *substituted contract*.
4. **Recission**—A remedy that allows contract parties to terminate the agreement and act as though the contract never existed. It is often used in the event of a material mistake or fraud.
5. **Release**—A written agreement where one contract party releases the other from performance.

G. Breach of Employment Contracts

1. **At-Will Contracts**—The employer may fire an employee at any time for almost any reason.
2. **Contracts for a Definite Term**—A contract for a definite term sets the term of employment for a specified time. For example, "You are hired for one year from January 1 to December 31."

VII. REMEDIES

A. Expectation Interest: Direct, Incidental, and Consequential Damages*

1. **Direct Damages**—Damages that are a direct result of the breach of contract. Sometimes referred to as the *benefit of the bargain*.
2. **Incidental Damages**—Expenses the nonbreaching party incurs as a result of the breach—for example, the costs of mitigating the damage.

3. **Consequential Damages**—Damages that naturally result from the breach of contract, like lost profits or loss of customer goodwill.

4. **Lost Profits**—Damages for the loss to net profits caused by the breach of a contract.

B. **Causation, Certainty, and Foreseeability***

1. **Causation**—Damages can only be recovered for a breach if the breach caused the damages.

2. **Certainty**—Any alleged damages from a breach must be proven with reasonable certainty.

3. **Foreseeability of Consequential Damages**—Consequential damages must be foreseeable at the time of contracting.

4. **Different Ways to Calculate Damage Award**—Damages are intended to put the plaintiff in the position they would have been in had the contract been performed. Under the UCC, if a buyer receives defective goods, the damages are the difference between the value of perfect goods and the value of the defective goods. If the seller has the goods and the buyer refuses to buy them, the seller may resell the goods and get the difference between the contract price and the resale price, plus incidental damages. If the seller does not resell the goods, the damages are the difference between the contract price and the market price at the time of the breach. If the seller is a lost volume seller (meaning the seller has a virtually unlimited amount of goods to sell), the damages are the seller's lost profits.

C. **Liquidated Damages and Penalties***

1. **Liquidated Damages Clauses**—A contract can state the amount of damages owed in the case of breach, so long as the actual damages would be difficult to calculate and the amount is reasonable.

2. **Penalties**—An unreasonably high liquidated damages clause may be construed as a penalty that will not be enforced.

3. **Enforceability of Agreed-To Remedy Limitation**—The enforceability of any agreed-to remedy depends on its reasonableness.

4. **When Disclaimers of Consequential Damages Are Unenforceable**—A disclaimer of consequential damages is unenforceable if it is unconscionable or violates public policy.

D. **Avoidable Consequences and Mitigation of Damages***

1. **The nonbreaching party to a contract has a duty to avoid those consequences that are avoidable and attempt to mitigate the damages.**

E. **Reformation**

1. **Reformation**—A court-ordered change to a contract to reflect the parties' true intentions.

2. **Equitable Defenses**—A defense the breaching party may use if the nonbreaching party has acted in some unfair way. For example, the idea of "unclean hands."

F. **Specific Performance and Injunction***

1. **Specific Performance**—Can be ordered where money damages may be inadequate, for example, where the money damages cannot be calculated or the

property is unique (like real property or singular personal property—like the *Mona Lisa*). Specific performance may not be ordered in a personal services contract because the Thirteenth Amendment prohibits involuntary servitude. Also, imagine how difficult it would be to enforce—think of trying to get a teenager to clean their room, who will only do half of it to get you off their back.

2. **Injunction**—A court may order a party to do or refrain from doing something called for in the contract. For example, if an employee leaves a company and tries to take the company's clients with them.

G. Reliance and Restitution Interests

1. **Reliance**—When one of the parties changes their position in reliance upon the contract being performed.
2. **Restitution**—A party who has provided a benefit to the other party in a contract is entitled to compensation from the other party.
3. **Restitution for the Party in Breach**—The breaching party may also recover restitution damages if they have provided a benefit to the nonbreaching party.
4. **Circumstances Where Appropriate**—Damages based on reliance or restitution are appropriate where standard damages may not fully compensate one of the parties.

H. Remedies Under the UCC

1. The same types of remedies are available under the UCC as under the common law.

VIII. THIRD-PARTY RIGHTS AND OBLIGATIONS

A. Third-Party Beneficiaries

1. **Intended**—A third party who is intended to benefit from the contract—for example, a creditor or a person receiving the contract performance as a gift. An intended beneficiary may sue to enforce the contract if they justifiably and materially change their position in reliance on the contract.
2. **Incidental**—A person who indirectly benefits from a contract. An incidental beneficiary may not sue to enforce the contract.

B. Assignment and Delegation

1. **Assignment of Rights**—A party to a contract may assign their rights under the contract.
2. **Delegation of Duties**—A party to a contract may delegate their duties under the contract unless the other party has a substantial interest in having that party perform. For example, a contract calls for a Taylor Swift concert. Taylor could not delegate her obligation to play the concert to Metallica.
3. **Clauses Prohibiting Assignment or Delegation**—The law generally disfavors such clauses, but they may be enforced if included in the contract.
4. **Revocation of Gratuitous Assignments**—If the person receiving the assignment has not paid for it, that assignment may usually be revoked.

C. Assignment of Rights and Delegations of Duties Under the UCC

1. The same rules regarding assignment and delegation apply to the UCC.

PRACTICE MULTIPLE-CHOICE QUESTIONS

1. A woman was employed as a creative director for an advertising agency. She created an advertising campaign that went viral, resulting in a new popular catchphrase and a 300 percent increase in the client's sales. Due to the campaign's popularity, the agency's client list tripled, resulting in new profits of over $10 million. The agency's owner called the woman into her office and said that, due to the woman's campaign, the advertising agency was going to expand internationally, and that all this good fortune was a direct result of the woman's efforts. The woman told the owner that the idea for the campaign had been in her mind since college, long before she took the job at the agency. The owner said that she would give the woman a $20,000 bonus at the end of the year in thanks for all her good work and because she would never want to lose her as an employee. Over the next six months, the owner and the woman began to clash after the woman was invited to speak at many advertising conferences and even appeared on television talk shows. Consequently, at the end of the year, the owner stated that she would not be giving the woman the $20,000 bonus after all, as she was taking all the credit for herself and not being a team player. The woman came to your office and asked whether the promise for the bonus was enforceable.

   Is the promise for the $20,000 bonus enforceable? **Select one.**

   (A) Yes, because the owner specifically stated that she did not want to lose the woman as an employee.
   (B) Yes, because the woman had the idea for the campaign before the agency employed her.
   (C) No, because the bonus was a modification of the woman's employment contract and had to be in writing.
   (D) No, because the bonus involved work already performed by the woman.

2. You are an associate doing research for a partner who is interested in the statute of frauds. In which of the following cases is the agreement least likely to be found unenforceable due to the statute of frauds? **Select two.**

   (A) A caretaker orally agrees to take care of a 70-year-old woman for the rest of her life.
   (B) A man orally agrees to transfer an easement to his neighbor.
   (C) A defendant testifies in court that there was an oral agreement to sell his farm.
   (D) A woman orally agrees to buy a new sports car.
   (E) Before getting married, a man and woman orally agree to divide their property 50/50 in the event of divorce.
   (F) A father's oral agreement to pay his son's debt in the event of the son's default.

3. A merchant from the United States visited a parts company in a foreign country. The merchant signed a contract prepared by the company that stated, "In consideration of One Hundred Thousand Dollars ($100,000), the company agrees to provide the merchant with 10,000 Class E metal joints, to be delivered on or before June 16." The merchant received the joints at his factory in the United States and sent the company an international money order for $100,000 in the foreign country's "dollars," which amounted to about $75,000 U.S. dollars. The company wrote to the merchant arguing that the contract was for U.S. dollars and that the merchant still owed the company $25,000 in U.S. dollars. The merchant refused to send any more money, and the company sued the merchant in a U.S. court. The merchant hired you to defend it. At trial, the company owner testified that, before executing the written contract, the parties had agreed that the price would be in U.S. dollars.

Should you object to the company owner's testimony? **Select one.**

- **(A)** Yes, because the written agreement was integrated entirely by providing the parties, goods, price, and time of delivery.
- **(B)** Yes, because the company prepared the written agreement.
- **(C)** No, because the company's testimony does not modify or contradict the written agreement's terms.
- **(D)** No, because the written agreement did not state that the merchant bore the responsibility for loss.

4. An employee worked as a driller for a large oil company. His contract was for a five-year term fixed at $75,000 per year. The employee had worked for two years before the oil company decided to restructure, and as a result, the employee's position was terminated. The employee spent six months searching for a new job, even spending several hundred dollars on the assistance of a staffing service. Although the employee was offered several jobs during this time, none of those jobs were similar to his prior job as a driller. At the end of six months, the employee finally found a similar job as a driller. The employee came to your office and asked whether it was likely a court would award him damages against the oil company.

Is the employee likely entitled to damages? **Select one.**

- **(A)** Yes, for a sum equal to the salary the employee would have received during the balance of the contract term.
- **(B)** Yes, for a sum equal to six months' salary under his employment contract, plus the amount he paid the staffing service.
- **(C)** No, because the employee turned down several job offers during his job search.
- **(D)** No, because the company restructuring terminated the employee's position.

5. A farmer signed a written contract to supply a fruit juice company with several tons of grapes on September 1. Due to heavy rains and a hurricane in June, the farmer did not think he would have enough grapes to fulfill the fruit juice company's order. The farmer called the fruit juice company owner and said that he would be unable to provide more than one ton of grapes on September 1. The company owner said, "If you have anything on September 1, I'll probably take what you have." Immediately after the call, the owner found another landowner who had been unaffected by the rains and hurricane and agreed to deliver all the necessary grapes on September 1. Despite his fears, on September 1, the farmer arrived at the company with all the grapes specified in the contract. The owner informed the farmer that the company would not purchase any of the farmer's grapes because he had already bought them from the landowner. The farmer came to your office to ask about a potential lawsuit against the company.

Is a lawsuit against the company likely to succeed? **Select one.**

- **(A)** Yes, because the farmer's statement that he would not be able to fulfill the contract was not in writing.
- **(B)** Yes, because the company owner did not expressly state that the contract was terminated when he was told that the farmer might be unable to deliver.
- **(C)** No, because the company owner found another supplier after the farmer told him that he would be unable to deliver the grapes.
- **(D)** No, because the farmer told the company owner that he would be unable to deliver the grapes.

6. A farmer hired a farm worker to help him with his wheat harvest. The contract was for a five-year term and paid the farm worker the market price of each bale of wheat harvested.

The contract also provided that the farm worker agreed to harvest a minimum of 1,000 bales of wheat per year, and that if the farmer needed less than 1,000 bales harvested, a liquidated damages clause provided that the field hand would still be paid for at least 1,000 bales at market price, regardless of whether the farm worker actually had to do any work. The following year, the farmer's wheat crop was too small to provide any work for the farm worker. The farm worker sued for breach of contract and requested damages based on the liquidated damages clause. The farmer came to your office and asked if he had a viable defense.

Is the farm worker entitled to judgment in his favor? **Select one.**

(A) Yes, because both parties agreed to the liquidated damages clause.
(B) Yes, because the liquidated damages clause guaranteed that the field hand would receive the benefit of the bargain.
(C) No, because the liquidated damages clause acted as an unenforceable modification without consideration.
(D) No, because the liquidated damages clause was an unenforceable penalty.

7. After recreational marijuana was made legal in her state, a woman looked for property to lease for a marijuana shop. The woman found a suitable recently closed coffeeshop downtown and signed a one-year lease with the landlord. The landlord came by a few times and offered some advice about serving coffee. A month before the store was going to open, the city changed the zoning code so that marijuana shops were not allowed to operate downtown. The woman immediately called your office and asked if she could cancel the lease.

   May the woman cancel the lease? **Select one.**

   (A) No, because the parties had a valid contract to lease the coffeeshop.
   (B) No, because the zoning law was changed after the contract was signed.
   (C) Yes, because the zoning law change made the lease voidable under frustration of purpose.
   (D) Yes, because the zoning law change made the lease void because of impossibility.

8. A woman was engaged to be married and entered a contract to buy a house. Her father wanted to help her financially, so he told her that he would build her a house in a new subdivision that his friend, a builder, was building in a neighboring town. The father gave his daughter a copy of a contract he had signed with his friend to build her a large new house. The woman was delighted and cancelled her contract to buy the other house. At the wedding, the woman and her father had a fight. The father told her that his friend had already refused to build the new house because the woman did not invite the friend to the wedding. The woman told her father that he had terrible friends, and her father responded that he would never deed the realty to the woman or build a house for her because she was spoiled. The woman contacted your office to see if a lawsuit to enforce the agreement with her father would be successful.

   Is a court likely to rule in the woman's favor? **Select one.**

   (A) Yes, because she was a third-party beneficiary of the original contract.
   (B) Yes, because she cancelled her contract to buy the other house.
   (C) No, because there was no consideration for the father's promise.
   (D) No, because the father made a gratuitous gift.

9. A man walked into an art gallery and saw a painting he immediately recognized as being by a famous artist. The man approached the gallery owner and inquired about the painting. The owner stated that he received the painting from another art dealer, who claimed it was one of the last works done by the famous artist and that he was selling it for $1 million. The man

agreed to buy the painting and immediately handed a personal check to the gallery owner. The owner delivered the painting to the man's home. A week later, another artist attended a party at the man's house and claimed the painting was a forgery worth only $100. When the man asked how the artist knew it was a forgery, the artist replied that he had created the forgery himself and showed his signature, hidden in the painting. The man stopped payment on this $1 million check to the gallery owner the next day before the owner had a chance to cash it. The gallery owner sued the man for breach of contract. The man hired you as his defense attorney.

Is a court likely to rule in the man's favor? **Select one.**

(A) Yes, because the man and the gallery owner thought the painting was by the famous artist.
(B) Yes, because $1 million for a painting worth $100 was unconscionable.
(C) No, because there was adequate consideration to support the agreement.
(D) No, because the man, as buyer, bore the risk of loss.

10. A homeowner hired a contractor to build a new bathroom for $10,000. The written contract stated that the contractor would build a new bathroom that met the homeowner's "complete satisfaction." When the bathroom was finished, the homeowner told the contractor that she was not pleased with the result because the cabinets were not square and the bathtub had a noticeable tilt. The homeowner said, "It will take me an extra $1,000 to fix these mistakes, so I'll pay you $9,000 for your work and we'll call it even." The contractor thought the homeowner was being unreasonable but agreed to accept the $9,000. The contractor came to your office to ask about recovering the remaining $1,000.

Is a lawsuit against the homeowner likely to be successful? **Select one.**

(A) Yes, because the modification in payment was not in writing.
(B) Yes, because the contractor thought the homeowner was being unreasonable.
(C) No, because the homeowner offered to pay less for what he thought was an unsatisfactory job.
(D) No, because the modification in payment did not require consideration to be enforceable.

11. A client came into your office and said that she had seen a sign at a county fair that said, "Keep the Fair clean! Pick up a garbage bag of trash, leave it at the front gate, and get $50." A woman next to the sign handed out empty garbage bags. Your client told the woman, "We accept!" Your client then instructed all 10 members of her family to take two empty garbage bags each and fill them as they walked around the fair. At the end of the night, they were walking toward the front gate with their full bags. They saw a man standing in front of a large pile of full garbage bags. He waved and yelled, "You might as well drop those bags! The garbage bag deal is off! We're out of cash!" Your client was upset because her family had spent much more money at the fair than they would have if they had known they would not be receiving the $50 per bag as promised. Your client would like to bring a claim for $1,000 against the fair.

Which of the following two legal concepts would be most useful to research to determine the potential success of your client's claim? **Select two.**

(A) Unilateral contract
(B) Bilateral contract
(C) Option contract
(D) Firm offer
(E) Promissory estoppel
(F) Restitution

12. A buyer, your client, wanted to buy an old house from a seller who had lived there for over 50 years. The seller kept getting cold feet about the sale and pushing back the closing date. You agreed to all the date changes, but the buyer was getting frustrated. As another closing date approached, the seller asked for a ten-day extension. You decided to agree, but you wanted to include language in your agreement email to ensure that another extension would not result in a breach of contract.

Which two phrases should you add to the email to make sure that the seller will be in breach of contract if he fails to deliver the property on the new closing date? **Select two.**

(A) There is a reasonable amount of time between this notice and the new closing date.
(B) Any deviation from this agreement will result in immediate breach.
(C) No further modifications of this sales agreement will be valid.
(D) Time is now of the essence.
(E) This agreement is governed by the Restatement (Second) of Contracts §90.
(F) This agreement is governed by the Restatement (Second) of Contracts §30.

13. Your client, a building contractor, was adding a new air conditioning system to a historic building downtown. She came to your office after the building owner informed her that he would no longer make any payments under the contract and also instructed her to stop working immediately.

Your client was considering filing a lawsuit and asked you what the largest amount of damages she could recover for the building owner's breach of contract was.

In determining your client's potential damages, which two questions would be most useful to ask her? **Select two.**

(A) Why could the building owner no longer make payments on the contract?
(B) How long has the contractor been working on the air conditioning project?
(C) How much has the contractor spent on the project?
(D) How much did the building owner agree to pay the contractor?
(E) What was the contractor's anticipated profit on the project?
(F) How close to complete was the project?

14. On January 17, a woman hired a disc jockey to play at her husband's 60th birthday party for $500. The birthday was on February 27, and the contract stated that she would pay the disc jockey by February 10.

On February 1, the woman received a text from the disc jockey saying that he could no longer play at the birthday party. On February 3, the woman hired another disc jockey for $1,000. On February 6, the woman received another text from the original disc jockey. The original disc jockey said that he revoked his earlier text. Now he was good to play and was looking forward to being paid $500 on February 10.

The woman did not pay the original disc jockey on February 10 and has come to you for advice on whether she will have to pay him eventually.

Which of the following legal topics are most relevant to woman's situation? **Select two.**

(A) Discharge
(B) Modification
(C) Repudiation
(D) Retraction
(E) Unjust enrichment
(F) Breach

15. A man hired an expert musical instrument maker to build him a guitar. In a written contract, the man agreed to pay the instrument maker $15,000 upon delivery of the guitar. When the guitar was delivered, the man did not like it. The man argued in good faith that the instrument maker's building plans were defective, making the guitar unplayable, although there were no problems with the building plans. The man orally offered to pay the instrument maker $8,000 in full settlement of the instrument maker's claim for the original fee. The instrument maker orally accepted the offer. The man paid the instrument maker $8,000. The instrument maker has come to you for advice about whether a claim against the man for the other $7,000 would be successful.

Which of the following legal topics should you research in answering the man's question? **Select two.**

(A) Preexisting duty
(B) Accord
(C) Statute of frauds
(D) Novation
(E) Unjust enrichment
(F) Consideration

16. A woman hired a man to add an extension to her house. The man had a lot of clients and had a construction bid pending for another house. The man orally agreed to build the woman's extension if his pending bid on the other house was not accepted. The woman agreed. The man wrote up an agreement that both parties signed. Although the agreement contained a merger clause, it said nothing regarding the pending bid on the other house.

Two weeks later, the man's bid on the other house was accepted. The man told the woman that he would not be able to build the extension. In response, the woman sued the man for breach of contract.

The man hired you as his attorney. He told you the story and asked if it was likely the court would consider evidence of the party's oral agreement regarding the pending construction bid.

Which of the following legal topics should you research to determine if the evidence of the pending construction bid is admissible? **Select two.**

(A) Illusory contracts
(B) Duty
(C) Accord
(D) Condition
(E) Parole evidence rule
(F) Satisfaction

17. A husband owned a very expensive racing car that he had inherited from his late father. Although his brother often asked to buy the car, the husband always refused.

The husband's wife died, leaving the husband with three children. On the day after the wife's funeral, the brother showed up at the husband's house with an attorney. The brother said that he wanted to buy the car, but this was his final offer, and the husband needed to accept it quickly because the brother had found a similar vehicle at a car dealership. The brother noted that now that the husband's wife was dead, the husband would need to think about saving for his children's college with just one income. Selling the car would provide the husband with money for a college fund. The attorney had already prepared a sales document. The brother offered a price that was lower than the car's accepted value. The husband said, "I don't know if I want to do this." Even so, the husband eventually signed the contract to sell the car to his brother.

Two days later, the husband came to your office for advice on how he could rescind the sales contract.

Which of the following facts would be most useful in rescinding the contract? **Select two.**

(A) The brother's claim that the husband had to accept the purchase quickly.
(B) The husband's statement, "I don't know if I want to do this."
(C) The fact that the brother's attorney wrote the sales contract.
(D) The fact that the brother asked the husband to sign the contract the day after the wife's funeral.
(E) The fact that the husband got the car through devise.
(F) The fact that the brother offered a price lower than the car's accepted value.

18. A man wearing sunglasses walked into a barbershop and sat down in an empty barber chair. Without saying anything to the man, one of the barbers who worked in the shop put a sheet over the man and cut his hair. When the haircut was over, the man stood up and started walking to the front door. The barber stopped him by yelling, "Hey! You owe me $100!" The man responded, "I just stopped in for a rest. I'm blind, and I didn't realize this was a barbershop. I didn't agree to anything. Once you started cutting my hair, I figured it would be worse to stop you because it wouldn't be finished. I didn't want it. And $100 is crazy for a man's haircut! I would never pay that!" The man left. A fellow patron of the barbershop said he knew the man and told the barber his name.

The barber came to your office and asked whether the man owed him $100 for the haircut.

Which of the following legal issues would be most useful for you to research to answer the barber's question? **Select two.**

(A) Statute of frauds
(B) Unilateral contract
(C) Implied-in-fact contract
(D) Unjust enrichment
(E) Objective theory of contracts
(F) Promissory estoppel

19. A seller entered into a contract to sell her motorcycle to a buyer for $20,000. The contract stipulated that time was of the essence and that payment and delivery of the motorcycle were to occur on January 8. The buyer said that the motorcycle was not exactly what he was looking for, but that it was a good deal for that type of motorcycle. On January 3, the buyer texted the seller and said that he might not have the $20,000 by January 8. The seller did not respond to the text. On January 6, the seller sold the motorcycle to a local lawyer for $10,000. She then texted the buyer and said that she planned to sue the buyer for breach of contract to recover the difference in the purchase price.

The buyer came to your office to ask for your help in defending him from the seller's threatened lawsuit.

Which of the following facts would be most useful in defending the buyer from the seller's suit? **Select two.**

(A) The buyer stated that the motorcycle was not exactly what he was looking for.
(B) The seller stated that time was of the essence.
(C) The buyer stated that he might not have the $20,000 by January 8.
(D) The buyer refused an option contract.
(E) The seller's failure to respond to the buyer.
(F) The seller is selling the motorcycle on January 6.

20. A man came to your office and said a woman had offered to buy a restaurant space from him if the woman could get the necessary permits. Three weeks later, the woman informed the man that she could not obtain the permits, so she would not be purchasing the space. However, the man had a friend who worked in the city permitting office and told him that, as far as he knew, the woman never applied for any permits.

The man is considering a lawsuit against the woman for breach of contract.

Which of the following two legal terms would be most useful to research in determining the potential success of the man's lawsuit? **Select two.**

(A) Conditions
(B) Frustration of purpose
(C) Parole evidence rule
(D) Obligation of good faith and fair dealing
(E) Impossibility
(F) Impracticability

ANSWERS

1. The correct answer is (D). A promise generally needs consideration to be enforceable. Importantly, past consideration is not sufficient consideration to support a promise. Here, the owner's promise to pay the bonus was made for work already done by the woman, and that work was part of the woman's job. The simple fact that the woman did her job particularly well in this instance would not make the owner's promise enforceable. (A) is incorrect because, although the owner said she did not want to lose the employee, there is no indication that the employee stayed at the agency longer than she might have based on the bonus (which could have provided sufficient consideration). (B) is incorrect because although the woman had the idea before the agency employed her, there is still insufficient consideration to support the owner's promise. (C) is incorrect because this bonus would not need a writing if it were supported by consideration. Importantly, it would not be a modification of the employment contract, would not be a promise incapable of being fulfilled in one year, and would not involve the sale of any goods. Be cautious of questions where the promise appears morally justifiable but is ultimately gratuitous.

2. The correct answers are (A) and (C). The statute of frauds requires certain agreements to be in writing. It applies to contracts in anticipation of marriage, contracts that cannot be completed within one year, land sales, executory agreements to pay the debt of another, the sale of goods exceeding $500, or suretyship. There is also an exception to the statute of frauds if one of the parties testifies in court to the existence of a contract. Here, (A) is correct because the woman may live less than a year; consequently, the contract is capable of being performed within one year. (C) is correct because the defendant testified that there was an oral agreement to sell his farm, which is an exception to the statute of frauds. (B) is incorrect because it involves a land sale. (D) is incorrect because a car is a good, and a new sports car is unlikely to cost less than $500. (E) is a contract in anticipation of marriage. Finally, (F) is an agreement to pay the debt of another.

3. The correct answer is (C). Parol evidence prohibits introducing evidence of prior or contemporaneous oral agreements that contradict, change, or modify a written agreement. However, parol evidence can always be used to interpret ambiguous contract terms. Here, the contract was ambiguous regarding the type of dollar it referred to. Since the evidence is being presented to clarify this ambiguous term, the court would overrule your objection. (A) is incorrect because parol evidence can be used to explain an ambiguous term in an agreement, even if the agreement is completely integrated. (B) is incorrect because the fact that the company prepared the written agreement does not change the analysis. (D) is incorrect because an agreement stating that one party or another bore the risk of loss would be irrelevant to the analysis.

4. The correct answer is (B). A nonbreaching employee is entitled to receive the entire contract price for the balance of the term plus consequential damages, less any damages avoided by mitigation. Here, since the employee mitigated his damages by taking the new job after six months of searching, he is entitled to compensation for the period between his termination and the start of his new job. He is also entitled to recover the fee he paid the staffing company as consequential damages. (A) is incorrect because the employee mitigated his damages by accepting a similar job. (C) is incorrect because although the employee had a duty to mitigate damages, this did not mean he had to accept absolutely any job he was offered. (D) is incorrect because the reason the employee was terminated does not change the analysis.

5. The correct answer is (C). If one of the parties to a contract tells the other that they will not perform their contractual duties, the other party may treat the statement as an anticipatory repudiation and immediate breach of the contract. However, a party may retract the repudiation before the time for performance, provided the other party has not relied on it. Here, because the company owner relied on the farmer's repudiation and found another supplier, the farmer may not withdraw his repudiation, and the company is relieved of any obligation under the contract. (D) is incorrect because the farmer could have withdrawn his repudiation if the company had not acted upon it. (A) is incorrect because an anticipatory repudiation does not need to be in writing. (B) is incorrect because the company did not have to expressly state that the contract was terminated before acting on the anticipatory repudiation.

6. The correct answer is (D). A liquidated damages clause will not be enforced if it is a penalty intended to punish one of the parties for breaching the contract. In determining whether a liquidated damages clause is an unenforceable penalty, courts look to whether the clause is tied to lost gross revenues, lost profits, or something else not tied to actual losses. Here, the farm worker receives the same pay whether they work or not. Consequently, it is not tied to any actual loss the farm worker might suffer. Since the clause acts as a penalty, a court will not enforce it. (A) is incorrect because a liquidated damages clause may still act as an unenforceable penalty even if both parties agree to it. (B) is incorrect because the clause acts as a penalty. (C) is incorrect because a liquidated damages clause does not act as a contract modification.

7. The correct answer is (A). Here, the parties had a valid agreement to rent the coffeeshop. Importantly, the landlord had no reason to know that the woman intended to use the coffeeshop as a marijuana store. Consequently, when the zoning law changed, there was no reason for the landlord to suspect anything was wrong regarding the lease. If the question had stated that the landlord knew of the woman's plan, she might have avoided enforcement of the agreement through frustration of purpose. (B) and (C) are incorrect because the landlord did not know why the woman was renting the coffeeshop. (D) is incorrect because impossibility refers to situations where performance of the contract is literally impossible (for example, the coffeeshop was destroyed by an 18-wheel truck driving into it).

8. The correct answer is (B). Promissory estoppel may be used to enforce an agreement not supported by consideration if the promisee reasonably relied on the promisor's promise to their detriment. Here, since the woman reasonably relied on her father's promise and cancelled the contract for the sale of the house to her detriment, she may be permitted to enforce her father's promise. (A) is incorrect because the fact that the woman was a third-party beneficiary would not give her special rights to enforce her father's promise. (C) and (D) are incorrect because the father's promise may be enforced through promissory estoppel.

9. The correct answer is (A). If both parties are acting under a mutual mistake regarding the subject of the contract, either party may choose not to perform. Here, since both parties wrongly believed that the painting was by the famous artist, neither party will be forced to perform the agreement. (B) is incorrect because unconscionability would only come into play if the parties were in unequal bargaining positions and one of them deliberately withheld information from the other. (C) is incorrect because the parties were acting under a mutual mistake. (D) is incorrect because there is no rule stating that a buyer automatically assumes the risk of loss.

10. The correct answer is (C). An accord and satisfaction is when the parties agree to lesser obligations under the contract. Like other agreements, an accord and satisfaction must be supported by sufficient consideration. Here, the homeowner received the benefit of a lower price. The contractor benefited from the homeowner not seeking damages for the poor work, as his belief that the job was unsatisfactory was likely reasonable, considering the cabinets were not square and the bathtub had a noticeable tilt. Consequently, the parties here entered into an accord and satisfaction, and the second agreement between the parties was enforceable. (A) is incorrect because there was a valid accord and satisfaction. (B) is incorrect because the homeowner's belief appeared to be reasonable. (D) is incorrect because the parties had a valid accord and satisfaction.

11. The correct answers are (A) and (C). Under the Restatement (Second) of Contracts §45, the fair's poster was an offer for a unilateral contract, which became an option contract once the client's family began performance. Once the family started picking up garbage, the fair could not revoke the offer. (B) is incorrect because a bilateral contract is a promise for a promise, not a promise for an action. (D) is incorrect because a firm offer is an offer for the sale of goods between merchants. (E) is incorrect because this unilateral contract can be enforced without resorting to promissory estoppel. Additionally, the offer here does not meet the requirements of promissory estoppel. (F) is incorrect because restitution is a concept associated with unjust enrichment, which is not occurring here.

12. The correct answers are (A) and (D). Because the original closing date kept changing, the initial contract did not state that time was of the essence. A later writing can make time of the essence if it states that time is now of the essence, and if the new agreement gives a reasonable amount of time between the notice and the new closing date. Including these two phrases would be most useful for achieving your goal. (B) is incorrect because it does not address the two things needed to make time of the essence in a later writing. (C) is incorrect because a change in the closing date would be a modification of the sales agreement. (E) is incorrect because this is the Restatement section dealing with promissory estoppel. (F) is incorrect because this is the Restatement section that deals with proper acceptance.

13. The correct answers are (C) and (E). If the contractor recovers the amount she has paid for the project plus her anticipated profit, she will be put in the position she would have been if the breach had not occurred. Thus, (C) and (E) are correct under Restatement (Second) of Contracts §347. (A) is incorrect because the building owner's reason is likely irrelevant, and (C) and (E) are much better answers. (B) is incorrect because it is also irrelevant. The costs of labor and materials are relevant, as reflected in answer (C). The time spent is not necessarily indicative of anything. (D) is incorrect because the amount the contractor expected to be paid is not the clearest calculation of damages. (F) is incorrect because this is irrelevant to damages.

14. The correct answers are (C) and (D). Here, the original disc jockey tried to repudiate his agreement with the woman, making (C) correct. A repudiating party may generally retract a repudiation so long as the other party has not materially changed their position in reliance on the repudiation.

This makes (D) correct, and the retraction was invalid because the woman hired another disc jockey before the original disc jockey wrote to retract his repudiation. These will be the two most important issues in this situation. (A) is incorrect because discharge refers to an occurrence that releases the parties from their contractual obligations. (B) is incorrect because modification refers to a change in the original agreement. (D) is incorrect because unjust enrichment occurs when one party gives a benefit to another without that party receiving compensation. (F) is incorrect because the big issue here is whether the disc jockey successfully retracted his repudiation.

15. The correct answers are (B) and (F). An oral agreement to accept a lesser payment in a contract is an accord. To settle an agreement with an accord, there must be a good-faith dispute as to the amount owed under the contract. The dispute gives the agreement the appropriate consideration to support it. Since both accord and consideration were present, the agreement was discharged through accord and satisfaction, and the instrument maker may not recover. (A) is incorrect because the preexisting duty rule states that part payment of an undisputed debt will not discharge the debt because there is no consideration. (C) is incorrect because the statute of frauds would not apply in this situation. (D) is incorrect because a novation occurs when a party to a contract is replaced by a third party, which is not happening here. (E) is incorrect because unjust enrichment occurs when one party gives a benefit to another without that party receiving compensation.

16. The correct answers are (D) and (E). The parol evidence rule generally prohibits evidence of writings or discussions that were not included in the final contract. However, there is an exception that allows evidence of any conditions to be added to the contract. Consequently, the two big issues here will be (D) and (E). (A) is incorrect because the parties made clear commitments to each other, so the contract was not illusory. (B) is incorrect because duty is not an issue in this case. (C) and (F) are incorrect because the parties are not trying to settle a prior agreement, which would bring in the issues of accord and satisfaction.

17. The correct answers are (A) and (D). Here, it looks like the husband has a pretty good claim for undue influence in the making of the contract. When determining whether a party signed a contract under undue influence, courts look at whether one party sought to manipulate the other party by approaching the other party at an unusual time, using multiple people to persuade the other party, or by alleging that there was time pressure on the deal. Here, (A) and (D) are examples of facts that would be useful in claiming that the contract should be rescinded due to undue influence. (B) is incorrect because this ambiguous statement does not really support a claim of undue influence. (C) is incorrect because the authorship of the contract would not add to the undue influence analysis. (E) is incorrect because the fact that the husband got the car through devise is irrelevant. (F) is incorrect because the brother offering a lower price would not support undue influence.

18. The correct answers are (C) and (E). An implied-in-fact contract can be created by intentional conduct by the parties that objectively appears to show that an agreement has been made. Here, the man sitting in the barber chair, the barber cutting his hair, and neither saying anything would likely create an implied-in-fact contract for the haircut. (E) is correct because courts look at whether the situation objectively appeared as if the parties intended a contract. (A) is incorrect because the statute of frauds would not apply to this situation. (B) is incorrect because this situation was not necessarily a unilateral contract that could only be accepted by performance. (D) is incorrect because an otherwise unenforceable agreement can be enforceable if it results in one party's unjust enrichment. Here, the implied-in-fact contract is likely enforceable. (F) is incorrect because promissory estoppel only comes in if there is an unenforceable contract.

19. The correct answers are (C) and (F). Here, the seller would likely argue that the buyer anticipatorily repudiated the contract by stating that he might not have the money by January 8. To cancel a contract through anticipatory repudiation, a party must clearly communicate an intention not to perform or commit an action that shows the party does not intend to perform. Here, "I might" does not clearly repudiate the contract when the money and delivery was not due until several days later. Thus, the buyer did not repudiate. However, the seller did repudiate the contract when she sold the motorcycle to the lawyer. Consequently, the buyer cannot be found liable for the difference in purchase price. (A) and (B) are incorrect because they would be irrelevant to the buyer's defense. (D) is incorrect because that might actually hurt the buyer's defense. (E) is incorrect because the seller's failure to respond was irrelevant.

20. The correct answers are (A) and (D). Here, the most important concepts to research would be conditions because there was a condition on the contract that the woman get the required permits, and the obligation of good faith and fair dealing because the woman had an obligation to actually try and get the necessary permits. (B) is incorrect because frustration of purpose is when both parties know the purpose of the contract and that contract may no longer be performed because of an unforeseeable event. (C) is incorrect because promissory estoppel only comes into play when there is no potentially enforceable contract, making this not as strong an answer as (A) and (D). (E) is incorrect because it refers to when a contract has been made impossible by some event. (F) is incorrect because it refers to a situation where a contract becomes impracticable, which is not the case here.

Criminal Law and Constitutional Protections of Accused Persons

4

Topics with asterisks (*) require you to know the black letter law cold; topics without an * require you to recognize the topic as part of the fact scenario or require you to analyze and apply legal resources provided for the topic efficiently.

MAIN POINT OF CRIMINAL LAW—MAKING SURE THAT THE STATE PROVES ITS CASE AGAINST THE ACCUSED

OUTLINE

I. GENERAL PRINCIPLES

A. Acts and Omissions

1. **Voluntariness**—To be liable for a criminal act, the act must be physical and voluntary. Consequently, acts done while sleepwalking, under hypnosis, due to convulsions, etc., do not create criminal liability.
2. **Omission as an Act**—Failing to do an act creates criminal liability only if the act is imposed by a statute (*e.g.*, filing taxes), imposed by a contract (*e.g.*, being a lifeguard), created by a special relationship (*e.g.*, parent/child), left the victim in a worse condition than the victim was found in, or when a person fails to aid the victim after causing the danger in the first place. Just like in torts, mere bystanders have no duty to act to save anyone.
3. **Possession as an Act**—Knowingly possessing an unlawful item is considered a criminal act.

B. **State of Mind**

1. **Intent or Purpose**

   a. **Specific**—The defendant must want to accomplish the prohibited crime (*e.g.*, first-degree murder).

   b. **General**—The defendant must want to perform an unlawful act (*e.g.*, kidnapping—A defendant does not necessarily want to commit a crime in that case; they just want to carry off the victim).

   c. **Motive**—The reason someone wants to commit the crime. Motive has nothing to do with intent.

2. **Knowledge**—The defendant is aware that their conduct is of the type required for the crime.

3. **Recklessness**—The defendant acts with a conscious disregard of a substantial and justifiable risk that a crime will result from his or her conduct.

4. **Criminal Negligence**—The defendant should have known of a substantial and unjustifiable risk that a crime would result from their conduct.

5. **Mistake of Law or Fact**

   a. **Mistake of Law**—Ignorance of the law is not a defense unless the defendant relied on an official decision, the statute defining the not obviously wrong crime was not reasonably available, or the defendant's honest mistake of law negated the specific intent required for the crime.

   b. **Mistake of Fact**—An honest, unreasonable mistake of fact is a defense to a specific intent crime. In contrast, an honest, reasonable mistake of fact is a defense to a general intent crime.

C. **Defenses**

1. **Provocation**—Where a defendant is provoked to commit a criminal act out of passion. While mere words or insults are not considered adequate provocation, battery, threats of the use of deadly force, or discovering a spouse committing adultery count. The most common example is the defendant murdering someone in bed with their spouse. In that case, murder is reduced to voluntary manslaughter.

2. **Intoxication**—Voluntary intoxication is a defense to specific intent crimes if the intoxication negates the necessary intent. However, voluntary intoxication is not a defense if the person forms the intent to commit the crime and then gets intoxicated (*e.g.*, a person decides to murder a rival, then drinks to get brave enough to do it). Involuntary intoxication is a defense when it negates an element of the crime. However, the intoxicating substance must have been ingested without knowing it was intoxicating or taken under duress.

3. **Self-Defense**—A defendant may defend themselves from imminent harm. However, the defendant may only use the amount of force necessary to stop the attack. Deadly force may be used to prevent death or serious bodily injury.

4. **Defense of Others**—A defendant may defend another person according to the same rules that apply to self-defense.

5. **Defense of Property**—A defendant may use reasonable force to defend property, but deadly force may only be used to prevent an intruder from forcibly entering their home.

D. Jurisdiction

1. **Federal**—The federal government has jurisdiction over crimes involving federal law, crossing state lines, or occurring on federal property.
2. **State**—The majority of criminal law is state law.

E. Burdens of Proof and Persuasion*

1. **Presumption of Innocence**—A defendant is considered innocent until proven guilty beyond a reasonable doubt.
2. **Reasonable Suspicion**—A police officer must have an objectively reasonable suspicion, based on the totality of the circumstances, that criminal activity is about to occur, is occurring, or has occurred. Reasonable suspicion is a lower standard than probable cause and is used in determining the reasonableness of an investigative stop.
3. **Probable Cause**—The facts and circumstances of the situation would warrant a reasonably prudent person to believe a crime had been committed or was being committed. Probable cause most often appears in questions involving arrests or search warrants.
4. **Proof Beyond a Reasonable Doubt**—The evidence convinces the jury that there is no other reasonable explanation.
5. **Prosecution Burden of Proof**—The prosecution must prove every element of a crime beyond a reasonable doubt.
6. **Defense Burden of Proof**—The defendant has no burden to prove their innocence.
7. **Defendant's Right to Present Evidence**—The defendant has the right to present evidence that may create reasonable doubt as to an element of the alleged crime.

II. STATUTORY CRIMES

A. Homicide (Including Felony Murder)

1. **Intent**
   a. **Homicide**—The defendant had the intent to kill.
   b. **Felony Murder**—An unintended killing proximately caused by the defendant engaging in an inherently dangerous felony. Those felonies are **b**urglary, **a**rson, **r**ape, **r**obbery, and **k**idnapping. Remember the felonies with the acronym BARRK: Imagine a dangerous dog, who is also a pirate (to get the double Rs). Usually, the goofier the memory aid, the more effective it tends to be.
   c. **Vehicular Manslaughter**—When a person's illegal or negligent use of a motor vehicle kills someone.
2. **Homicide Offenses**
   a. **Intentional Murder**
      i. **Premeditated**—The defendant planned to kill the victim.
      ii. **Impulsive**—When the defendant kills the person out of sudden anger, jealousy, etc.
   b. **Manslaughter**
      i. **Provocation**—Sufficient provocation will lower an intentional murder to manslaughter. Remember, for voluntary manslaughter, the defendant totally meant to kill the victim but was just acting out of extreme emotion. Most of the time, it is the defendant who catches their spouse in bed with someone else.

ii. **Extreme Emotional Disturbance**—A similar defense to provocation. Basically, the defendant defends their actions by claiming they committed the crime out of extreme fear, anger, or sadness.

c. **Unintentional Murder**

i. **Depraved Indifference**—Also known as *depraved heart murder*, occurs when the defendant acts in such a way that they are very likely to kill or seriously injure someone (*e.g.*, driving on a crowded sidewalk).

ii. **Recklessness**—basically the same as *depraved indifference*

iii. **Criminal Negligence**—When a defendant kills another person through criminal negligence. For example, a train engineer failing to check the train's brakes properly and killing a commuter crossing the tracks.

B. **Theft**

1. **Statutory Theft**—Also known as *larceny*, theft is the trespassory taking of another person's personal property with the intent to deprive that person of the property permanently.
2. **Aggravated Theft**—Theft with additional factors, such as force, threats, coercion, or high-value property. Different from robbery in that the force or threats may not necessarily threaten direct and imminent harm.
3. **Defenses to Theft**—entrapment, lack of intent to steal, intent to borrow, mistaken belief as to ownership of the property, believing the property is one's own, and the property owner's consent

C. **Burglary**

1. **Statutory Burglary**—breaking and entering a building with the intent to commit a crime therein
2. **Aggravated Burglary**—burglary with additional factors, such as the defendant had a deadly weapon with them or assaulted or battered someone
3. **Defenses to Burglary**—entrapment, alibi, consent, and lack of intent

D. **Robbery**

1. **Statutory Robbery**—taking another person's property through direct and imminent force or threat of violence
2. **Aggravated Robbery**—robbery with additional factors, such as using a deadly weapon or other serious threats of violence
3. **Defenses to Robbery**—no intent to steal, duress, belief that the property belongs to the defendant, and no actual force or intimidation

E. **Assault and Battery**

1. **Statutory Assault and Battery**—Assault is either the attempt to commit a battery or intentionally placing another person in apprehension of imminent bodily harm. In contrast, battery is the unlawful application of harmful force to another person. Many modern criminal codes combine the two.
2. **Aggravated Assault and Battery**—Assault and battery with additional factors, such as use of a deadly weapon or intentionally causing serious bodily harm.
3. **Defenses to Assault and Battery**—self-defense, defense of others, lack of intent, consent, and accident

F. **Possession and Trafficking Offenses**

1. **Statutory Possession Crimes**—the possession of unlawful items, such as the unlawful possession of a firearm or possession of unlawful drugs
2. **Possession with Intent to Distribute**—possession of controlled substances with the intent to sell or distribute them
3. **Contraband Trafficking Crimes**—the unlawful transporting, selling, or distributing of controlled substances
4. **Defenses to Possession and Trafficking Offenses**—entrapment, duress, lack of intent, and police misconduct

G. **Operating a Motor Vehicle While Impaired or Under the Influence and Vehicular Manslaughter**

1. **Driving While Impaired or Under the Influence**—operating a motor vehicle while under the influence of an intoxicating substance
2. **Vehicular Manslaughter**—when a driver's negligent or illegal operation of a motor vehicle causes the death of another person
3. **Defenses to Driving While Impaired or Vehicular Manslaughter**—sudden medical emergency, hazardous road conditions, and lack of negligence or impairment

III. INCHOATE CRIMES AND PARTIES TO A CRIME

A. **Attempt**

1. **Elements**—a substantial step toward the commission of a crime with the specific intent to commit the crime
2. **Defenses**—abandonment, lack of intent, mistake of fact, excuse, and legal impossibility
3. **Actus Reus**
   a. **Substantial Step**—Must be more than mere preparation for crime; however, actions like lying in wait for a victim, unlawful entry into a place where the crime is intended to occur, possession of materials designed specifically for the crime, and possession of criminal materials near the place of commission of the crime are generally considered to be more than mere preparation.
4. **Intent**
   a. **General**—Specific intent must generally be shown even if the underlying crime is a general intent or strict liability crime.
   b. **Specific**—The defendant must have the specific intent to perform the crime.
5. **Lesser Included Offenses**—Most jurisdictions consider an attempt to be a lesser included offense of the completed crime.
6. **Merger Doctrine**—Historically, if a defendant's actions constitute both a misdemeanor and a felony, the misdemeanor merges into the felony, meaning the defendant may only be convicted of the felony. Modern criminal law does not apply the merger doctrine when considering misdemeanors and felonies, but it does apply it to solicitation (persuading someone to commit a crime) and attempt. Consequently, a defendant can only be convicted of solicitation

and the completed crime or attempt and the completed crime. Finally, a defendant may be concurrently prosecuted but not punished for more than one inchoate crime connected to the same completed crime.

B. Conspiracy

1. **Elements**—An agreement between two or more persons to commit a crime. Modern criminal law generally requires an overt act to commit the crime as well.
2. **Defenses**—lack of an agreement, withdrawal, duress, and lack of intent
    a. **Withdrawal**—To withdraw from a conspiracy, a defendant must do some affirmative act to withdraw, must communicate that withdrawal to all coconspirators, and must withdraw before the conspiracy's goal is completed.
3. **Liability of Coconspirators for a Substantive Crime**—Coconspirators may be found guilty of substantive crimes committed by their coconspirators.

C. Parties to Crime

1. **Accomplice**—A person who intentionally aids another in committing a crime. An accomplice is subject to the same liability as the defendant and is typically present when the crime is committed.
2. **Accessories Before the Fact**—a person who intentionally aids or encourages a crime but who is not present when the crime is committed
3. **Accessories After the Fact**—a person who helps a defendant who has already committed a crime, with the intention of having them avoid arrest

IV. CONSTITUTIONAL PROTECTIONS OF ACCUSED PERSONS

A. Arrest, Search, and Seizure (Fourth Amendment)

1. **Search***
    a. **Reasonable Expectation of Privacy**—A search occurs when the government intrudes upon a person's reasonable expectation of privacy. Look for questions where a defendant lacks standing to challenge the search, like when another person's car is searched and produces evidence against the defendant. Also, look if the government is using a private actor to conduct the search, such as asking a principal to search a child's locker.
    b. **Open Fields**—A person does not have a reasonable expectation of privacy in property outside the curtilage of one's home—for example, a farmer's fields.
    c. **Surveillance**—The government may not conduct warrantless surveillance using devices that are not in use by the general public and reveal information that would not be accessible without a physical search, such as a thermal-imaging device. The use of a device to eavesdrop on a private phone conversation may also constitute an unlawful search.
    d. **Technological Information Gathering**—Installing a physical device to track a car or person may result in a search. A technological search that intrudes on a person's reasonable expectation of privacy is also a search—for example, opening someone's cell phone to look at the pictures on it.
    e. **False Friends**—There is no reasonable expectation of privacy when talking to others, even if that person is a government agent or informant.

f. **Dog Sniffs**—In the absence of physical intrusion onto private property, a dog sniff is not a search.

g. **Curtilage**—The area immediately around a person's home where the person has taken steps to protect the area from the view of a passerby

h. **DNA Evidence**—The police are authorized to take DNA samples from persons arrested for serious crimes. The police may also store the DNA samples in a government database and compare them to unsolved crime scene samples.

2. **Reasonable Suspicion and Probable Cause***

a. **Reasonable Suspicion**—The level of suspicion needed for an investigative stop by police. More than a "hunch"—specific and articulable facts, looking at the totality of circumstances, that lead a reasonable person to believe a crime has occurred, is occurring, or is about to occur.

b. **Probable Cause**—The higher level of suspicion needed for arrests and search warrants. For arrest, there needs to be a reasonable belief that a crime has been committed. For search, a reasonable belief that evidence of a crime will be present in the place to be searched.

3. **Search Warrant and Exceptions***

a. **Requirements for Obtaining a Valid Search Warrant**

i. A search warrant must be issued by a neutral magistrate based on probable cause, supported by a police officer's oath or affidavit, and describe the place to be searched and items to be seized.

b. **Exceptions to the Warrant Requirement**

i. **Search Incident to a Lawful Arrest**—If valid in scope and incident to a lawful arrest. May search the person arrested and the immediate "wingspan" of that person. A container on the person may be searched if it is large enough to hold a weapon or evidence of the crime for which the person is being arrested.

ii. **Automobile Exception**—A vehicle may be searched when evidence may be removed from the scene, and it is not practical to get a warrant under the circumstances. Locked containers may not be searched unless there is separate probable cause to believe evidence is hidden within.

iii. **Plain View**—A police officer may seize property that is obviously unlawful and visible from a place the officer may lawfully stand. Look for situations where a police officer unlawfully stops a car and then sees a bunch of weed on the backseat. In that case, the plain view exception will not apply because the police officer was not lawfully standing in a place where they could see the weed.

iv. **Consent**—A person with apparent authority over the property may consent to a search. Two common scenarios involving consent are when a hotel manager gives permission to search a room and when a homeowner gives permission to search a child's locked room. In both cases, the consent would be invalid. For the hotel manager, remember that renters have a reasonable expectation of privacy in their hotel room (people cannot just barge in on you when you are staying at a hotel). For the homeowner, clearly, the child putting a lock on their door signals that they expect privacy in their room (and the homeowner has allowed it).

v. **Stop-and-Frisk**—An officer may pat down a person's outer clothes for weapons during a stop if the officer has reason to believe the person is armed. Look for questions where a police officer pats down a person and feels something that is obviously not a weapon but seizes it anyway.

vi. **Hot Pursuit**—If the police are in hot pursuit of a person who may have committed a felony, the officers may enter private buildings while in pursuit, search those private buildings for evidence, and seize any evidence found there. Think of movies where police chase a suspect through a bunch of private residences.

vii. **Exigent Circumstances**—Police may enter a place in an emergency in which a person might be in danger or evidence might be destroyed. For example, officers knock on the door of a suspected drug lab and start hearing the toilet flush repeatedly.

viii. **Community Caretaking**—If police officers enter a place to render aid, that entry would not involve an unlawful search. For example, family members and friends say someone has been missing for several days, and the police enter that person's home.

c. **Requirements for Proper Execution of Warrant**

i. **"Knock and Announce"**—Generally, police officers executing a search warrant must knock, state that they are police officers, and wait a reasonable amount of time for the people inside to answer the door.

ii. **Exceptions**—If knocking-and-announcing is unreasonable, officers are not required to do so—for example, if doing so would expose the officers to danger or destroy evidence.

iii. **Proper Scope of Search**—Any limitation on the warrant or a person's consent to the search must be respected by the police. For example, if the warrant allows the officers to search for a rifle, they cannot open up a microwave because a rifle would not fit in it.

iv. **Methods that "Shock the Conscience"**—If the execution of the warrant is grossly unfair and wrong. For example, the officers fail to knock and come flying through every window in the place.

4. **Seizure of Persons (*Terry* stop and arrest)***

a. A police officer may temporarily stop a person if the officer has reasonable suspicion (see above). Such stops are frequently referred to as "Terry" stops, based on the case from which the rule originates (such as *Miranda*). A police officer may arrest a person if the officer has probable cause (see above).

5. **Administrative and Suspicionless Searches**

a. **Border Searches**—Border officers may reasonably search people crossing the border without any suspicion of wrongdoing.

b. **Inventory Searches**—If the police impound a person's vehicle, the police may search the vehicle to make an inventory of its contents so long as the police follow a standard search procedure. Evidence found during the inventory is admissible in court.

c. **Airport Searches are treated like border searches and do not require suspicion.**

d. **Checkpoints**—A police checkpoint is lawful if done for valid purposes (like checking for drunk drivers). If a stop results in an arrest or sufficient probable cause, a search of the person and vehicle may be lawful.

e. **Searches of Government Offices**—Privacy concerns also extend to workers in government offices.

f. **Public School Searches**—A search conducted by school authorities must only be reasonable.

6. **Exclusionary Rule and Exceptions***

   a. **Fruits Doctrine**—Evidence seized as a result of a Fourth Amendment violation may not be admitted at trial.

   b. **Independent Source**—Evidence that was unlawfully obtained may become admissible if it is later obtained through lawful means.

   c. **Inevitable Discovery**—Evidence that was unlawfully obtained may become admissible if its discovery was inevitable. For example, police find a victim's body after an unlawful confession, but the body was in the exact area where a massive search for the victim was underway.

   d. **Good-Faith Doctrine**—Evidence unlawfully obtained due to police mistake (even police negligence) is admissible if the mistake was made in good faith. For example, the police execute a warrant that seems lawful but is actually flawed.

   e. **"Knock-and-Announce" Exception**—If knocking-and-announcing is unreasonable, officers are not required to do so—for example, if doing so would expose the officers to danger or result in the destruction of evidence.

   f. **Use of Evidence for Impeachment**—The use of unlawfully obtained evidence may be used to impeach the defendant on cross-examination if the defendant is testifying on his or her own behalf.

7. **Standing to Object**

   a. **Coconspirators and Third Parties**—Third parties and coconspirators do not have standing to object to the search of their coconspirators or other third parties.

   b. **State Action Doctrine**—Constitutional concerns regarding searches only apply to state parties. Consequently, if a private person decides to search someone's house on their own and then gives the evidence to police, there is no constitutional violation.

B. Confession and Privilege Against Self-Incrimination (Fifth Amendment)

1. **Triggering the Fifth Amendment Privilege Against Self-Incrimination***

   a. **Testimonial Standard**—A defendant cannot be compelled to act as a witness against themselves in a criminal trial. The privilege only applies to testimonial evidence.

   b. **Nontestimonial Standard**—Because the privilege only applies to testimony, physical evidence, such as blood samples, does not count.

   c. **Incrimination Standard**—A defendant cannot be compelled to give incriminating testimony against themselves. Often referred to as *the right to remain silent*.

2. **Triggering *Miranda* Rights***

   a. ***Miranda***—Unless a suspect is informed of their *Miranda* rights, any incriminating statements obtained in a police interrogation cannot be used against them at trial.

   b. **Custody**—*Miranda* does not apply unless the suspect is in custody. The test is whether a reasonable person would feel free to leave from police presence. For example, if the suspect is told that they can leave at any time. A suspect already in prison is not necessarily in custody for *Miranda* purposes. For example, if the suspect is simply wandering around in the prison yard, that is essentially their everyday life.

c. **Interrogation**—*Miranda* only applies to police actions or questions that the police know or should know could elicit an incriminating response. For example, asking a suspect if they want a "Coke," and the suspect responds with "Yes, I sold all of the cocaine!" would be unlikely to count as interrogation. Courts will consider the age, intelligence, education, and intoxication of the suspect, as well as any potential police coercion, in determining whether a suspect has made a voluntary statement.

3. **Adequacy of *Miranda* Warnings***

a. A police warning is adequate if the officer informs the suspect of their right to remain silent, that any statement they make may be used in court, that the suspect has the right to consult an attorney or have an attorney present during interrogation, and that an attorney will be appointed if the suspect cannot afford one. Basically, if you have watched any police shows, you probably have this memorized as it is.

4. **Invoking and Waiving *Miranda* Rights***

a. **Fifth Amendment Right to Counsel**—As stated below, a suspect must affirmatively invoke their *Miranda* rights.

b. **Sixth Amendment Right to Counsel**—The right to have counsel automatically attaches at all critical stages of a criminal prosecution.

c. **How a Person Must Assert *Miranda* Rights**—The suspect must make a specific, unambiguous statement that the suspect wants an attorney. For example, "Do you think I need an attorney?" does not count.

d. **When *Miranda* Rights Properly Waived**—The government must prove by a preponderance of the evidence that a suspect has knowingly, intelligently, and voluntarily waived their *Miranda* rights. After a suspect receives and understands their rights, those rights are waived if the suspect makes a voluntary statement to the police.

e. **Subsequent Law-Enforcement Conduct Allowed**

i. **Resuming Questioning After Lapse of Time**—If the suspect is released from custody, questioning may resume after 14 days, even if the suspect had previously invoked their rights.

ii. **Questioning About Other Crimes**—A suspect's invocation of *Miranda* applies to any suspected crimes.

iii. **Questioning by Informants**—*Miranda* is not required if an informant does the questioning. A common situation is a suspect confessing to an informant placed in their jail cell.

5. **Involuntariness Under the Fifth and Fourteenth Amendments***

a. An involuntary statement occurs when the police use coercion to obtain it.

6. **Exclusionary Rule and Exceptions***

a. A coerced confession cannot be used at trial for either substantive or impeachment purposes. However, a statement taken in violation of *Miranda* may be used against the defendant for impeachment purposes if they take the witness stand and make a statement that conflicts with the previous statement.

C. **Right to Counsel (Including Ineffectiveness of Counsel) (Sixth Amendment)**

1. **When the Right Attaches***—The right attaches automatically at all critical stages of trial.

2. **Waiver of the Right to Counsel***—A defendant may refuse counsel and defend themselves pro se, unless the request is untimely or the defendant cannot follow court rules.

3. **Ineffective Assistance of Counsel***—A defendant may reverse a conviction if the defendant shows that their attorney's representation fell below an objectively reasonable standard and that the representation prejudiced the defendant.
    a. **Immigration status**—A defense counsel must inform a defendant that a guilty plea will affect immigration status.
4. **Right to Counsel of One's Choice**—A defendant who does not require appointed counsel may choose who represents them.
5. **Exclusionary Rule**—Any evidence gathered by the government in violation of the Sixth Amendment may not be used at trial except for impeachment.

D. **Right to Disclosure of Exculpatory and Impeachment Evidence**

1. The prosecution must disclose to the defense any evidence that tends to prove the defendant's innocence.

E. **Due Process Implications Related to Identification**

1. **Lineups**—The Sixth Amendment's Right to Counsel Clause attaches to lineups. A lineup may not be unduly suggestive, such as when only the suspect is wearing a certain type of clothing.
2. **Showups**—The Sixth Amendment and issues of fairness also apply to showups, where a witness is asked to identify a suspect who is standing alone.
3. **Voice Exemplars**—The compelling and taking of a voice exemplar of the suspect does not violate any constitutional right.
4. **Photo Arrays**—Photo arrays must be administered fairly. Consequently, the photos being shown to a witness may not be unduly suggestive.

F. **Right to Jury Trial**

1. In all criminal prosecutions, the defendant has a right to an impartial jury.

PRACTICE MULTIPLE-CHOICE QUESTIONS

1. You are representing a criminal defendant who has been charged with unlawful possession of a firearm by a convicted felon. According to the police reports, a police officer stopped a car for failing to come to a complete stop at a stop sign. The car traveled two blocks with the police officer behind it before finally coming to a stop. The defendant's girlfriend was driving the car, and the defendant was sitting in the passenger seat. During the stop, the police officer discovered an outstanding warrant for the girlfriend's arrest due to her failure to appear in another court proceeding. The officer immediately removed her from the car and placed her under arrest. While the officer was removing the defendant's girlfriend, he thought he detected the odor of marijuana. The pistol was discovered during an ensuing search of the vehicle in the backseat immediately behind the defendant in a closed brown paper bag.

    Which of the following topics are most important for you to research in determining whether you can get the pistol suppressed? **Select two.**

    (A) Hot pursuit
    (B) Exigent Circumstances
    (C) Standing
    (D) Probable Cause
    (E) Reasonable Suspicion
    (F) Search incident to arrest

2. A law school had an ongoing problem with textbook theft. At the request of the law school, the local police department deployed two uniformed officers on campus. The dean believed he saw a student take a textbook off a table and disappear into the women's bathroom with it. He called the officers. One of the officers, who was female, went into the bathroom and saw that several of the stalls were occupied. The officer looked under the stall doors and saw the student inside one of the stalls, placing the missing textbook in her bag. The officer ordered the student to leave the stall, took the textbook out of her bag, and placed her under arrest. The student hired you as her defense attorney.

Should you move to suppress the textbook? **Select one.**

- **(A)** Yes, because the student had a reasonable expectation of privacy in the bathroom stall.
- **(B)** Yes, because the student had a reasonable expectation of privacy in her bag.
- **(C)** No, because the officer's search of the stall was valid under the plain view exception.
- **(D)** No, because the officer's search of the bag was incident to a lawful arrest.

3. The police obtained a warrant to search the suspect's small firearms business for a stolen A-type rifle. While executing the warrant at the store, the officers recognized a marijuana plant on the shelf behind the cash register. They then searched a display case containing a rifle. The officers realized the rifle was not an A-type rifle, so they ran the rifle's serial number through their computer and found that the rifle was a B-type rifle that had been reported stolen from another store. The officers found the A-type rifle behind a flag pinned to the wall behind the cash register. After finding the A-type rifle, one of the officers walked down a short hallway and noticed that the storage room door was open. He looked around the corner and into the open door. He saw another rifle inside the storage room. This rifle was a C-type rifle and was still wrapped in packaging that clearly indicated it had been stolen from a large commercial hunting store. Next to it on the shelf was a large, clear bag of heroin. The officers arrested the store owner. As the officers were walking the store owner to their patrol car, they walked past the store owner's car. Based on the arrest, they opened the car door, and a bag of cocaine immediately fell out onto the street. The store owner hired you as his defense attorney. You are considering challenging the introduction of the evidence found at the store.

Which of the following pieces of evidence are most likely to be admissible? **Select Two.**

- **(A)** A-type rifle
- **(B)** B-type rifle
- **(C)** C-type rifle
- **(D)** The marijuana plant
- **(E)** The heroin
- **(F)** The bag of cocaine

4. A police officer applied for a warrant based on a tip that she received from a reliable confidential informant who had provided her with correct information leading to several past arrests. According to the tip, the informant had been to the defendant's house three months before and seen a large amount of cocaine being packaged for sale. The officer wrote an affidavit and included all the information she had regarding the tip. A neutral magistrate then granted a search warrant. A group of officers went to the defendant's house and executed the warrant. Inside, the officers discovered cocaine sitting on the living room coffee table. The defendant hired you as his defense attorney.

Is a motion to suppress the cocaine likely to be granted? **Select one.**

(A) Yes, because the informant stated he had seen the cocaine three months before.
(B) Yes, because the mere statement of a single confidential informant creates insufficient probable cause for the search warrant.
(C) No, because the confidential informant was known and reliable.
(D) No, because the cocaine was sitting in plain view.

5. The police suspected a man of murdering his neighbor and hiding his body. Two officers went to the man's home. The man was sitting on his front porch when the officers arrived. One officer sat in the patrol car with the engine running, in case the man decided to flee, while the other officer approached and asked to speak with the man. The man invited the officer onto the porch and offered him a beer, which the officer declined. The officer sat down and asked if the man had seen his neighbor recently because the neighbor's family was looking for him. The man said that he had not. The officer then asked, "Wasn't it true that the two of you were out drinking at a bar last night? Did you two have a fight? You don't have to say anything if you don't want or if you want to get an attorney or something." The man laughed and said, "My neighbor was being ornery. I just needed to do what needed to be done. I helped him go swimming in that pond over there." The officer walked to the pond. At the bottom of the pond was the neighbor's body with his head bashed in. The man was ultimately arrested for murder. The man hired you as his defense attorney. At trial, the government sought to enter the man's statements into evidence.

Is a motion to suppress the man's statements likely to be successful? **Select one.**

(A) Yes, because the man was a suspect at the time of his conversation with the police officer.
(B) Yes, because the officer did not give the man sufficient *Miranda* warnings.
(C) No, because the man was not in custody at the time of his conversation with the police officer.
(D) No, because the officer did not ask the man if he was involved with the neighbor's murder.

6. Police officers on patrol were notified over the radio that a woman's wallet had just been stolen. The officers saw a man running down the street and decided to stop him. One of the officers asked what the man was doing, and the man said he was jogging. The officer was suspicious because the man was wearing dress slacks. The officer inquired about the slacks, and the man stated that they were the only clean pair of pants he had, and he was not planning on going on a long run. The officer ordered the man to raise his hands and frisked him to see if he had a wallet. During the frisk, the officer felt a baggie in the man's pocket. Inside the baggie was marijuana. The officers arrested the man for unlawful drug possession. The man hired you as his defense attorney.

Should you move to suppress the marijuana? **Select one.**

(A) Yes, because the officer did not frisk the man to look for marijuana.
(B) Yes, because the frisk was unlawful.
(C) No, because there was sufficient reasonable suspicion to support a frisk.
(D) No, because there was sufficient probable cause to support a frisk.

7. A woman was sitting in an airport waiting for her plane. Unbeknownst to her, the man sitting next to her was an undercover police officer who was surveilling the woman for possible drug trafficking. The woman got up to use the bathroom and asked the undercover officer if he would be willing to watch her bag for her for a moment. The undercover officer agreed to watch the bag, and when the woman went to the bathroom, he opened it. Inside the bag were several pill bottles full of marijuana. The woman hired you as her defense attorney.

Is a motion to suppress the marijuana likely to be successful? **Select one.**

(A) Yes, because the woman asked the officer to watch her bag for her.
(B) Yes, because there was insufficient probable cause for the search.
(C) No, because the woman abandoned her bag with the officer.
(D) No, because the officer was acting as a false friend.

8. A man was parked next to a mobile camper at a public rest area. The man watched as the driver of the camper and his passenger left the vehicle and went inside the restroom. As the man sat in his car, he caught the smell of marijuana drifting from the camper. The man was a narcotics counselor who hated drug use. Because he hated drug use, the man got out of his car and tested the door of the camper, discovering that the driver and passenger had left it open. The man went inside and saw a large bag of marijuana on the floor of the camper. The man grabbed the bag and immediately ran over to a police car parked at the rest area. The man turned the marijuana over to the police, who then arrested the camper driver and passenger for drug crimes. The camper driver asked you to be his defense attorney.

Is a motion to suppress the marijuana likely to be successful? **Select one.**

(A) Yes, because the man acted as a *de facto* agent of the police.
(B) Yes, because the camper driver had a reasonable expectation of privacy in the camper.
(C) No, because the marijuana smell created probable cause for a search.
(D) No, because the man entered the camper because he hated drug use.

9. A college student lived with a roommate in a fraternity house that the university owned. The housemother, whom the university employed to manage the fraternity house, believed that the student was dealing unlawful drugs. The housemother called the police and explained her concerns. When the police arrived, they asked to search the student's room. The housemother explained that neither the student nor his roommate was at home, but she had a master key that opened every room in the fraternity house. She led the officers upstairs to the student's room and let the officers inside with her key. In the room, the officers found a large amount of marijuana and other drugs. You worked as a prosecutor for the state. At trial, the student moved to suppress the evidence found in his room.

Which of the following is the prosecution's strongest argument in opposition to the student's motion? **Select one.**

(A) The housemother's tip provided sufficient probable cause.
(B) The university owned the fraternity house.
(C) The housemother had a master key that opened every room in the fraternity house.
(D) The housemother had apparent authority to allow entry into the student's room.

10. A band that was well known for having fans who engaged in unlawful drug use staged a show on the outskirts of a small town. On the day of the show, the local police force set up a checkpoint where they randomly stopped vehicles driving in the direction of the concert. A woman was driving a car that the officers randomly stopped. When an officer questioned her, she stated that she was on her way home, which just happened to be in the direction of the concert. The officer questioning the woman looked in the backseat of the car. In the backseat, the officer, who was trained in drug enforcement, saw a large, clear bag of marijuana. The officer arrested the woman for unlawful drug possession. The woman hired you as her defense attorney.

Should you move to suppress the evidence? **Select one.**

(A) Yes, because the woman was not driving to the concert.
(B) Yes, because the marijuana was discovered in an illegal search.
(C) No, because the marijuana was in plain view on the back seat.
(D) No, because the officer was trained in drug enforcement.

11. You work as a city prosecutor. A city neighborhood was well known for drug trafficking. Neighborhood residents reported to a police officer that they saw a man in a straw cowboy hat driving a silver hatchback stop several times near the neighborhood park, where he would talk to people for only a short period before driving away again. Later that day, the officer saw a man wearing a straw cowboy hat walking from a fast food restaurant to a silver hatchback in the parking lot. The officer stopped the man and frisked him for weapons. The officer then asked what he was doing in the area, and the man immediately said, "I wasn't anywhere near the park." A plastic baggie of drugs then fell out of the man's pocket, and the officer arrested him.

The lead prosecutor in the case has asked you to research the legal issues that the defendant will most likely raise in his defense. **Select two.**

(A) Probable cause
(B) Reasonable suspicion
(C) *Miranda*
(D) Fifth Amendment
(E) Plain view
(F) Stop and frisk

12. You work for an immigration firm. A woman came to your office after she served a short prison sentence for burglary. The woman told you that her defense attorney advised her to accept a plea bargain because there was "a lot of circumstantial evidence against her" and that going to trial was likely to result in a much longer sentence. The woman inquired about calling her brother as an alibi witness, but the defense attorney advised against it, stating that he would likely make a bad impression on the jury and that a jury was unlikely to believe him due to his lengthy criminal record. All in all, her defense attorney thought she was getting a great deal from the prosecution. The woman repeatedly asked the defense attorney about whether pleading guilty could lead to her deportation, but the defense attorney assured her that the plea bargain would not affect her immigration status. The woman told her defense attorney that she would reject the plea deal if it could lead to her deportation, but with the defense attorney's assurances, she decided to accept. When the woman was released from prison, she was immediately informed by immigration authorities that her guilty plea required her deportation. She asked you what she could do to keep from being deported. You decided that you could likely get the woman's plea vacated based on ineffective assistance of counsel.

Which of the following facts would be most useful to support your motion to vacate the defendant's plea based on ineffective assistance of counsel? **Select two.**

(A) The defense attorney told the woman he thought the woman was getting a great deal from the prosecution.
(B) The woman served time in prison.
(C) The defense attorney did not want to call the woman's brother as a witness.
(D) The defense attorney assured the woman that a guilty plea would not affect her immigration status.
(E) The defense attorney told the woman that going to trial was likely to result in a much longer sentence.
(F) The woman would not have agreed to the plea deal without the defense attorney's assurances.

13. A probationer was called by his probation officer to come by her office. The probationer went by the probation officer's office on his way home from work, and the probation officer questioned him about a burglary that the probation officer believed he might be involved in. It was a hot day, and after about 20 minutes of questioning, the probation officer asked the probationer if he wanted a "Coke." The probationer apparently misheard the probation officer and said, "If Bill says I know anything about dealing coke, he's a liar." "Bill" was a known drug dealer who had recently been arrested. After talking to Bill, other police officers asked the probation officer if she knew anything about the probationer's involvement in drug trafficking. The probation officer told the other officers what the probationer had said to her. Ultimately, the probationer was arrested.

You worked for the prosecution. At trial, the defense moved to suppress the probationer's statement to his probation officer.

Which of the following facts would be most useful in opposing the motion? **Select two.**

(A) The probationer came to the office voluntarily.
(B) The probationer was not in custody.
(C) The probationer had a general obligation to answer the probation officer's questions.
(D) The probation officer only questioned the probationer for 20 minutes.
(E) The probation officer asked the probationer if he wanted a Coke.
(F) The probation officer only asked the probationer about a suspected burglary.

14. A man was arrested for robbing a bank. The man was immediately taken to the police station, fingerprinted, and required to appear in a lineup. He was not given *Miranda* warnings, nor was the man given the option to refuse to participate in the lineup. The lineup contained the man and four other men. The man was the only bald man and the only one with an English accent. The lineup was viewed by one of the bank's clerks, who heard the robber say, "I'm going to gut you!" Each person in the lineup was made to say, "I'm going to gut you!" The clerk identified the man as the robber after each person had spoken the phrase. The man hired you as his defense attorney, and you decided to try to suppress the identification.

At the suppression hearing, the clerk stated that he did not see the robber's face because the robber was wearing a bandana over his mouth. However, the clerk was certain the man was the robber because he recognized his voice at the lineup.

Which of the following facts would be most useful in your motion to suppress the identification? **Select two.**

(A) The man was required to utter the phrase, "I'm going to gut you!"
(B) The man had an English accent.
(C) The man was not read his *Miranda* rights before the lineup.
(D) The man was bald.
(E) The man was not given the option to refuse to participate in the lineup.
(F) The robber wore a bandana over his mouth.

15. Neighbors called the police after hearing several screams coming from a house. The police responded and heard loud screaming coming from inside. They knocked on the door, but when they received no response and the screaming continued, the officers entered the home. Inside, they found the homeowner yelling, waving a gun, and overturning furniture. The officers restrained the homeowner and quickly opened several closed doors. Behind one of the closed doors, the officers found a large methamphetamine laboratory. The officers then arrested the homeowner.

You are a public defender assigned to represent the homeowner.

If you move to suppress the officers' testimony at trial, alleging that the warrantless search of the home violated the homeowner's rights, which two legal concepts would be most helpful for you to research in developing your argument? **Select two.**

(A) Exigent circumstances
(B) Implied consent
(C) Express consent
(D) Plain view
(E) Protective sweep
(F) Search incident to arrest

16. A defendant, your client, was arrested for arson after she allegedly burned down a bowling alley. Under state law, serious crimes, such as arson, require officers to obtain DNA samples from those arrested and store them in a state facility for later testing and registration. The arresting officers told the defendant about the state law and took a cheek swab of her DNA. The defendant did not object.

You secured an acquittal for the defendant at trial. Six months after the acquittal, the police matched the defendant's DNA to an unsolved murder. You are representing the defendant again in the murder case.

When you met with the defendant, you told her that it was unlikely that you could get the DNA sample suppressed.

Which of the following facts are most relevant to the admissibility of the DNA evidence? **Select two.**

(A) The defendant failed to object to the taking of his DNA sample.
(B) The defendant was arrested for a serious crime.
(C) The police may test and store DNA profiles in a government database.
(D) The police acted in good-faith reliance on the DNA collection law.
(E) The Fourth Amendment does not allow DNA collection except in certain circumstances.
(F) DNA evidence is nontestamentary evidence.

17. A defendant, your client, took his 8-year-old son to a Little League lacrosse game one morning. The defendant's son played poorly, so the coach benched him and yelled at him until he cried. That evening, the defendant saw the coach at a gas station. The defendant walked up behind the coach and hit him in the head as hard as he could with a wrench. The coach bounced off the gas station pump, cracked his head open, and died from his injuries. You met with the defendant to discuss whether the defendant is likely to be found guilty of murder for the coach's death.

Which of the following concepts will be most relevant to the defendant's potential guilt for murder? **Select two.**

(A) The father intended to inflict serious injury
(B) Heat of passion
(C) Malice aforethought
(D) Intent to kill
(E) Dangerous instrumentality
(F) A wrench is likely a deadly weapon.

18. Your client lived in an apartment building with two friends. The police had been surveilling one of the friends for a month based on an anonymous tip that the friend was dealing in illegal rifles. The police received a warrant to search the apartment for rifles and decided to conduct the search early one morning. The officers quietly approached the apartment front door and listened to hear if anyone was moving inside. One of the officers tried the door and discovered that it was unlocked. The officer thought he heard a loud crash, so he entered the apartment. Your client was eating breakfast in the front room when the officers entered. They yelled for him to put his hands up, and he did so immediately. The officers fanned out and conducted a protective sweep, finding several rifles in a bedroom. Also during the sweep, an officer opened a kitchen cabinet and saw several clear plastic bags of cocaine. Only your client was in the apartment. Your client told the officers that his two friends had moved out the day before, and now he was the only one renting the place. He also stated that he had no idea the cocaine was in the cabinet, and he did not know that his friends were involved in drug dealing. The state charged your client with drug conspiracy charges, and your client hired you to defend him.

Which of the following legal doctrines should you research in crafting your client's defense? **Select two.**

- **(A)** Fruits doctrine
- **(B)** Independent source
- **(C)** Inevitable discovery
- **(D)** Good-faith doctrine
- **(E)** Knock-and-announce exception
- **(F)** Use of evidence for impeachment

19. You work as a prosecutor for the state. An 18-year-old murder suspect was brought into a police station for questioning. At the same time as the questioning, other officers were searching the suspect's apartment according to a valid search warrant. The interrogating officers brought the suspect into an interrogation room, but they left the door open and were not wearing uniforms. The suspect had previously visited the police station and had a lengthy criminal record. The suspect, who knew the officers from prior interactions, asked, "Do you think I need an attorney?" The officers did not respond but started questioning the suspect about the murder. After a few minutes, the suspect confessed. At the same time, the officers searching his apartment called the interrogating officers and said that they had discovered the murder weapon. At the suspect's subsequent trial, the suspect moved to suppress his confession, arguing that it was taken in violation of his *Miranda* rights.

Which of the following facts would be most useful in supporting the lawfulness of the suspect's confession? **Select two.**

- **(A)** The suspect was 18 years old.
- **(B)** The door to the interrogation room was open.
- **(C)** Officers were already searching the suspect's home at the time of interrogation.
- **(D)** The suspect had a lengthy criminal record.
- **(E)** The interrogating officers were not wearing uniforms.
- **(F)** The suspect asked, "Do you think I need an attorney?"

20. Your client is charged with several crimes related to a drug and weapons conspiracy. All the evidence was discovered during a search of the area near his home and an isolated shed located in the woods adjacent to his property. The officers used a new X-ray and infrared camera to inspect the inside of the shed. With the camera, they could see a handgun and drugs inside, which they seized. They then used a dog to sniff the contents of your client's trash can, which was on the curb for pickup. The dog alerted, and the officers discovered rags inside the trash can covered in methamphetamine residue. The officers then took the dog around your client's car, which was parked on the street. The dog alerted to the trunk, where drugs were eventually discovered. Finally, the officers looked over your client's backyard fence and saw a rifle on a picnic table and a knife leaning against a chair on the back porch.

Which of the following pieces of evidence do you have the best chance of getting excluded? **Select two.**

(A) The handgun in the shed
(B) The drugs in the shed
(C) The rags in the trash can
(D) The drugs in the car trunk
(E) The rifle in the backyard
(F) The knife on the porch

ANSWERS

1. The correct answers are (C) and (D). Standing is likely to be an issue in this case because the defendant was a passenger in the car, and his girlfriend was driving. Consequently, there is likely to be an issue as to who owns the car and who has a reasonable expectation of privacy in its contents. Probable cause is also an issue. While the automobile exception allows warrantless searches of vehicles, an officer may only conduct a search if they have probable cause. Additionally, containers within a vehicle cannot be searched under the automobile exception without probable cause. Consequently, a major issue will be whether the traffic stop or the smell of marijuana created sufficient probable cause for the search of the paper bag in the back seat. (A) is incorrect because hot pursuit allows officers to enter private buildings while in pursuit, search those private buildings for evidence, and seize any evidence found there. Here, there is no evidence of any pursuit, even though it took the girlfriend two blocks to stop the car. (B) is incorrect because there is no evidence of exigent circumstances, such as emergency or destruction of evidence, that would justify a warrantless search. (E) is incorrect because reasonable suspicion is a lower level of suspicion than probable cause, and probable cause is the necessary level for a valid vehicle search. (F) is incorrect because the pistol would not be in plain view, considering it was inside a paper bag.

2. The correct answer is (A). The Fourth Amendment prohibits searches of places where people have a reasonable expectation of privacy. Here, a bathroom stall would likely be such a place. (B) is incorrect because the officer's search of the stall was likely unlawful. As such, the evidence should be suppressed under the fruit of the poisonous tree doctrine before the court even considers the search of the bag. (C) is incorrect because looking under the stall door would not be excused by the plain view exception. A person clearly has an expectation of privacy in a bathroom stall, and the mere fact that a police officer could physically bend down and peer under the door without touching anything does not change the analysis. (D) is incorrect because the arrest is likely unlawful, as it was based on evidence obtained through an unlawful search.

3. The correct answers are (A) and (D). The officers had a search warrant specifically allowing them to search for the A-type rifle, so the rifle would be admissible. The marijuana plant would be allowed in under the plain view exception because it is sitting behind the counter, where anyone entering the store could see it. (B) is incorrect because the officers knew that the rifle was not an A-type rifle when they ran the serial number. Since they knew it was not the rifle they were looking for, they could not run the number to find out if it was stolen. Once officers find the subject of the warrant, the search should stop. Instead, after the officers found the A-type rifle, one of them continued to look around the store. Consequently, his poking his head around the corner and into the storage room was an unlawful search, making (C) and (E) incorrect. Importantly, because the officer no longer had a lawful right to search the storage areas of the building, the C-type rifle and the heroin would not be valid under the plain view exception. Finally, (F) is incorrect because the officers had no right to open the store owner's parked car based on the incident of arrest.

4. The correct answer is (A). To obtain a search warrant, an officer must demonstrate that the information they possess creates probable cause that evidence will be found at a specific location. Here, the fact that the informant saw the drugs three months ago is likely too far away in time to provide sufficient probable cause that drug evidence is likely to be discovered there (a lot could happen in three months). (B) is incorrect because a reliable informant's statement could create sufficient probable cause for a search warrant. Here, the problem is that the drugs were seen three months before. (C) is incorrect because the drugs were seen three months before. (D) is incorrect because even if the cocaine was sitting in plain view, the officers' entry to execute the warrant was unlawful because it was based on stale information. Thus, the officers did not see the cocaine from a place where they were lawfully entitled to be.

5. The correct answer is (C). For *Miranda* to apply, the suspect must be in the custody of police (which means their freedom of movement is restricted). Here, the officers did not inform the man that he was not free to leave, did not handcuff or restrain him, and did not give any indication that he was not free to end the officer's conversation with him at any time. Consequently, the man was not in custody. (A) is incorrect because the mere fact that the man was a suspect does not change the analysis. (B) is incorrect because the man was not required to receive *Miranda* warnings since he was not in custody. (D) is incorrect because if the man were in custody, the officer asked questions that he should have known could elicit an incriminating response, whether he directly asked if the man was involved in the neighbor's murder.

6. The correct answer is (B). If an officer stops a suspect and has reason to believe they may be armed, it is lawful for the officer to frisk the suspect for weapons. However, an officer may not frisk a suspect solely for the purpose of gathering evidence. Here, since the officer specifically frisked the man in search of a wallet, the frisk was unlawful. (A) is incorrect because the officer could only lawfully frisk the man in search of weapons. (C) and (D) are incorrect because the officer unlawfully frisked the man in search of a wallet.

7. The correct answer is (A). The government may not conduct a warrantless search of a person's bag in which they have a reasonable expectation of privacy. While she did leave the bag with the officer, she did ask him to watch it for her until she returned. As such, she likely retained a reasonable expectation of privacy in the bag's contents, and the officer's search was unlawful. (B) is incorrect because the issue here is not one of sufficient probable cause, but whether the woman retained a reasonable expectation of privacy in the bag. (C) is incorrect because the woman did not abandon the bag. In fact, she sought to retain control over the bag by asking someone to watch it and promising her return. (D) is incorrect because "false friend" refers to situations where a suspect makes incriminating statements to an informant or undercover police officer.

8. The correct answer is (D). The Fourth Amendment protection against unreasonable searches only applies to government searches. Here, since the man had no apparent connection to the police and only entered the camper because he hated drugs, there was no government involvement in the search, and the search cannot be found to be unlawful. (A), (B), and (C) are incorrect because there was no connection between the government and the man's decision to search the camper.

9. The correct answer is (D). The big issue in this question is whether the student had a reasonable expectation of privacy in his room and whether anything could have overridden that reasonable expectation of privacy. A person who has apparent authority over an area or thing can consent to its search, and such consent would be the only thing in question that could allow the search that occurred. Consequently, the prosecution's best argument is that the housemother had apparent authority to consent to searches of the fraternity's rooms. (A) is incorrect because probable cause alone would not negate the need for a search warrant. (B) and (C) are incorrect because neither fact would negate the student's reasonable expectation of privacy in his room.

10. The correct answer is (B). Here, the police stopped the woman's car at random. As such, the traffic stop was unlawful, making the marijuana the fruit of an unlawful stop. Consequently, the marijuana should be suppressed. (A) is incorrect because where the woman was going does not change the analysis. (C) is incorrect because the officer unlawfully stopped the vehicle, making the marijuana the fruit of an unlawful traffic stop. (D) is incorrect because the officer's training does not change the analysis.

11. The correct answers are (B) and (C). The man is most likely to challenge the officer's investigative stop, which would require reasonable suspicion, and the use of his statement about the park, since he made it before receiving any *Miranda* warnings. (A) is incorrect because there is no issue here for probable cause for the arrest, since the man dropped the drugs in front of the officer. (D) is incorrect because the Fifth Amendment covers testimonial privilege. (E) is incorrect because there is not really an issue involving the discovery of the dropped drugs. (F) is incorrect because the officer did not frisk the man.

12. The correct answers are (D) and (F). A defendant may reverse a conviction if the defendant shows that their attorney's representation fell below an objectively reasonable standard and that the representation prejudiced the defendant. Additionally, courts have ruled that defense counsel must inform a defendant that a guilty plea may impact their immigration status. Here, (D) is correct because the defense attorney told the woman that the guilty plea would not affect her immigration status. (F) is correct because the woman would not have accepted the plea if she had known it could lead to her deportation, so the representation prejudiced the defendant. (A) is incorrect because tactical decisions are not examples of ineffective assistance of counsel. (B) is incorrect because the simple fact that she had an adverse result would not support an ineffective assistance of counsel claim. (C) is incorrect because tactical decisions do not support ineffective assistance of counsel claims. (E) is incorrect as an example of another tactical decision by the defense attorney.

13. The correct answers are (B) and (E). The probationer's motion to suppress the statements would be based on the probation officer's failure to provide any *Miranda* warnings before the probationer made the incriminating statement. For *Miranda* to apply, the suspect must be in custody and subject to interrogation. Subject to interrogation means that the police officer asked a question likely to elicit an incriminating statement. Here, if the probation officer only asked the probationer if he wanted a Coke, her question was not something likely to elicit an incriminating statement. As far as custody goes, there was no indication that he wasn't free to leave. (A) is incorrect because the relevant issue would be custody, not voluntariness. (C) is incorrect because probationary status does not negate the requirements of *Miranda*. (D) is incorrect because there is nothing special about 20 minutes of questioning. (F) is incorrect because the relevant issue is whether the probationer's statement was the result of interrogation.

14. The correct answers are (B) and (D). A lineup cannot be overly suggestive, and the fact that the man was the only bald man in the lineup and the only one with an English accent would likely be overly suggestive. (B) is correct because the man was required to say the robber's phrase, which he would likely utter with an English accent when no one else in the lineup would do so. (D) is correct because even with a bandana over his mouth, the clerk would likely be looking for a robber with a bald head. (A) is incorrect because suspects may be compelled to utter the phrase as a means of physical identification. (C) is incorrect because the man was not facing custodial interrogation, so *Miranda* does not apply. (E) This is incorrect because the man did not need to be given the option to refuse participation. (F) is incorrect because the police could still do a lineup even if the bank robber wore a bandana over his mouth.

15. The correct answers are (A) and (E). Because the officers entered without a warrant, the main issue will be their initial entry and search of the home. (A) is correct because the screaming likely allowed the officers to enter the home in case the homeowner needed emergency aid. (E) is correct because the officers opened a door to discover the meth lab, which they could lawfully do as part of a protective sweep. (B) and (C) are incorrect because there is no evidence of any homeowner consent. (D) is incorrect because the meth lab was behind a closed door, and waving around a gun at police officers does not require the use of the plain view exception. (F) is incorrect because the homeowner was not arrested until after the entry into the home and the discovery of the meth lab.

16. The correct answers are (B) and (C). The police are authorized to take DNA samples from persons arrested for serious crimes. The police may also store the DNA samples in a government database and compare them to samples from unsolved crime scenes. This makes (B) and (C) correct. (A) is incorrect because the defendant did not object to the taking of the sample. Even if she had not, she could have challenged the potential Fourth Amendment violation later. (D) is incorrect because there is no need to use the good-faith exception. (E) is incorrect because this statement is incorrect. (F) is incorrect because it also fails to address the collection of DNA evidence, which is the primary issue.

17. The correct answers are (A) and (F). Here, to prove murder, the prosecution only needs to show that the defendant intended to inflict serious bodily injury by hitting the coach on the head with a deadly weapon, the wrench. As such, he could likely be convicted of murder for the coach. (B) is incorrect because there was likely a sufficient cooling-off period between the morning game and the later hitting, which would make heat of passion irrelevant. (C) is incorrect because the intent to inflict serious bodily injury could be used to establish malice aforethought. (D) is incorrect because the prosecution would not need to show intent to kill under these circumstances. (E) is incorrect because the defendant's use of the wrench as a deadly weapon does not require the court to get into dangerous instrumentality analysis.

18. The correct answers are (A) and (E). Under the fruits doctrine, evidence seized as a result of a Fourth Amendment violation is not admissible at trial. A protective sweep is lawful to discover potential threats to officers conducting a search, specifically threats from someone who might attack them. While opening doors and looking under beds would be lawful, opening a kitchen cabinet is unlikely to count as a lawful part of a protective sweep. Also, since the warrant was for illegal rifles, which could not fit in a kitchen cabinet, opening the kitchen cabinet might not have been a valid part of the search under the warrant. Consequently, you may be able to exclude the cocaine based on a Fourth Amendment violation. (E) is correct because the officers did not knock and announce their presence before entering the apartment, so you may be able to claim the entry was unlawful. (B), (C), (D), and (F) are incorrect because those concepts would not help craft a potential defense.

19. The correct answers are (B) and (F). To trigger *Miranda*, a suspect must be in custody. (B) could be useful to show that the suspect was not in custody at the time of questioning (cases have found that an open interrogation room door is enough to show a suspect is not in custody for purposes of

Miranda). (F) would be useful because a suspect must clearly invoke *Miranda* rights. Here, asking, "Do you think I need an attorney?" is not a clear invocation of those rights. (A) is incorrect because this would not address the issue of custody or invocation of rights. (C) is incorrect because this would be irrelevant to the lawfulness of the confession. (D) is incorrect because this would not address custody or invocation. (E) is incorrect because the simple fact that the officers were not wearing uniforms would not necessarily indicate whether the suspect was in custody.

20. The correct answers are (E) and (F). The Fourth Amendment protects searches of places where a suspect has a reasonable expectation of privacy. People have a reasonable expectation of privacy in the curtilage of their home. Here, the fact that the rifle was in the backyard behind the fence and the knife was on the back porch (also probably behind the fence) likely protected these two items as being within the curtilage of the client's home. Consequently, you have the best chance of getting these two items excluded. (A) and (B) are incorrect because they were discovered in an "isolated" shed, which would be unprotected by the Fourth Amendment, whether the police used some weird camera or not. (C) and (D) are incorrect because a dog sniff is not generally considered a search.

Evidence

5

Topics with asterisks (*) require you to know the black letter law cold; topics without an * require you to recognize the topic as part of the fact scenario or require you to analyze and apply legal resources provided for the topic efficiently.

TWO MAIN POINTS OF EVIDENCE—(1) GUARANTEEING THE TRUTH AS MUCH AS HUMANLY POSSIBLE, AND (2) IF A PERSON IS FOUND LIABLE OR GUILTY, IT IS FOR THE ACTUAL THING ALLEGED, NOT FOR SOME OTHER REASON (LIKE BEING GENERALLY UNLIKABLE)

OUTLINE

NextGen tests the federal rules of evidence

I. RELEVANCE AND REASONS FOR EXCLUDING RELEVANT EVIDENCE

A. Probative Value

1. **Relevance* (including offers to stipulate)**—Evidence is relevant if (1) it makes a fact more or less probable, and (2) the fact is of consequence in determining the action. Evidence can still be admitted even if the opposing party offers to stipulate to it. However, a court may consider an offer to stipulate when determining evidence's probative value.
2. **Exclusion***—Relevant evidence may still be excluded if the danger of unfair prejudice substantially outweighs its probative value, confuses the issues, or wastes time. Remember that the point of evidence is to make sure the jury makes their judgment based on the actual thing alleged, not simply because they do not like the accused or get confused by the issues.

B. Character and Related Concepts

1. **Admissibility of Character Evidence**—not allowed to prove conformity with the party's character on a particular occasion

   a. **Direct Examination**

      i. **Criminal Trial**—Prosecution cannot initiate evidence of the defendant's character. Otherwise, prosecutors might open with evidence of the defendant's consistently poor behavior.

      ii. **Civil Trial**—Generally not admissible, unless character is directly at issue. Examples include child custody cases or defamation actions, because in those cases, character is a significant factor. For example, if parties are arguing about who would be a better parent, the character of the parents would certainly be a critical issue.

   b. **Cross Examination**

      i. **Criminal Trial**—The defendant can introduce evidence of their good character to prove innocence. But once the defendant does so, it can open the door to evidence of their bad character. It can also be used to impeach the defendant or a witness.

      ii. **Civil Trial**—can only be used to impeach a party or a witness

2. **Crimes, Wrongs, or Other Acts***—In a criminal case, they can be used to prove motive, opportunity, intent, preparation, common scheme or plan, knowledge, identity, and absence of mistake or accident. It can be remembered with MIMIC-KOP—Think of classic detective books or shows where the detective goes through the murderer's motive, opportunity, etc. Remember, we do not want to incarcerate people solely for being bad individuals, so courts must be cautious about admitting evidence of other crimes.

3. **Methods of Proving Character**—Generally, a person's reputation in the community or a witness's opinion of the person's character can be used when character evidence is admissible. Usually, the proponent of the evidence cannot just use one single event to prove character. Basically, it takes a lot of time to build up community reputation (so the community's belief about character is more likely to be true), while being nice to a puppy once does not prove that you do not spend the majority of your life kicking puppies.

4. **Habit and Routine Practice**—Evidence of a person's habit is admissible to show the person acted in accordance with that habit on a particular occasion (for example, he always drives home the same way). A business's routine practice may be used in the same manner (for example, the business always sends out late payment notices to customers on the 15th of the month). If I walk to work, I always go the same way, so if I disappear on my walk, evidence of this habit would be pretty significant.

C. Opinions and Expert Testimony

1. **Lay Opinion***—A lay opinion is admissible if it is (1) rationally based on the witness's perception; (2) helpful to clearly understand the witness's testimony or determine a fact in issue; and (3) not based on scientific, technical, or other specialized knowledge. For example, a layperson could say, "I saw that car that got into a wreck going really fast down the street."

2. **Qualification of Expert Witness**—A witness qualifies as an expert if they have the requisite knowledge, skill, experience, training, or education necessary to qualify as an expert on a particular matter. For example, I qualify as an expert on law school exams, but I know nothing about snails except that they look slimy.

3. **Proper Subject Matter for Expert Testimony***—The expert's special knowledge must assist the trier of fact, and the expert's testimony must be based on sufficient facts or data, be the product of reliable principles and methods, and reflect a reliable application of the principles and methods to the facts of the case.
4. **Reliability of Expert Testimony***—To determine the reliability of the testimony, courts look at whether the expert's principle or technique has been tested, whether it has been subjected to peer review, whether there is a known or potential error rate, and whether it is generally accepted in the scientific community. So, if the expert is the only person to believe something in their field, it is probably not super reliable.
5. **Bases of Expert Opinion Testimony**—An expert's opinion may be based on facts or data in the case that the expert has been made aware of or observed. The facts that the witness relies on in court do not need to be admissible themselves. Essentially, the primary purpose of having an expert is that they have spent a lifetime absorbing facts to become an expert, and there is no way every single fact they have ever learned will be otherwise admissible on its own.
6. **Ultimate Issue Rule**—While an expert can testify about their opinion on an ultimate issue in a case, the expert may not offer an opinion regarding the requisite mental state of a criminal defendant.

II. PRESENTATION OF EVIDENCE

A. Foundation, Authentication, and Identification, Best Evidence Rule*

1. **Foundation**—Laying a foundation means presenting facts that the evidence is admissible because it tends to prove or disprove an element of the claim or defense. This connects to the rule that evidence must be relevant and not just waste time or confuse issues.
2. **Authentication and Identification**—Except for testimony, all evidence must be authenticated or identified with proof that the evidence is what the proponent claims it to be. Examples include an opinion about a voice, testimony of a witness with knowledge, or comparison by an expert witness or the trier of fact.
   a. **Photographs and Signatures**—For photos, a witness is needed who can testify that the photograph fairly and accurately represents what it is supposed to be a photo of. For signatures, a witness must be familiar with the person's signature to say the signature looks like that person's signature.
   b. **Self-Authenticating Documents**—Seven things do not need any outside authentication, and they can be remembered with OIL CANS. These seven things are: (1) official publications issued by a public authority; (2) instruments—negotiable and commercial paper; (3) label, tag, or trademark fixed in the ordinary course of business; (4) certified public documents (certified by a clerk or court that had custody); (5) acknowledged documents signed before a notary; (6) newspapers; and (7) sealed documents.
3. **Best Evidence Rule**—To prove the contents of a writing, the original writing must be produced. Photocopies are allowed unless the original's authenticity is disputed. If the original or a photocopy is unavailable through no fault of the proponent, other evidence of the writing's contents may be admitted at the judge's discretion. Examples are photos, X-rays, and contracts. This makes sense because if the argument is about the actual contents of something, the court should see that actual thing and not just listen to people talk about it.

B. **Competency of Witness**—Every person is competent to be a witness unless the rules of evidence prove otherwise. To be competent, a witness must testify using their personal knowledge and understand the importance of testifying truthfully.

C. **Juror's Competency as a Witness**—A juror may not testify as a witness in the case in which the juror is sitting. This seems like a sensible rule.

D. **Refreshing Recollection**—If a witness does not remember something, you can show them anything to jog their memory. For example, if I were on the stand testifying about a student's grade in 2010, I am pretty sure I would have no memory at all. But if I am shown my gradebook from 2010, I would probably remember and could testify to it.

E. **Objections and Offers of Proof**—If opposing counsel objects to the admission of evidence, a lawyer may respond with an offer of proof. To make an offer of proof, the lawyer describes the evidence, explains its purpose, states the grounds for admissibility, and argues the potential consequences of not allowing the evidence.

F. **Judicial Notice**—A court may take judicial notice of a fact that is not subject to reasonable dispute. For example, it would be a waste of time for a party to need to provide evidence that Columbia is the capital of South Carolina.

G. **Limited Admissibility**—Upon request, a court may instruct the jury to limit evidence as admissible to only one party or for one purpose.

III. PRIVILEGES AND OTHER POLICY EXCLUSIONS

A. **Spousal Immunity and Marital Communications**—Because of the social interest in preserving marriages, a spouse cannot be compelled to testify against the other spouse in a criminal case, and a spouse may not disclose confidential communications with the other spouse made during the marriage. However, these privileges do not apply in claims between the spouses, when one spouse is charged with a crime against the other spouse or their children, or when communications were made to plan a crime. Additionally, a spouse loses the confidential communication privilege if they disclose that communication to a third party.

B. **Attorney-Client and Work Product***—Clearly, a big issue in professional responsibility, but also an issue in evidence. A client may prevent the disclosure of any confidential communication between the client and attorney that was made while obtaining legal advice. The client does not need to pay the attorney for this advice. The privilege does not apply if the advice was intended to be used to commit a crime or fraud. If evidence protected by the attorney-client privilege is accidentally disclosed, only that specific evidence loses the protection of the attorney-client privilege.

   1. **Work Product**—"Work product" is the documents and other tangible things prepared by the attorney for their own use in conducting the case, such as witness lists, citation lists, emails regarding trial strategy, etc. While the privilege does not cover work product, it cannot be sought through discovery unless the requesting party demonstrates a need for the information. Most of the time, a court will not let the other side discover it.

C. **Physician/Psychotherapist-Patient**—There is no doctor-patient privilege in federal courts. However, there is a privilege for confidential communications made to a psychotherapist to obtain treatment.

D. **Insurance Coverage**—It cannot be used to show negligence or ability to pay damages but can be used to show ownership. This makes sense because if you could use insurance coverage as evidence of negligence or ability to pay damages, no one would buy insurance.

E. **Subsequent Remedial Measures**—Subsequent remedial measures are when the defendant fixes the thing that injured the plaintiff. It cannot be used to show negligence, but can be used to show ownership or that the thing is, in fact, fixable. This makes sense because if you could use fixing things as evidence of negligence, no one would fix anything after it injured someone.

F. **Compromise and Payment of Medical Expenses**—Offers to settle or pay medical expenses are not admissible. However, if the defendant makes an admission of fact along with the offer to pay medical expenses, that admission of fact is admissible. Basically, society wants to encourage settlement and people getting their injuries taken care of.

IV. HEARSAY AND CIRCUMSTANCES OF ITS ADMISSIBILITY

A. **Definition of Hearsay***—Hearsay is an out-of-court statement used for the truth of the matter asserted. The primary issue with hearsay is that while a party can challenge the testifying witness because they are present in court, there is no way to challenge the out-of-court person who made the statement the witness is testifying about.

1. **Out-of-Court**—Remember that the entire issue is that the party cannot challenge the statement. Consequently, if the statement was made in court or during a deposition (see below), it is admissible because someone was there to challenge the statement.

2. **Truth of the Matter Asserted**—If the truth of the statement does not matter, it is not hearsay. For example, imagine students tell me another student is coming to kill me. Later that day, the student shows up in my office, and I immediately clobber him with a chair. The student later sues me for battery. I defend myself by saying, "I thought he was coming to kill me, so I hit him." The reason I thought he was coming to kill me was that the other students told me he was. In that case, it does not matter at all if he was actually coming to kill me (the truth of the statement). Even if it was a lie that he was coming to kill me, it gives me a defense for my actions.

B. **Statements That Are Not Hearsay**

1. **Declarant-Witness's Prior Statement***

a. **Prior Inconsistent Statement**—Admissible to impeach and for its truth. Think about movies where someone is on the stand, looks up, sees the mobster staring, and changes their story.

b. **Prior Consistent Statement**—Admissible to rebut a charge of lying or improper motive for testifying.

c. **Prior Identification**—Can show that a witness identified a person earlier. For example, in the case where the defendant had a gigantic beard and then shaved it off for trial. If you could not do this, defendants would be growing and chopping off beards and changing their hair color all day long.

2. **Opposing Party's Statement***—Any statement made by a party may be used against that party. Keep in mind that this applies to employees and agents of companies. Remember that uncle who told you never to say, "It's my fault!" after a fender bender.

C. **Right to Confront Witnesses**—Under the Sixth Amendment Confrontation Clause, a criminal defendant has the right to confront witnesses. This means that the defendant may be at trial and may cross-examine witnesses.

D. **Hearsay Within Hearsay**—If an individual statement includes more than one instance of hearsay, all instances must meet one of the exceptions to the hearsay rule. For example, a business record might contain a hearsay statement of an employee. In that case, the business record must meet the business record exception, and the hearsay statement has to meet an exception (for example, maybe it was an excited utterance).

V. EXCEPTIONS TO THE RULE AGAINST HEARSAY

V. EXCEPTIONS TO THE RULE AGAINST HEARSAY—Hearsay exceptions are based on the idea that a person would be very unlikely to lie under the circumstances, or at least not have the time to make up a lie. Do not start thinking about murder mysteries. Just think that, if this scenario happened, how likely would it be for a normal person under normal circumstances to lie?

A. **Hearsay Exceptions**—Regardless of Whether the Declarant is Available as a Witness—Always pay close attention to whether the witness is available because this could eliminate some incorrect answer choices.

1. **Present Sense Impression and Excited Utterance***

   a. **Present Sense Impression**—The statement describes an event or condition and was made while the declarant was perceiving it or immediately thereafter. For example, the declarant was watching a guy at a bar and said, "Wow. That guy's hammered."

   b. **Excited Utterance**—The statement relates to a startling event and is very close in time to that startling event. These questions will always include a quote from the witness and may or may not have an exclamation mark, so do not be misled by this trick. Look for yelled, exclaimed, etc. Remember that the event does not need to be particularly exciting, so even something as mundane as tripping over a curb counts. The idea is that the declarant would not have time to make up a lie.

2. **Statement of Then-Existing Mental, Emotional, or Physical Condition**—It must be a statement of the then-existing state of mind, not a memory. For example, if a person said, "I plan on going to town today," "I'm cold," "I'm sad," or "My foot hurts," their statement is, at that moment, the most likely truth we will hear about the situation. Generally, reasonable people do not tell others they feel hot when they are actually feeling cold.

3. **Statement Made for Medical Diagnosis or Treatment**—This can come in because of how likely a person is to lie to their doctor if they want effective medical treatment. This exclusion is not based on the doctors themselves or any privilege; therefore, statements made to nurses and other individuals in the doctor's office in an attempt to obtain medical help are also considered. Think about all the people you may have to talk to when getting a doctor's appointment.

4. **Recorded Recollection***—The written record of a matter that the witness once knew but then forgot may be read into evidence—for example, my gradebook from 2006. I have not looked at it in years and have no memory of what it says, but I can read it into evidence since I knew the information at that time. As a matter of trial timing, if an attorney has a witness who cannot recall something, the attorney should first show the witness the recorded recollection and see if it jogs their memory. If it does, the attorney can then question the witness normally, assuming they now remember what happened. If the declarant still cannot remember, then the attorney can enter the recorded recollection. We would rather have a live human on the stand to question, if possible.

5. **Business Records; Absence of Business Record*—**Records kept in the regular course of business by someone with knowledge and no indication of a lack of trustworthiness. The absence of something that should have been in the business record also counts. However, if a business knows litigation is coming, its business records suddenly become highly suspect because the holder of the business records has every reason to manipulate them. For example, I have drawers full of student records that I use in my research. I have no reason to lie in them, because that would screw up my research. But if a student decides to sue me, and I make new records from that point forward, I have every reason to cook those new records to cover my tracks.
6. **Public Records and Reports; Absence of Public Record—**If the person making the record has a legal duty to report, then the record is admissible. Again, the idea is that it would be very unlikely for someone to lie in that situation.
7. **Statement in Learned Treatise, Periodical, or Pamphlet—**Again, there's no reason for someone to lie in a learned treatise, periodical, or pamphlet on the off chance that the lie might be useful for litigation later.
8. **Reputation Concerning Character—**A person's reputation is not necessarily the truth. A person may have a reputation as a great person, but spend all day being mean to puppies. Consequently, a witness may testify regarding a person's reputation under certain circumstances because truth is not really part of it.

B. **Hearsay Exceptions—**When the Declarant is Unavailable as a Witness—Remember to note whether the declarant is available or unavailable. Things that make a declarant unavailable are privilege, refusing to testify, lack of memory, death or illness, or being beyond the reach of a subpoena.

1. **Former Testimony*—**If the witness made the statement at trial, a hearing, or during a lawful deposition against a party who had a similar motive to develop the witness's testimony by direct, redirect, or cross-examination. The idea is that the witness would not be able to lie without some pushback.
2. **Statement Under the Belief of Imminent Death—**A statement about the cause of a person's death while believing that death was imminent. The romantic rule for this is "Who would want to meet their maker with a lie upon their lips?"
3. **Statement Against Interest*—**A statement against the declarant's proprietary, criminal, or pecuniary interest supported by circumstances that make it seem true. For example, a reasonable person would be unlikely to say, "I just killed my neighbor and stole his golden retriever" unless it were true.
4. **Statement Offered Against a Party That Wrongfully Caused the Declarant's Unavailability—**If a party wrongfully gets rid of the declarant, the declarant's statements may be admitted into evidence. For example, a party gives the declarant a one-way ticket to Brunei to get the declarant beyond subpoena jurisdiction.

VI. IMPEACHMENT, CONTRADICTION, AND REHABILITATION

A. **Ability to Observe, Remember, or Relate Accurately—**The opposing party may challenge a witness's ability to observe, remember, or relate the facts accurately.

B. **Contradiction—**Evidence of contradiction may be used to impeach a witness in the same way as inconsistent statements and conduct. A contradiction would be something like the witness stating that they do not like guns while owning several rifles.

C. **Inconsistent Statements and Conduct**—Evidence of inconsistent statements and conduct may be used to show that the witness is lying now. However, the witness must be allowed to explain or deny the inconsistent statement or conduct.

D. **Bias and Interest**—Evidence that the witness is biased or has an interest in the outcome may be used to impeach, for obvious reasons.

E. **Character for Truthfulness or Untruthfulness**

1. **Impeachment with Bad Acts**—Specific bad acts that show untruthfulness. For example, filing a false insurance claim would count, but kicking puppies has nothing to do with honesty. Although we can all agree that the puppy-kicker should go to prison forever.

2. **Impeachment with Convictions**—Can impeach using a crime involving dishonesty. In that case, the court has no discretion to exclude, and there is no time limit on the age of the crime. For felonies not involving dishonesty, courts have discretion and usually do not allow evidence of felonies that are over 10 years old.

F. **Religious Belief or Opinion**—Evidence of a witness's religious belief or opinions is not admissible to attack or support the witness's credibility.

G. **Rehabilitation of Impeached Witness**—Evidence supporting a witness's credibility may only be offered after their credibility has been attacked.

H. **Impeachment of Hearsay Declarant**—The credibility of a hearsay declarant may be challenged in the same way as a regular witness.

PRACTICE MULTIPLE-CHOICE QUESTIONS

1. As a prank, a group of students told their professor that another student was coming to kill him. Later that day, the student arrived at the professor's office hoping to ask some questions. The moment the professor saw the student, he hit him with a stapler. The professor was arrested and charged with criminal battery. You are a prosecutor working on the case. At trial, the professor claimed that he was acting in self-defense and testified about what the students had told him.

   If you object to the professor's testimony regarding what the students had told him, what is the likely outcome? **Select one.**

   (A) The statement is admissible because it is not hearsay.
   (B) The statement is admissible because it is a statement of the students' present sense impressions.
   (C) The statement is inadmissible because it is hearsay without any exception.
   (D) The statement is inadmissible because the professor is testifying in a criminal trial.

2. A teacher was driving to work. As the teacher pulled into the school's parking garage, a student who was late for class crashed into the back of the teacher's car. The teacher's back was seriously injured, and she sued the student. The student's parents hired you as her defense attorney. During the trial, the teacher alleged that the student was speeding and sleep deprived because of an exam she had that day and was not watching where she was going because she was a new driver and playing with her cell phone. You want to introduce

the testimony of a school security officer who saw the accident and immediately went to the teacher's car to see if she was injured. According to the officer's testimony, when he asked the teacher if she was hurt, the teacher said, "I should not have cut off that kid who was driving behind me." Part of the officer's official duties was writing reports regarding any accidents, injuries, or criminal activities on campus.

Will your attempt to introduce the officer's testimony be successful? **Select one.**

- **(A)** Yes, because the officer is reporting what the teacher said.
- **(B)** Yes, because the officer has a duty to make an accident report.
- **(C)** No, because the teacher's statement is hearsay without any exception.
- **(D)** No, because there is no indication that the teacher is unavailable to testify.

3. You represent an environmental nonprofit that sued a hazardous waste company for unlawfully dumping hazardous waste in a sewer that went straight to the city's harbor. The sewer was at the end of a street with four houses on it. You called one of the homeowners to the stand and asked her about how many times she had seen the company's trucks on her street and how long those trucks stayed there. The homeowner said she was not sure, but she kept a handwritten list of every time that she saw a company truck on her street. You showed the homeowner the list, but she still could not remember the exact number. You then asked the court to admit the homeowner's list at trial.

Is it likely that the court will admit the list? **Select one.**

- **(A)** Yes, the homeowner can read the list into evidence.
- **(B)** Yes, the homeowner can read the list into evidence or have it received as an exhibit.
- **(C)** No, because the homeowner's memory was not refreshed when she saw the list.
- **(D)** No, because there were no further guarantees of the list's truth.

4. A toy company was aware that a consumer protection nonprofit was planning a lawsuit against it regarding an allegedly defective toy that injured several children. The toy company hired you as its attorney, and you began gathering several pieces of evidence that could be useful in defending the toy company against the allegations.

Which of the following pieces of evidence are least likely to be admissible at trial? **Select two.**

- **(A)** Business records relating to the toy's manufacture and the possible lawsuit.
- **(B)** A mailman's statement that he heard one of the nonprofit leaders say, "I do not think anything is wrong with the toy."
- **(C)** A photocopy of a contract of sale between the toy company and a toy store linked to several injuries caused by the toy.
- **(D)** A bartender's statement that he overheard a toy company employee at the bar looking at one of the toys say, "The lines, screws, and seals on this toy are pretty near perfect."
- **(E)** A wife's statement that 24 hours after her husband, a toy company employee, was served to testify, her husband yelled, "There's nothing wrong! There's nothing wrong with the toy!"
- **(F)** A deceased toy company employee's statement made during a deposition that he thought the toys were some of the safest toys in the industry.

5. You represent a retailer that sued a manufacturer. The retailer claimed that the two parties had entered into a contract for $50,000 worth of cashmere sweaters, and the manufacturer failed to deliver the requested sweaters as promised. At trial, a retailer's employee testified that he had negotiated the contract in question. He also testified that the contract could not be provided because the original and all copies had been destroyed in a recent flood at the retailer's offices. However, he was familiar with the contract's substance and could testify to its contents. You began to question the employee about the contract's contents, but the manufacturer objected.

Is the court likely to sustain the manufacturer's objection? **Select one.**

(A) Yes, because the testimony violates the best evidence rule.
(B) Yes, because the contract was destroyed in the retailer's offices.
(C) No, because the testimony of someone deeply familiar with the document is satisfactory, so long as they can be cross-examined.
(D) No, because the retailer explained that the contract and its copies had been lost in a flood.

6. After a local sports match, a bar erupted into a giant fight where many people were injured, and several thousand dollars' worth of property was damaged. Everyone involved managed to escape before the police arrived. Soon thereafter, the police arrested the bar's owner, believing he had orchestrated the entire fight as a scam against his insurance company. You are working as a prosecutor on the case. At trial, you want to use the testimony of the girlfriend of one of the bar employees. According to her, the employee came home two hours after the fight and yelled, "Let's go to Vegas! The bar owner just gave me $1,000 to start a fight and get the bar trashed!" The employee died in a boating accident two days before the trial.

Is the girlfriend's testimony admissible? **Select one.**

(A) Yes, because it is a statement against penal interest.
(B) Yes, because it is an excited utterance.
(C) No, because there are no circumstantial indications of trustworthiness.
(D) No, because it is hearsay without any exception.

7. You represent the family of a man killed in a motorcycle accident. The family sued the motorcycle manufacturer for wrongful death. The family claimed that a defect in the wheel mounts caused the accident. Pursuant to a subpoena, you called upon the manufacturer to produce records of tests it had done on the motorcycle wheel mounts before it was sold to the public. The manufacturer's attorney objected, arguing that the test records had been turned over to her in preparation for trial.

Should the trial court require the manufacturer to produce the test records? **Select one.**

(A) Yes, because they are relevant to the facts at issue.
(B) Yes, because they are a statement against interest.
(C) No, because they are privileged as attorney work product.
(D) No, because they are being used to prepare for litigation.

8. A man was charged with driving under the influence. You worked as a prosecutor on the case. At the man's trial, the police officer who arrested the man testified that she was a highway patrol officer who was very familiar with the highway the man was driving on. She also testified that she had years of experience estimating the speed of vehicles driving on that highway and had stopped over 1,000 drivers for speeding. She said that she was driving on the highway when she saw the man pass her car at what appeared to be an excessive rate of speed. You asked the officer whether she had formed an opinion regarding the man's speed at the time she stopped him, and she replied that she had. You asked the officer to state that opinion, and the man's attorney objected.

Should the objection be sustained? **Select one.**

(A) No, because the officer established that she was an expert regarding the speed of moving vehicles.
(B) No, because a layperson may testify as to an opinion regarding the speed of moving vehicles.
(C) Yes, because the officer had not established that she was an expert regarding the speed of moving vehicles.
(D) Yes, because the officer's opinion would not be the best evidence regarding the speed of moving vehicles.

9. A defendant hired you to defend him in a murder case. The defendant was alleged to have poisoned his grandmother. You called a law professor to testify as an expert. During the law professor's testimony, he stated that he had taught criminal law for over 20 years, written several books on the subject, hosted a popular true-crime podcast, and was recognized in his field as the leading expert on the legal standards of mens rea and actus reus.

Which of the following opinions of the law professor are least likely to be admissible? **Select two.**

(A) An opinion based on several books that are no longer in print or available
(B) An opinion based partly on the hearsay statements of several witnesses to the crime
(C) An opinion regarding the defendant's mens rea
(D) An opinion regarding an ultimate issue in the case
(E) An opinion regarding the chemical makeup of the poison
(F) An opinion regarding the number of murders committed by poison each year

10. A husband and wife were eating at a restaurant when the wife had a severe allergic reaction to peanuts in her meal. The wife hired you to sue the restaurant. She claimed that she was never told peanuts were used to make her dinner. The husband died of a heart attack before the trial. At trial, the restaurant owner denied negligence and testified that he had personally informed the wife that peanuts were included in all meals prepared by the restaurant. You offered into evidence the husband's earlier deposition testimony that he never heard the restaurant owner say anything about peanuts.

Is the husband's deposition testimony admissible? **Select one.**

(A) Yes, as former testimony.
(B) Yes, as a dying declaration.
(C) No, because the husband is unavailable for cross-examination.
(D) No, because the husband's statement is inadmissible hearsay.

11. You represented an employee who sued his employer over injuries he sustained while working in a factory. At trial, the employee took the stand to testify that the employer had told him during a loud and heated argument that he needed to be careful around the machines. The employer's attorney learned that the employee had secretly recorded the private conversation on the employee's phone. The employer's attorney objected to the employee's testimony, arguing that the recording of the conversation had to be introduced because the conversation had been recorded. The recording was in your possession and had been given to you by the employee.

Which of the following legal issues are most relevant to the admission of the recording? **Select two.**

(A) Excited utterance
(B) Statements by a party opponent

(C) Best evidence rule
(D) Attorney-client privilege
(E) Statement against interest
(F) Relevance

12. You represent a woman who sued a restaurant for personal injury after she slipped and fell on the restaurant's premises. During a jury trial, a waitress at the restaurant testified on behalf of the restaurant. She testified that the woman drank a glass of wine before she slipped and fell down the stairs to the restaurant bathroom. You cross-examined the waitress, who admitted that probably a dozen people have fallen down those stairs, including many patrons who had not consumed any alcoholic drinks at all. You moved to strike the waitress's testimony that the woman had a glass of wine before falling.

Which of the following two statements are correct regarding the motion to strike the testimony? **Select two.**

(A) The evidence is not admissible because the waitress could not state that the woman was under the effects of alcohol when she fell.
(B) The evidence is admissible because it has limited probative value.
(C) The evidence is not admissible because probably a dozen people have fallen down those stairs.
(D) The evidence is not admissible because sober people have fallen down the stairs.
(E) The evidence is admissible because the waitress worked at the restaurant.
(F) The jury decides how much weight to give the evidence.

13. A jogger was seriously injured when a motorcyclist hit her. A witness, who was robbing a car parked nearby, saw the accident and immediately called 911. After the witness called 911 and described the scene, he ran over to the jogger. The jogger said, "I think I might die!" The witness looked at the motorcyclist lying on the street and said, "I think he's dead, too!" The witness panicked, yelled for help, and then ran four doors down the street to the local fire station. He and a firefighter ran back to the injured jogger. As the firefighter was aiding the jogger, the motorcyclist got up, jumped back on his motorcycle, and sped off. The witness chased him for a block but gave up after memorizing the motorcyclist's license plate number.

The jogger hired you to sue the motorcyclist. You wanted to call the witness at trial. The witness would testify that he called 911 and accurately described what he had just seen, but that he no longer remembered the details of the accident. You had the recording of the 911 call. You wanted to offer the recording into evidence, but you were afraid that it might be excluded on hearsay grounds.

Which of the following hearsay exceptions would best support the admission of the 911 recording? **Select two.**

(A) Present sense impression
(B) Excited utterance
(C) Statement against interest
(D) Dying declaration
(E) Recorded recollection
(F) Best evidence rule

14. A plaintiff hired you to represent him in an action to recover damages that he sustained in a car crash. Several local citizens witnessed the crash.

Which of the following statements are LEAST likely to be admissible at trial as lay opinion testimony? **Select two.**

(A) "I think the defendant's car must have had bad brakes."
(B) "It was a really loud crash."
(C) "The defendant looked drunk."
(D) "I think the defendant was trying to beat the red light."
(E) "The defendant was driving the car that crashed into the plaintiff's car."
(F) "The defendant was speeding."

15. A man was charged with murdering a gas station clerk late on July 5. According to officers who investigated the scene, the clerk was shot with a .45 caliber handgun during a botched robbery. The man was arrested at his home on July 8. During the arrest, the arresting officers discovered an illegal rifle and a large amount of cocaine. You are a prosecutor assigned to the case.

Which of the following pieces of evidence are most likely to be admitted as relevant evidence in the man's criminal trial? **Select two.**

(A) The man's checking account statement showing a negative balance on July 4
(B) A plane ticket to Australia that the man bought on July 6
(C) The cocaine found during the man's arrest
(D) The man's savings account statement showing a withdrawal of $10,000 on July 6
(E) The illegal rifle found during the man's arrest
(F) The gas station owner's testimony that criminals often targeted the gas station

16. You represented a client who was involved in a fight on an airplane. There were many witnesses to the fight, and you were unsure which particular witnesses you would use at trial. You narrowed the list down to ten and discovered that all of them would be available as witnesses at trial. After you interviewed the witnesses, you realized that most of their statements involved hearsay, but you believed you could use exceptions to the hearsay rule to get their statements admitted.

If all the witnesses are available to testify, which hearsay exceptions would be unavailable to you? **Select two.**

(A) Present sense impression
(B) Excited utterance
(C) Statement against interest
(D) Former testimony
(E) Recorded recollection
(F) Statement made for medical treatment

17. You represented an Environmental Protection Agency employee who was charged with taking bribes from clothing manufacturers in the area who were dumping chemicals in a local river.

At trial, which of the following pieces of evidence will require outside authentication to be admissible? **Select two.**

(A) A newspaper
(B) A clothing label
(C) An Environmental Protection Agency newsletter
(D) A negotiable instrument given to the employee
(E) A clothing manufacturer's signature
(F) A clothing manufacturer's business records

18. You were a prosecutor working on a burglary case. The burglar was seen by a security guard, who described the burglar as having long, bleached-blond hair and a mustache. After the burglary, the security guard had identified the burglar in a photo lineup. At trial, the burglar appeared with a shaved head and no longer wore a mustache. You showed the security guard a selection of photographs. The security guard testified that the first photograph was a picture of the burglar, and that photograph showed the burglar with long, bleached-blonde hair and a mustache.

Which of the following facts needs to be true for the security guard's statement to be admitted? **Select two.**

- **(A)** The security guard no longer remembers seeing the burglar.
- **(B)** The photograph of the burglar was made soon after the burglary.
- **(C)** The security guard testifies at trial and is subject to cross-examination.
- **(D)** The security guard adopted the photograph as a correct identification of the burglar shortly after the burglary.
- **(E)** The security guard perceived the burglar earlier.
- **(F)** The photograph of the burglar is corroborated by another witness.

19. You brought suit on behalf of your client, who sued a truck driver for injuries caused in a multivehicle accident. You hoped to call as a witness a woman who was a passenger in the truck at the time of the crash. However, before you had the chance to depose the woman, she died in a similar car accident. You discovered that a doctor had also sued the truck driver for his injuries in the same crash and that the doctor had deposed the woman two days before she died. During that deposition, the woman made the statement, "The truck driver was playing with his phone just before the crash."

Which of the following facts would best support a motion that the woman's statement should be admitted at trial? **Select two.**

- **(A)** The woman made the statement at a deposition.
- **(B)** The woman was a party-opponent.
- **(C)** The doctor's lawsuit involved the same accident as your client.
- **(D)** The woman's statement was a statement against interest.
- **(E)** The woman was biased in favor of the truck driver.
- **(F)** The woman was killed in a car accident.

20. Your client was charged with being involved in a conspiracy with two friends, a man and a woman, to commit a robbery of a local car dealership. During the robbery, a large plate-glass window was shattered, and a clerk was shot. All three members of the conspiracy were tried separately. The man's trial was held first, and he was acquitted. At your client's trial, the man's father would testify that after the man was acquitted, the man told him that he had committed the robbery with his friends. A doctor would testify that the man came to his office with large cuts that required stitches, and the man told the doctor that he had gotten the cuts while breaking a plate-glass window. An EMT would testify that the clerk told him, whispering, "I'm ready to die. I'm not scared at all. The man shot me. I wish the woman well." In fact, the clerk did not die, but he told you that he would not testify because he feared the man. A witness to the robbery would testify that he saw the robbery, saw the woman walk out of the car dealership, and that she exclaimed, "This robbery wasn't supposed to go down like this." Finally, the woman's mother would testify that, three days after the robbery, she heard the woman say, "I can't believe the man got me to rob the car dealership."

Which of the following statements are most likely to be inadmissible hearsay? **Select two.**

(A) The doctor's statement that the man told him he had gotten the cuts while breaking a plate-glass window.
(B) The father's statement that the man told him he had helped his friends commit a robbery.
(C) The EMT's statement that the clerk told him, "The man shot me!"
(D) The clerk's statement that "I wish the woman well."
(E) The woman's statement that, "This robbery wasn't supposed to go down like this."
(F) The mother's statement that, "I can't believe the man got me to rob the car dealership."

ANSWERS

1. The correct answer is (A). Here, the students' statement is not hearsay because it is not being offered for the truth of the matter asserted (that the student actually was coming to kill the professor). It is only being used to explain why the professor hit him. (B) is incorrect because the students' statement is not related to a present sense impression. (C) is incorrect because the statement is not hearsay. (D) is incorrect because the fact that this is a criminal trial does not change the analysis.

2. The correct answer is (A). A party-opponent's statement offered against that party is not hearsay—Federal Rule of Evidence 801. Here, the teacher is a party to the suit, and her statement that she cut off that kid is admissible against her. The idea is that she would not have said that unless it were true. (B) is incorrect because the officer's duty to report accidents is irrelevant. (C) and (D) are incorrect because the teacher's statement was admissible as a statement by a party-opponent.

3. The correct answer is (A). Here, the homeowner's list would qualify as a past recollection recorded. As such, the homeowner may read the list into evidence since looking at its contents has failed to jog her memory. (B) is incorrect because the homeowner may only read the list into evidence. However, if the adverse party was offering the list, the list could also be received as an exhibit. Here, the homeowner is a witness of the nonprofit, so it cannot be offered as an exhibit. (C) is incorrect because the witness could still read the list into evidence. (D) is incorrect because the issue is not whether there are additional guarantees regarding its truth.

4. The correct answers are (A) and (E). The business records would not be admissible because they were prepared with litigation in mind, and the business has every reason to cook the books. (E) is hearsay, so it needs to be admissible under an exception. Under the circumstances, the only possible exception seems to be excited utterance; however, his statement was made 24 hours after the startling event and is likely too far in time to be considered an excited utterance. (B) is incorrect because it would be the statement of a party opponent that would later be used against that declarant. (C) is incorrect because it would likely be relevant as to whether the toys were put into interstate commerce. (D) would be admissible because the bartender is simply relating the present-sense impression of what the employee is looking at. (F) is incorrect because a statement made during a deposition is generally admissible if the declarant is not available.

5. The correct answer is (D). If the terms of a writing are in issue, the best evidence rule requires that the original writing or photocopies must be offered into evidence. However, if the original and all copies of the document are destroyed without any evidence of bad faith, oral testimony to its contents is admissible. (A) is incorrect because the original and copies are destroyed, and there is no evidence of bad faith. (B) is incorrect because there was no evidence of bad faith, even if the documents were destroyed in the retailer's offices. (C) is incorrect because the best evidence rule requires a copy of the original document unless there is some valid excuse for it being missing.

6. The correct answer is (A). If a declarant is unavailable for trial and has made a statement against penal interest, that statement is admissible in court. Here, the employee died in a boating accident, and her statement that she helped commit insurance fraud would be against her penal interest. Consequently, the statement is admissible. (B) is incorrect because an excited utterance must take place very close in time to the startling event. Here, the startling event took place two hours before, which is unlikely to be close enough in time. (C) is incorrect because circumstantial guarantees of trustworthiness are irrelevant to the analysis. (D) is incorrect because the statement is a statement against penal interest, which is an exception to the hearsay rule.

7. The correct answer is (A). The test records are relevant because they tend to establish the manufacturer's knowledge regarding problems with the wheel mounts. (B) is incorrect because a statement against penal interest is a statement subjecting the declarant to some liability, and the test records themselves would not do that. (C) and (D) are incorrect because the tests do not contain the attorney's mental impressions regarding the litigation and were conducted for purposes other than litigation.

8. The correct answer is (B). A layperson may give opinions regarding matters within the competence of an ordinary person. The layperson must show that they had experience that would enable them to form an opinion, that they could perceive, and that they formed an opinion based on that perception. Since the officer established that she had experience with speeding vehicles, her opinion may be admitted as a lay opinion. (A) and (C) are incorrect because there is no rule stating that only experts may testify as to the speed of moving vehicles. (D) is incorrect because a layperson may testify to the speed of moving vehicles, and the best evidence rule is not applicable in this situation.

9. The correct answers are (C) and (E). (C) is correct because while an expert can testify about their opinion on an ultimate issue in a case, the expert may not offer an opinion regarding the requisite mental state of a criminal defendant. Consequently, the expert could not testify regarding the defendant's mens rea. (E) is correct because there is nothing in the facts showing that the expert is qualified to give an expert opinion regarding the chemical makeup of a substance—all his expertise is in criminal law, not chemistry. (A) is incorrect because nothing is preventing an expert from basing their opinion on works that are unavailable to the court. (B) is incorrect because the basis of an expert's testimony does not in itself need to be admissible. (D) is incorrect because the prohibition regarding ultimate issues has been relaxed, so long as the opinion does not involve the requisite mental state of a defendant. (F) is incorrect because the expert's expertise would likely involve such statistics.

10. The correct answer is (A). Former testimony is an exception to the hearsay rule if the witness is unavailable and the party against whom the testimony is offered had an opportunity to develop the testimony. Here, the husband is unavailable at trial and was subject to examination by the restaurant owner at the deposition. Consequently, the former testimony is admissible. (B) is incorrect because, although the husband is dead, this is not a dying declaration. (C) is incorrect because the husband does not need to be available for cross-examination. (D) is incorrect because former testimony is an exception to the hearsay rule.

11. The correct answers are (B) and (C). Here, because the employer is a party to the claim, his statements are admissible over a hearsay objection. Consequently, (B) is correct. (C) is correct because the employer's attorney's demand for the recording is likely based on a misunderstanding of the best evidence rule. Here, the best evidence rule would not apply because the employee is not seeking to prove the content of the recording itself. (A) is incorrect because even if the employee and employer were having a fight when the conversation occurred, there would be nothing to support the excited-utterance exception to the hearsay rule. (D) is incorrect because you do not appear to be protecting the recording from discovery, so arguments about attorney-client privilege are likely irrelevant. (E) is incorrect because a simple admonishment to be careful does not seem to be against any particular interest of the employer, and in fact, might help him. (F) is incorrect because any conversation about the machine between the employee and employer is likely to be relevant.

12. The correct answers are (B) and (F). (B) is correct because evidence is admissible even if it has limited probative value, and here the fact that the woman drank a glass of wine might have contributed to her falling down the stairs. (F) is correct because the jury decides how much weight to give the evidence. (A), (C), and (D) are incorrect because the fact that the woman drank a glass of wine was still probative as to whether alcohol might have contributed to the fall. (E) is incorrect because the mere fact that the waitress worked at the restaurant would not make any evidence she offered admissible (for example, if she had not actually seen the woman at the restaurant and only worked driving the restaurant's delivery truck).

13. The correct answers are (A) and (E). (A) is correct because the recording is of the witness describing the accident scene while he was perceiving it. Thus, the witness's description would be admissible as a present-sense impression. (E) is correct because the recording concerns a matter about which the witness once knew, but he cannot now remember; it was recorded when the event was fresh in the witness's memory, and it accurately reflected the witness's knowledge at the time. Thus, the recording is admissible as a recorded recollection. (B) is incorrect because there is no fact indicating that the witness was excited when he made the 911 call. (C) is incorrect because the witness did not say anything against his interest. (D) is incorrect because the witness never thought he was dying. (F) is incorrect because the best evidence rule only applies when the actual contents of a record are at issue.

14. The correct answers are (A) and (D). A fact cannot be supported by lay opinion when it requires specialized knowledge. (A) is correct because it would take expert or specialized knowledge to know that the defendant's car had bad brakes. A lay opinion also cannot be used when it is based on pure conjecture. (D) is pure conjecture because how would a witness know what the defendant was intending to do unless they could read minds? In any event, the four remaining answers are clear examples of allowable lay opinion. (B) is incorrect because a layperson may testify that something is loud. (C) is incorrect because a layperson may testify that a person looked intoxicated. (E) is incorrect because a layperson can identify another person. (F) is incorrect because a layperson may judge a moving vehicle's speed.

15. The correct answers are (B) and (D). Evidence of a defendant's intent to flee is relevant because it shows the defendant's consciousness of guilt and makes the defendant's guilt more probable. Here, (B) and (D) are correct because buying a plane ticket to Australia and withdrawing a large amount of money soon after the murder shows an intent to flee, which makes the man's guilt more probable. (A) is incorrect because the fact that the man had a negative bank balance would not make it more likely that he murdered the clerk (although this could show a motive, this evidence on its own is not necessarily relevant). (C) is incorrect because the fact that the man had cocaine at his home would not make the man's murder of the clerk more probable. (E) is incorrect because the illegal rifle would not make the man's murder of the clerk more probable. (F) is incorrect because the fact that many crimes occurred at the gas station would make it more probable that this man murdered the clerk.

16. The correct answers are (C) and (D). The hearsay exceptions for statements against interest and former testimony require the declarant to be unavailable at the time of trial. (A), (B), (E), and (F) are valid exceptions regardless of the declarant's availability.

17. The correct answers are (E) and (F). Seven things do not need any outside authentication, and they can be remembered with OIL CANS. These seven things are: (1) official publications issued by a public authority; (2) instruments—negotiable and commercial paper; (3) label, tag, or trademark fixed in the ordinary course of business; (4) certified public documents (certified by a clerk or court that had custody); (5) acknowledged documents signed before a notary; (6) newspapers; and (7) sealed documents. Consequently, (A), (B), (C), and (D) are incorrect.

18. The correct answers are (C) and (E). Without a hearsay exception, the security guard's statement would be inadmissible as hearsay because the security guard is testifying to an out-of-court statement used to establish the truth of the matter asserted. Here, the security guard's statement would be admissible as a prior identification, which requires the declarant to testify and be subject to cross-examination, and the declarant's statement to identify a person the declarant perceived earlier. Consequently, (C) and (E) are correct. (A), (B), (D), and (F) are incorrect because they are not necessary parts of a prior identification, nor do they support the admission of the security guard's statement either alone or in some combination.

19. The correct answers are (C) and (F). Suppose an unavailable witness made a statement at trial, a hearing, or during a lawful deposition against a party who had a similar motive to develop the witness's testimony by direct, redirect, or cross-examination. In that case, the statement is admissible as former testimony. Here, (C) is correct because the doctor would have the same motive to develop the woman's testimony as your client would, since your client and the doctor are both suing the truck driver for injuries caused in the same accident. (F) is correct because the fact that she died in a car accident makes her unavailable. (A) is incorrect because if the woman were available, the statement would not be admissible simply because she made it at a deposition. (B) is incorrect because your client is not suing the woman, so she is not a party opponent. (D) is incorrect because no one was suing the woman, so any statement she made was not against her interest. (E) is incorrect because there is no indication that the woman was biased in favor of the truck driver, nor would it matter to admissibility if she was.

20. The correct answers are (B) and (D). (B) is correct because the man was already acquitted, so it could not be admitted under the hearsay exception for a statement against interest. It would generally be excluded due to double jeopardy concerns. (D) is correct because a dying declaration only applies to the circumstances of the person's possible death (for example, who shot the person). Here, "I wish the woman well" does not have any connection to the causes of what the clerk believed was his impending death. (A) is incorrect because the statement could be used in a medical context, as a person is likely to inform a doctor about their injury to receive the correct care. (C) is incorrect because the statement could be considered a dying declaration. (E) is incorrect because the woman's statement is a statement against interest. (F) is incorrect because this is another statement against the woman's interest.

Real Property

6

Topics with asterisks (*) require you to know the black letter law cold; topics without an * require you to recognize the topic as part of the fact scenario or require you to analyze and apply legal resources provided for the topic efficiently.

MAIN POINT OF REAL PROPERTY—THE LAW FAVORS BENEFICIAL *USE* OF PROPERTY

OUTLINE

I. OWNERSHIP OF REAL PROPERTY

A. Present Estates

1. **Fee Simple Absolute***—Created by either "to A" or to "A and their heirs"—the largest interest in property, and the owner can do anything they want with it—can last for an infinite duration. This is the king of property rights.
2. **Defeasible Fees**—land ownership that is ended by a stated event—freely alienable, devisable, and descendible
   a. **Fee Simple Determinable**—Created by either "so long as," "while," "during," or "until"—interest automatically terminates when the stated event happens.
      i. **Grantor retains "Possibility of Reverter"**—Grantor gets property back when the stated event occurs. Remember it as sounding like "possible reverse."
      ii. Example: A conveys Blackacre to "B and his heirs so long as Blackacre is used as a kangaroo farm." B has a fee simple determinable, and A has a possibility of reverter, which means A will regain ownership of the property if Blackacre is no longer used as a kangaroo farm.

b. **Fee Simple Subject to Condition Subsequent**—When the grantor retains the right to take back the property if the stated event occurs. The major difference between this and other defeasible fees is that the property does not automatically revert to the grantor; instead, the grantor must choose to take it back by bringing an eviction action.
   i. The grantor keeps a "right of reentry." Sometimes referred to as *power of termination*.
   ii. Example: A conveys Blackacre to "B and his heirs, but if Blackacre is no longer used as a kangaroo farm, A can reenter Blackacre." B has a fee simple subject to a condition subsequent; A has a right of reentry.

c. **Fee Simple Subject to an Executory Interest**—If a third party will get the property automatically when the stated event occurs. Conveyance can either use the same language as the fee simple determinable or "provided that," "on condition that," or "but if."
   i. Example: A conveys Blackacre to "B and his heirs, but if Blackacre stops being used as a kangaroo farm, then to C." B has a fee simple subject to an executory interest, C has an executory interest, and A has nothing.

3. **Life Estates**

a. **Life Estate**—"To A for life." A has the property for the duration of their life.

b. **Life Estate *Pur Autre Vie***—"To A for the life of B." A has the property for the duration of B's life. If you cannot remember the French, remember "for the life of another."

B. **Future Interests**

1. **Reversion**—The interest held by the grantor when the grantor conveys a life estate. Think "reverse."

2. **Remainder, Vested, and Contingent**

a. **Indefeasibly Vested Remainder**—An interest that has no preconditions and an ascertainable grantee—basically, nothing could stop the interest holder from taking when the prior interest ends.
   i. **Example: "To A for life, then to B and his heirs."**—B has an indefeasibly vested remainder because there is no circumstance that will stop B's interest from vesting.

b. **Vested Remainder Subject to Open**—A remainder interest that is granted to a group where at least one member of the group is ascertainable, but the group may expand in numbers.
   i. Example: "To A for life, and on A's death, to his children." If A has one child alive when the property is conveyed, A could have more children, so the child has a vested remainder subject to open. Look for a group with a living member that could gain more members in the future.

c. **Vested Remainder Subject to Total Divestment**—If a future condition can totally take away the remainder interest
   i. Example: "To A for life, and then to B; but if B does not have children at the time of A's death, then to C's children." In that case, B has a vested remainder subject to total divestment because if B does not have children at the time of A's death, the property will go to C's children.

d. **Contingent Remainder**—Remainder is contingent upon an event occurring.
   i. **Subject to Condition Precedent**—"To A for life, then to A's children who reach 18 years of age." Imagine A has a ten-year-old child—that child has a contingent remainder subject to a condition precedent. The child will only gain interest in the property once they turn 18.
   ii. **Subject to Unborn or Unascertained Person**—"To A for life, then to their children." A does not have any children at the time of conveyance. Consequently, A's unborn children have a contingent remainder subject to the unborn person because there is no living person that can take the interest yet.

e. **Effect on Marketability of Title**—Whether a purchaser is interested in buying a piece of property could be determined by remainders; however, a valid remainder does not affect overall marketability. Therefore, a person could purchase someone's life estate interest, even if it is subject to a following remainder.

f. **Transferability of Remainders**—Both vested and contingent remainders are alienable (you can sell them), devisable (you can will them), and descendible (they can go through the rules of intestacy). Remember that remainders are valuable property rights.

3. **Executory Interest**

   a. **Executory Interest**—Except for the executory interest that follows a fee simple determinable discussed above, an executory interest is a third-party interest that cuts short the prior estate.
      i. **Springing Executory Interest**—Ends a gap in possession when the property has reverted to the grantor. It "springs" into being when the stated event occurs, taking the property from the grantor.
         [a]. Example: "To A for life, then 12 months after A's death, to B." After A dies, the property will revert to the grantor for one year. When the year is up, B's interest will spring into being.
      ii. **Shifting Executory Interest**—When the stated event happens, a new grantee "shifts" in and gets the property.
         [a] Example: "To A, but if B returns to this city, then to B." If B returns to the city, A's interest is cut short and B shifts in to take possession.

   b. **Marketability of Title**—Generally, a purchaser of the property could be dissuaded from purchasing an estate that could be cut short by an executory interest.

   c. Transferability of executory interests is alienable (you can sell it), devisable (you can will it), and descendible (it can go through the rules of intestacy). An executory interest is a valuable property right like any other property right.

4. **Rules Affecting Future Interests: Survivorship, Class Gifts, and Waste**

   a. **Survivorship**—When a conveyance depends upon a donee being alive at the time of taking.
      i. **Express**—Example—"To A for life, then to his surviving children."
      ii. **Implied**—Example—"To A for life, then to his heirs." A has two children, but one dies before A. The property passes to the surviving child.

   b. **Class Gifts**—A gift to a class of people, like "children" or "heirs." Gifts to people in the class may change as more people join the class.
      i. **"Children"**—The gift only goes to that generation, and adopted children are included.
      ii. **"Heirs"**—The people who would inherit if the grantor had been a testator who died without a will.

iii. Generally, class members not born at the time the will was written are included. If you think about wills, for example, most people write them and leave things to their "children" when the first child is born. If others come along, it would be clear that they meant to include them.

iv. **Class Closes When No One Else Can Enter the Class**—For example, a class of "children" when the parent dies because the parent could not have children at that point without some sort of magical help.

v. Conditions placed on a class member before that member may inherit are generally enforceable.

vi. **Waste**—Obligations to pay taxes and make repairs, apportionment of costs for special assessments. Unnecessary rules to memorize, but you should recognize that these things might be an issue in a writing prompt.

C. Cotenancy

1. Tenancy in Common, Joint Tenancy (Four Unities), and Tenancy by the Entirety (Five Unities)*

a. **Tenancy in Common**—Two or more people have an equal right to possess the property, but they do not have a right of survivorship—each tenant can transfer, mortgage, lease, or devise their interest to a third party without affecting the property interests of the other tenants in common. Requires only unity of possession—meaning all tenants have an equal right to possess the property.

b. **Joint Tenancy (Four Unities)**—Two or more people own the property with a right of survivorship. When one tenant dies, the other tenants split up the dead tenant's interest and add it to their own. In addition to the right of survivorship, the joint tenancy requires four more unities to be valid: (1) Possession—equal right to use and possess property; (2) Interest—each interest must be equal to the other interests; (3) Time—interests created at the same time; and (4) Title—interests created by same document. You can remember this by using the mnemonic PITT and thinking about how the underside of many of your jointed areas have pits—armpits, knee pits, etc. Or, you may have lived in a "pit" with some roommates in college.

   i. Example: "To A and B, as joint tenants with right of survivorship."

c. **Tenancy by the Entirety (Five Unities)**—Tenancy by the entirety adds one more unity to a joint tenancy—the cotenants must be married. Can remember this with MyPITT—either body parts or if you have had a somewhat hellish apartment.

   i. Example: "To A and B, a married couple, as joint tenants with right of survivorship.

2. Partition*

a. **Remedy of Partition**—If cotenants no longer wish to be cotenants, they can partition the land into separate properties.

b. **Limitations on Partition**—Agreements not to partition are enforceable. Only a tenant in common or a joint tenant may partition unilaterally. A tenant by the entirety may not do so, which makes sense if you consider the marriage aspect.

c. Methods of partition may be done voluntarily if the cotenants agree in writing on how to divide the land, or it can be done involuntarily by a court.

3. **Severance***

   a. **Conveyance**—Because the sale of a cotenant's portion of the land necessarily destroys the time and title requirements of a joint tenancy, the sale will turn the joint tenancy into a tenancy in common. However, if there are more than two cotenants, a sale does not destroy the joint tenancy of the cotenants not involved in the sale because those cotenants still share time and title.

   b. **Judgment Liens**—If one joint tenant has a judicial lien against them, this will not sever a cotenancy in most states.

   c. **Mortgages**—In most states (lien theory states), a joint tenant may grant a mortgage on their interest without severance. In the minority of states (title theory states), granting a mortgage severs the joint tenancy because it constitutes a transfer of title, just as in a sale. Consequently, time and title are destroyed. Pay attention to whether the question tells you if the jurisdiction follows the majority or minority rule. If the question does not say, assume the jurisdiction follows the majority rule, and look out for answer choices that mix the elements of lien and title theory.

   d. **Leases**—There is a jurisdictional split on whether a lease severs a joint tenancy. Look to see if the question provides facts showing that one of the unities has been destroyed.

4. **Relations Among Cotenants**

   a. **Possession**—Cotenants have an equal right to possess the premises, unless they have an explicit agreement to the contrary.

   b. **Rent and Profits**—Cotenants do not have to pay rent to each other, nor do they have to share profits from business conducted on the land. However, rent from third parties must be split among the cotenants, less any expenses.

   c. **Cotenant's Encumbrance**—*See* mortgages and liens above.

   d. **Ouster**—When one cotenant bars another cotenant from access to the property. In that case, the ousted cotenant can sue for access and recover damages for the loss of use of the property. Think of ouster as one cotenant punching the other to keep him out, creating an "ouchie."

   e. **Contribution for Expenses**—Cotenants are responsible for expenses in proportion to their ownership interests in the property. This applies to taxes and mortgage payments but not to repairs or improvements, unless the other cotenants agree. This makes sense because repairs or improvements are necessary according to the eye of the beholder, not necessary in that the government will foreclose on the property if the taxes are not paid.

D. Landlord-Tenant Law

1. **Tenancies***

   a. **Tenancy for Years**—A tenancy that starts on a specific day and ends on a specific day. It can be for any length of time, so do not think there is a tenancy for years simply because the lease says it is for a "year" or several "years." No notice is required to terminate because the lease already specifies a specific termination date. If the agreement is over one year, the statute of frauds applies (M-Y [Contracts that cannot be completed in under a year]-L-E-G-S). For MYLEGS, you can remember it by noting that people often mistake "statute" for "statue," and you can visualize a statue with legs. I imagine the Statue of Liberty.

b. **Periodic Tenancy**—Continues from period to period with no set termination date until proper notice is given. Needs notice to terminate—usually a month. If the question has a particularly long rental period, such as a year, and inquires about what will happen if the parties fail to renew, courts are likely to treat the lease as a month-to-month lease until the parties can resolve their issues. If you see an automatic renewal, it is a periodic tenancy. More likely than not, every rental you have ever had was month-to-month.

c. **Tenancy at Will**—Continues as long as the landlord and tenant desire. This tenancy cannot be assigned or transferred and will end upon the death of one of the parties. When I was in law school, I let a friend live in my apartment as long as he wanted. I only did it because he was my friend. If he had assigned it to someone else, so someone I did not know was staying in my place, that would have been super bizarre.

d. **Tenancy at Sufferance**—If the tenant stays over after the lease expires without the landlord's permission. The landlord is "suffering" this person hanging around.

2. **Possession, Rent, and Actual and Constructive Eviction***

a. **Landlord's Duty to Deliver Possession**

i. **English Rule**—Common Law Rule—Majority Rule—the landlord must give the tenant both the legal right to possess the property and deliver actual possession of the property. If there are trespassers or squatters inside the property, the landlord needs to remove them. If the doors are locked, the landlord must unlock them so you can gain entry. Remember this by thinking this is the rule that makes sense. Usually, the majority rule makes the most sense, and we derive our common law from English common law because that law is logical and well-established. If you rented property, you would not expect to have to evict squatters yourself.

ii. **American Rule**—Minority Rule—The landlord only has to give the tenant the legal right of possession. If there are squatters on the property, the tenant has to deal with them. Remember this by thinking this rule does not make a lot of sense, and that is why it is the minority rule.

b. **Rent**—An implied lease is created in the situation where the lease is over, but the tenant gives the landlord the next month's rent, and the landlord accepts it. In that case, the lease is extended for another month even though there is no lease agreement. If the landlord wants the person out, they should not accept the rent.

c. **Actual Eviction**—The landlord breaches the lease's covenant of quiet enjoyment by intentionally doing something, such as telling the tenant they cannot go in a certain area of the property after the tenant rented it or leaving all of the landlord's stuff in a room so the tenant cannot use all of the property they signed a lease for. In that case, the tenant can remain in the property and no longer has to pay rent. Remember this by thinking that the landlord is acting like an "ass" and the law wants to punish the landlord. "Actual = ass." Be cautious of answer choices that state the tenant only receives a rent abatement or reduction.

d. **Constructive Eviction**—The landlord is being "clumsy" by accidentally allowing something to breach the lease's covenant of quiet enjoyment—like a tree hits the roof, the heater breaks, or anything that might make the property uninhabitable. In that case, the entire question will depend on whether the tenant moves out. If the tenant moves out, the lease is automatically terminated, and the tenant no longer has to pay rent. If the tenant remains, they must continue to pay rent. Think of the potentially bad places you have rented in the past—for example, maybe the heat was glitchy, but you wore a blanket and decided to stay because you did not want to find a new place, so why should you not continue to pay rent? Additionally, the landlord must have knowledge that something is wrong with the property and an opportunity to rectify it before the tenant can leave, as it would not be fair for the tenant to leave without the landlord having a chance to make the necessary repairs. In a question, you can assume the landlord has knowledge if their negligence led to the problem (e.g., they fell through the ceiling while working on the apartment upstairs). Remember this by thinking that the landlord is "clumsy = constructive eviction." Be careful of answer choices that imply the tenant must "terminate the lease." This implies that the tenant may need to provide notice. The correct statement is that the tenant can "treat the lease as terminated" and leave.

e. **Covenant of Quiet Enjoyment**—Every lease, whether commercial or residential, has a covenant of quiet enjoyment. This covenant is breached when the landlord or someone with a superior title interferes with the tenant's use of the property. Landlords are not liable for the actions of other tenants, but they are responsible for common areas and for the actions of other tenants that constitute a nuisance.

f. **If Landlord Fails to Fix Damage in Timely Manner**—If the tenant gets hurt because the landlord is negligent in failing to fix something they have a duty to fix, the tenant can sue the landlord for violating the lease and for regular negligence (*e.g.*, lease says landlord responsible for repairs, window breaks, tenant tells landlord, three weeks pass with no repair, tenant steps on glass).

3. **Statutory Remedies**

a. **Forcible Entry Statutes**—Local laws regarding eviction and what actions a landlord can take when a tenant refuses to leave. Just be aware of what they are in case they appear in a skills question.

4. **Assignment and Sublease***

a. **Assignment**—The tenant gives all their interest in the property to another person. For example, if six months are left on the lease, the tenant gives the other person those six months that are left. If a tenant fails to pay rent, the landlord can recover the unpaid rent from the original tenant who signed the lease (based on their signature on the lease agreement) and from anyone who has received an assignment.

b. **Sublease**—The tenant gives less than their entire interest to another person. For example, when the tenant gives someone four months of the lease when six months are left. The landlord can never get unpaid rent from the sublessee unless the sublessee expressly assumes the duty to pay rent. Think of the sublessee as a submarine hanging off the bottom of the other property interests, and the landlord is sailing on top of the sea of property interests and cannot get at them.

c. **Restrictions**—Restrictions on assignments and subleases are strictly construed. Consequently, if the lease prohibits assignments, the tenant can still sublease; if the lease prohibits subleases, the tenant can still assign it. A landlord can assign the right to rent to another person because this does not affect the tenant, who has to write a check to someone (unless the tenancy is an at-will tenancy, in which case neither the landlord nor the tenant can assign or sublet the property). Think back to the main point of property law and how it encourages people to make beneficial use of their property.

5. **Termination of Lease***
   a. **If Lease Says Only Landlord or Tenant Can Terminate**—Courts will interpret the lease as allowing either the landlord or tenant to terminate. If only one party had the right to terminate, you would have the set-up for a horror movie because one party could be held hostage by the other.
6. **Habitability and Suitability***
   a. **Affirmative Waste**—Tenant cannot trash the place, dig a salt mine, etc.
   b. **Permissive Waste**—Unless the lease or local law says the tenant does not have to do it, the tenant has to repair the premises to the extent necessary to maintain the premise's pre-rental condition. Think about filling the holes you made in the walls before you move out of a place. However, the tenant is not required to take any action regarding ordinary wear and tear on the property.
   c. **Ameliorative Waste**—When the tenant increases the value of the premises with a major permanent alteration. For example, if I rent out my house to you while I'm on sabbatical, I do not expect to come home and find a new pool in the backyard. I expect to get my house back in the same condition as I left it.
   d. **Modern Contract Theory of Leases**—Just like a contract, a landlord and tenant can covenant for anything they want in the lease. For example, the lease could stipulate that it is the tenant's duty to rebuild the property if it is destroyed. The leases we sign today are based on this theory. Remember this by thinking about the last lease you signed and how many things both you and the landlord explicitly agreed to.
      i. **If Premises Destroyed**—Tenant does not need to rebuild unless the tenant agreed to do so in the lease.
      ii. **If Express Covenant to Do Something Minor**—If the lease has an express covenant stating that the landlord will repaint the walls, replace the carpets, etc., every couple of years and the landlord does not do it, the tenant can fix the problem and take the cost out of the rent.
   e. **Common Law Lease**—If there is no information about the lease agreement or the question says that the common law governs the lease, it is a common law lease. In that case, the tenant is responsible for keeping out wind, rain, and raccoons. (Usually stated as only "wind and rain," but "raccoons" makes it easier to remember for me because I find raccoons delightful, and they basically get in the same way and cause the same problems as wind and rain.) Consequently, if a window is broken, there is a minor hole in the roof, or the screen door breaks, the tenant has the duty to repair it. The rule is beneficial for the landlord, as it ensures the property is protected from the elements. Conversely, the rule is advantageous for tenants, as they are not required to worry about the landlord inspecting the property daily.
   f. **Implied Warranty of Habitability**—Only applies to residential leases and cannot be waived by the tenant (because landlords would try to get tenants to do this all the time). Warrants that the landlord will keep the property in a habitable condition. If a lease is commercial, no implied warranty of habitability because no one is supposed to be living on the property. Just remember "habitat" means the place something lives.
   g. **Property Defects**—Landlord must inform a tenant of latent defects, which are defects the tenant would not see—think of an alligator under the water—two LLs in alligator, one L in latent. For obvious patent defects, the landlord is not required to provide warning. So, if the property has a giant, obvious wall of spikes, the landlord does not have to warn the tenant about it. If the tenant somehow impales themselves on the spike wall, that is their problem.

E. Alienability, Descendibility, and Devisability of Present and Future Interests

1. **Rule Against Perpetuities**—Do not have to worry about it because it is not covered on the bar exam. Breathe easy.
2. **Total Restraint**—Total restraints on the transfer of property are generally unlawful as a matter of public policy. Remember, property law wants the property to be used as beneficially as possible.
3. **Partial Restraint**—A partial restraint, like a right of first refusal in the sale of the property, is enforceable in most jurisdictions. Sometimes, a restraint like this is the best way to make sure the property is used as beneficially as possible.

F. Fair Housing and Discrimination*

1. **Fourteenth Amendment**—The Fourteenth Amendment prohibits the government from treating similarly situated individuals differently without sufficient justification. The particulars of this will be covered in Constitutional Law.
2. The Fair Housing Act prohibits discrimination in the sale, renting, or financing of housing.
3. **Retaliatory Eviction**—unlawful eviction of a tenant for reporting problems regarding a property
4. **Discrimination in Leasing**—A landlord may not discriminate against a potential tenant based on race, religion, national origin, sexual orientation, gender, disability, or family status. However, housing limited to older individuals, such as retirement communities, is allowed.
5. **Racially Restrictive Covenants**—Absolutely prohibited, which should be fairly obvious.
6. **Reasonable Accommodations for Tenants with Disabilities**—Landlords must make reasonable accommodations, such as making allowances for seeing-eye dogs. However, unless the property is a large-scale rental, the landlord does not have to install ramps, etc.

II. RIGHTS IN REAL PROPERTY

A. Easements and Licenses

1. Nature and Type of Easements and Licenses*

a. **Affirmative Easement**—The easement owner has an affirmative right to use the property, like crossing another person's property to get to the road.

b. **Negative Easement**—Must be expressly created in a writing signed by the grantor and prohibits the grantor from using their land to the detriment of the holder—for example, not interfering with the holder's support, light, air, or water flowing over the two properties. Remember it as an easement that does not actually use the other property.

c. **Easement Appurtenant**—There is judicial preference for this type of easement, which is an easement connected to and benefiting the use and enjoyment of land. The land that benefits from the easement is the dominant estate, while the land with the easement is the servient estate (because it serves the use of the other estate). Generally, when you think of an easement, you think of it being connected to another piece of land.

d. **Easement in Gross**—This is when the easement is granted to a specific person and is unconnected to any use of land. For example, letting a specific person who lives miles away drive across your lakeshore property for boat access. Think of it as "gross" to pick favorites like this.

e. **Difference Between an Easement and a License**—A license is freely revocable and does not require consideration or a writing. The most common example of a license is a ticket to a show or sporting event. Basically, a theater can toss you if you keep yelling, "I don't believe you!" during a play.

2. **Creation of Easements and Licenses***

a. Express easement must be in a writing signed by the grantor that identifies the parties and the interest transferred.

b. **Reserved Easement**—Under the common law, a seller could reserve an easement for their own use when they conveyed property. Modern law allows the seller to do this for third parties as well.

c. **Easement Implied from Existing Use**—Created when an owner of two parcels of land conveys the parcel of land that was used as the servient estate. If the buyer of the servient estate was aware of the easement's use or the easement was readily apparent, courts will assume that the parties intended the use to continue.

d. Easement implied from a subdivision plat can be implied without any existing use if recorded as part of a subdivision plan.

e. **Prescriptive Easement**—Created in the same way as gaining title to property through adverse possession. However, the use does not need to be exclusive, so it is OCAN instead of OCEAN. Think of it as "Oh, can I use the easement?" said in a snarky tone.

f. **Easement Arising from Estoppel**—Created by the user's detrimental reliance on the servient estate owner's permission to use the servient property. Similar to promissory estoppel in contracts.

g. **Easement by Necessity**—Created when a common owner owns both the dominant and servient estates, and the severance of the two estates leaves the dominant estate landlocked with no free and legal access to a public road.

h. **Expressly Created License**—express personal permission to use the property, like a concert ticket

i. **License Created by Failing to Create an Easement**—If someone orally tries to create an easement or if there is some problem with the writing purporting to create the easement, a license is created instead.

3. **Scope and Apportionment***

a. **Rules of Construction**—Courts first look at the terms of the easement document. If that is ambiguous, then courts will consider what is reasonable and infer the parties' intent from their actions.

b. **Consequences of Change in Use or Use Outside Scope**—The servient estate owner may stop the easement holder from going outside the scope of the easement, but such conduct will not terminate the easement itself.

c. **Duties to Repair**—The easement owner has the duty to maintain the easement, which is only fair.

d. **Effect of Subdivision of the Dominant Estate**—Generally, if the easement is appurtenant, the easement will remain for the benefit of every subdivided parcel.

4. **Effect of Transfer of the Dominant or Servient Estate and the Assignability of Easements and Licenses***

a. **Transfer of Dominant Estate**—An easement appurtenant is automatically transferred along with the transfer of the dominant estate.

b. **Transfer of Servient Estate**—A license is revoked when the servient estate is transferred. Usually, an easement appurtenant is transferred along with the transfer of the servient estate. However, if an unrecorded express easement exists, it may be unenforceable against a subsequent purchaser, depending on the recording act followed by the jurisdiction.

c. **Assignability of Easement**—Usually, it may be transferred dependent upon the easement's terms and whether the burden would increase for the servient estate.

d. **Assignability of License**—Usually, an attempt to transfer the license will revoke the license. Thinking of licenses as concert tickets does not really work for this point since people transfer concert tickets all the time.

5. **Termination of Easements and Licenses***

a. **Stated Conditions**—An easement may include express terms stating when the easement will terminate. This is similar to any other property rights.

b. **Unity of Ownership**—If a single owner acquires title to both the dominant and servient estate, the easement is terminated by "merger." Additionally, the easement will not automatically revive if the property is separated again.

c. **Abandonment**—The owner of an easement may terminate the easement by acting in a way that shows their intent to give up the easement—for example, by building a wall blocking it off.

d. **Estoppel**—If an easement owner appears to abandon the easement through words or conduct and the servient estate owner acts in detrimental reliance on those words or conduct, the easement may be terminated through estoppel.

e. **Prescription**—The owner of the servient estate can terminate the easement by engaging in activities that interfere with the easement in a way that is open, continuous, actual, and nonpermissive for the statutory period (remember OCAN). For example, if the servient owner builds a wall across the easement and the easement owner takes no action.

f. **Necessity**—If the need that created the easement by necessity ends, the easement is terminated.

g. **Condemnation**—A court may condemn an easement.

h. **Destruction of the Servient Estate**—If the easement is connected to access to a structure, and natural events destroy that structure, then the easement is terminated. For example, if an easement provides access to an oceanfront bathhouse and the bathhouse is washed away by a storm, the easement will terminate.

i. **Termination of License by Revocation**—Most licenses are freely revocable. Think of a license as permission. For example, James Bond has a license to kill. If Bond starts killing too many people, the folks who gave him the license should be able to yank it.

j. **License that Becomes Irrevocable**—A license can become irrevocable through detrimental reliance. In that case, there would need to be some agreement between the property holders that makes it fair to revoke it.

B. Restrictive Covenants

1. Nature and Type of Restrictive Covenants*

a. Affirmative covenant requires the landowner to do something, like pay dues to a homeowner's association or mow the yard. It is enforced through monetary damages.

b. Negative covenant prohibits the landowner from doing something, like putting the property up on Airbnb. It is enforced through monetary damages.

c. Equitable servitude is enforced by an injunction instead of money damages.

2. Creation and Enforceability of Restrictive Covenants and Equitable Servitudes

a. **Statute of Frauds**—both covenants and equitable servitudes have to be in writing. Remember the "L" of MYLEGS. The writing must clearly indicate that the parties intend for the rights or duties to be conveyed with the land. For example, referring to "Bob and his heirs" would imply that the parties intended the agreement to run with the land, not just be personal to Bob.

b. **Runs with the Land**—A covenant or equitable servitude runs with the land, which means it can be enforced against subsequent property owners. Both must also "touch and concern the land," which means that the covenant or servitude is not just personal against the promisee or promisor.

c. **Implied from Common Scheme**—Restrictive covenants and equitable servitudes cannot be implied from a common scheme.

3. Transfer of Restrictive Covenants and Equitable Servitudes

a. A purchaser must have notice before they can be required to do or not do something according to a covenant or equitable servitude.

4. Termination of Restrictive Covenants and Equitable Servitudes*

a. Termination of restrictive covenants can terminate in the same way as easements. Consequently, they can terminate through abandonment, waiver, estoppel, condemnation, merger, written release, or sale to a bona fide purchaser for value who is protected by the jurisdiction's recording act.

b. Termination of Equitable Servitudes

   i. **Unclean Hands**—If the plaintiff has intentionally engaged in the same conduct that the plaintiff is complaining about regarding the defendant, the plaintiff can be denied equitable relief.

   ii. **Acquiescence**—If one party knew about the other party's actions and acquiesced in that conduct, equitable relief can be denied.

   iii. **Estoppel**—As in all instances of estoppel, a party cannot induce another party's reliance and then benefit from that change in position at the other party's expense.

iv. **Changed Neighborhood Conditions**—If changed circumstances in the surrounding area have taken away the benefit of a property restriction, the restriction may no longer be enforced. For example, if a residential subdivision has become surrounded by industrial use since its founding, it may be possible that the subdivision will no longer enforce its residential restrictions. If a question gives you changed circumstances in the area, see if any land restrictions in the area continue to make sense.

III. REAL ESTATE CONTRACTS

A. Creation and Construction of Real Estate Contracts

1. **Statute of Frauds and Exceptions***—A contract for the sale of land must comply with the statute of frauds.

   a. Exceptions

      i. If there is evidence of part performance of the agreement, either party can demand full performance. Such evidence includes payment of all or part of the purchase price, possession of the property by the purchaser, or substantial improvement of the property by the purchaser. Most jurisdictions require proof of two of the three.

2. **Essential Terms***—A real estate contract must be (1) in writing, (2) signed by the party to be charged, and (3) contain all the essential terms (*i.e.*, who, property, price).

3. **Time for Performance***

   a. **Presumption That Time Is Not of the Essence**—Generally, a party does not have to deliver marketable title until the closing.

      i. **How to Overcome**—This can be overcome if (1) the contract specifically states time is of the essence, (2) if the parties' intentions indicate that time was of the essence, or (3) when one party gives notice to the other party that time is of the essence.

      ii. **Liability Issues**—If a party fails to render performance on the closing date, that party will be in breach and liable for damages.

4. **Remedies for Breach***

   a. **Specific Performance**—A buyer can demand specific performance of the land sale contract because all land is unique.

   b. **Part Performance**—If one of the parties has already done part of the agreement, a court could enforce the agreement. For example, if one of the parties made improvements to the property as specified in the real estate contract.

   c. **When Tender of Performance Is Excused**—When one party repudiates the real estate contract, the other party is excused from performance.

   d. **Liability for Defects**—If there is a defect in the title, the buyer may rescind and recover costs.

   e. **Damages (Including Liquidated Damages)**—Expectation damages are available for both the buyer and the seller. These damages represent the difference between the contract price and the market value as of the date of performance. Incidental damages are also recoverable.

i. Sometimes, a real estate contract states that a buyer's deposit can be seized as liquidated damages. However, the amount of liquidated damages must be reasonable.
ii. Most jurisdictions put the risk of any loss on the buyer for the time between the contract execution and the closing. However, the seller is liable if the damage is caused intentionally by the seller or due to their negligence. The minority of jurisdictions keep the risk of loss on the seller until the buyer takes title.

f. Distinctions Between Negligence of Builders and Sellers of Existing Property
   i. **Misrepresentation**—When the seller provides false or misleading facts concerning an aspect of the property. The buyer may seek to rescind the contract or seek damages. This can be done either intentionally or negligently.
   ii. **Fraud**—If intentional fraud can be shown, the buyer may seek rescission of the real estate contract and damages for losses caused by the fraud. If the seller's conduct is particularly egregious, the buyer may also be awarded punitive damages.
   iii. **Active Concealment**—Actively hiding a problem about the property can be grounds for nullifying the land sales contract.
   iv. **Failure to Disclose**—While *caveat emptor* (buyer beware) may protect some sellers, a seller's failure to disclose can also lead to a claim of misrepresentation or fraud.

g. Disclaimers of Liability
   i. A disclaimer of liability in a real estate contract can be legally binding if the recipient explicitly agrees to its terms.

B. Marketability of Title*

1. **Title "Reasonably Free from Doubt"**—reasonably free from doubt as to who is the owner of the property
2. **Defects in the Record Chain of Title**—A break in the chain of title is a serious title defect. This can be remedied by a suit to quiet title, where a judge examines the records to determine the valid owner of the property.
3. **Encumbrances**—A marketable title must be free from legal or physical restraints that affect the use of the property. Examples would be mortgages, zoning violations, and adverse possession claims.
4. **Waiver**—A buyer can waive issues regarding the marketability of the title.
5. **Timing of Marketability Requirement**—The seller is not required to deliver marketable title until the closing, which is when the sale is o ver, the ownership of the land is transferred, and the deed is delivered to the buyer. However, the buyer and seller can agree otherwise.
6. **Merger**—Under the common law, an obligation in the contract of sale is merged into the deed and can no longer be enforced unless it is also in the deed. Exceptions include when the parties intended the obligation to survive the deed or when the obligation is independent of the land sale itself.
7. **Remedies**—If there is a problem with the marketability of the title, the buyer's remedies include money damages, rescission, and specific performance.

IV. MORTGAGES AND FORECLOSURE

A. Mortgages and Deeds of Trust

1. **Definition of Mortgage and Deed of Trust**—A mortgage is a real property interest that acts as a security for an obligation—for example, most people get the money to buy a home by getting money from a bank and securing the repayment of the money by giving the bank a property interest in the house. In some states, instead of a mortgage, the state uses a deed of trust. In that case, the deed of trust is held by a third-party trustee to secure repayment to the lender.
2. **Purchase Money**—A purchase money mortgage has priority over other mortgages and liens. To be a purchase money mortgage, the mortgage is granted to the seller or a third-party lender, and the proceeds are used to buy the property or construct improvements.
3. **Future Advance**—This is a line of credit against the real property. The borrower gives a lender a mortgage on the property in exchange for money, for example, home equity loans.

B. Mortgage Theories

1. **Title**—In the minority of states, the lender (mortgagee) is treated as being the owner of the property, while the borrower (mortgagor) has the right to regain the property once they pay off the loan.
2. **Lien**—In most states, the borrower (mortgagor) is treated as being the owner of the real property, while the lender (mortgagee) is the holder of a lien on the property.
3. **Intermediate**—In this case, the borrower (mortgagor) retains the title, but the lender (mortgagee) can take the property back without a court order if the borrower defaults.

C. Foreclosure

1. **Judicial and Nonjudicial**—All states allow foreclosure through judicial means. More than half of the states also allow foreclosure through a private sale.
2. **Acceleration**—If a mortgage contains an acceleration clause, the entire amount of the mortgage obligation is due at default. Otherwise, the mortgagor may collect only the amount that is owed if the mortgagor brings a foreclosure action.
3. **Parties to the Process**—usually, the mortgagor, the mortgagee, and an auctioneer auctioning the property to the highest bidder
4. **Deficiency and Surplus**
   a. **Priorities of Senior and Junior Interests**—The rights of a senior interest are generally not affected by the foreclosure sale.
   b. **The Effect of Foreclosure on Junior Interests**—All junior interests to the foreclosed mortgage are destroyed.
   c. **Modification of Priorities (Failure to Record, Subordination Agreement)**—Mortgages are subject to the jurisdiction's recording acts. Additionally, a senior interest may agree to subordinate itself to a junior interest.
   d. **Distribution of the Proceeds of Sale**—Sale proceeds are applied to (1) costs that are part of the sale; (2) the foreclosed mortgage obligation; (3) junior interests in order of priority; and (4) the mortgagor.

e. **Deficiency Judgments**—In many states, the mortgagee may bring an action against the mortgagor or anyone else who has assumed the mortgage if the sales proceeds do not cover the mortgage obligation.

5. **Redemption After Foreclosure**—Some jurisdictions allow a property owner to reclaim property after a foreclosure sale if they pay all costs associated with the sale and the amount of the unpaid loan.

V. TITLES

A. Adverse Possession

1. **Elements**—A person can gain title to land if they use the land as a true owner would and their use is open, continuous for the statutory period, exclusive, actual, and nonpermissive. Remember the elements by using the word "OCEAN" and imagine an ocean wave washing away a house from its owner.
2. **Issues Affecting the Running of the Statutory Period**—If the actual owner is insane, an infant, or imprisoned at the time adverse possession starts, the period will not begin to run against the owner. This makes sense because adverse possession punishes actual owners who fail to take any action to protect their land. Someone who cannot defend themselves should not be subject to adverse possession.
3. **Tacking**—One adverse possessor can add or "tack" their period of possession onto another person's if there is privity between the two possessors. Privity is satisfied if the passing of the property interest between the two adverse possessors is by descent, devise, deed, or contract.

B. Transfer by Deed

1. **Requirements for Deed***

a. **Rules of Construction**—Deeds are meant to give effect to the intent of the grantor.

b. **Statute of Frauds**—Deeds must conform to the statute of frauds since they are a transfer of real property. Remember MY LEGS!

c. **Parol Evidence (Ambiguity, Grantor's Intent)**—Just like in contracts, parol evidence is generally not admissible to show the meaning of a deed.

d. **Proper Description of Land and Parties**—The grantor, grantee, and property must be identified. The description of the property must be reasonable and can be done by metes and bounds.

e. **Words of Intent**—Any language showing an intent to transfer the property is sufficient.

f. **Signature**—The grantor or grantors of the property must sign the deed.

g. **Consideration Not Required**—Property can be transferred without consideration.

h. **Void and Voidable Deeds**—A void deed does not pass title and cannot be enforced by a bona fide purchaser. However, a voidable deed may be enforced by a bona fide purchaser.

i. **Delivery and Acceptance Issues (Conditional Delivery and Relation Back of Acceptance)**—Acceptance of the deed is required for the transfer to be complete. Unless a bona fide purchaser or creditor of the grantor would be adversely affected, the acceptance relates to the time the deed was transferred. A grantee can reject the deed. In that case, the grantor keeps title to the land.

2. **Types of Deeds***

   a. **General Warranty Deed**—The holder of the deed guarantees that he holds all six covenants of title: seisin, the right to convey, no encumbrances, quiet enjoyment, warranty, and further assurances.

   b. **Covenants of Title**
      i. **Seisin**—The seller is the sole owner of the land.
      ii. **Right to Convey**—The seller has the right to convey the land.
      iii. **Against Encumbrances**—There are no encumbrances affecting the use of the land.
      iv. **Warranty**—The seller has a good and marketable title.
      v. **Quiet Enjoyment**—the right to use the property without interference from others
      vi. **Further Assurances**—Seller will do whatever is needed to remove title defects.

   c. **Breach of Covenant and Damages**—Either the grantor or the grantee may take action against the other for damages for breach of a covenant of title.

   d. **Statutory Special Warranty Deed**—A deed where the seller only guarantees that the property was free from any other claims during the seller's ownership.

   e. **Quitclaim Deed**—A quitclaim only prevents the grantor from claiming they have an interest in the property being sold. It does not state or guarantee that the grantor had valid ownership in the property in the first place.

C. **Recording Acts**

1. **Types of Recording Acts**

   a. **Notice**—Purchasers of the land are protected against those of whom they have no notice.

   b. **Race**—In the minority of states, the purchaser who records first prevails regardless of notice of any other interests.

   c. **Race-Notice**—A purchaser must take interest without notice and be the first to record.

   d. **Purchaser for Value**—A bona fide purchaser for value who has no notice of a defect in title is protected under property law.

2. **Indexes**

   a. **Title Searches**—Usually, a title company goes through public records to determine the history of property.

   b. **Grantor and Grantee Indexes**—The official documentation used by most counties in the United States to record property transfers.

   c. **The Effect of Recordation**—It gives subsequent purchasers of the property constructive notice that a prior conveyance of the property has occurred.

   d. **Issues Related to Mistakes by the Recorder**—Clerical mistakes on the deed may create issues with the property's title. These can be corrected by a corrective deed, an affidavit of correction, a scrivener's error, or a completely new conveyance.

   e. **Issues Related to Recording an Unacknowledged Instrument**—An unacknowledged deed may not be recorded.

3. **Chain of Title**—the official ownership record of a piece of property

4. **Undelivered and Forged Deeds**—Invalid deeds do not give title to the property.

PRACTICE MULTIPLE-CHOICE QUESTIONS

1. Your client, a tenant, and a landlord shared a house as roommates. Under the lease, both the landlord and tenant had access to the basement. One day, the landlord took the tenant's personal property from the basement, put a lock on the door, and informed the tenant that he was no longer allowed to use it. The tenant objected and asked the landlord why he could no longer use the basement. The landlord responded that the tenant's rental payments were less than half of the property's mortgage cost, so the landlord intended to use the basement as an extra room for himself to even things out. The tenant continued to live in the house, although he had to store his personal property that was taken out of the basement in his bedroom closet. The tenant has grown tired of the landlord. He would like to continue living in the house if he could, but he does not like the current arrangement. He asks you for advice.

In most jurisdictions, what relief is the tenant entitled to? **Select one.**

(A) The tenant no longer must pay rent because he has been constructively evicted.
(B) The tenant no longer must pay rent because he has been evicted.
(C) The tenant is only entitled to a rent abatement because he did not move out of the house.
(D) The tenant is not entitled to any relief because the landlord is paying more for the shared property.

2. A tenant comes to you for advice, wanting to know if he actually owed his landlord money after a neighbor's baseball came smashing through the front window of the tenant's apartment during a neighborhood potluck party. The tenant called the landlord immediately and informed her of the broken window. Two days later, the landlord returned the tenant's phone call and said that she would not fix the window because the lease agreement did not include any language regarding who was responsible for apartment repairs. In her view, the tenant was responsible for the window because he had hosted a potluck party and could have instructed the neighbors who were present to stop their children from playing baseball near the window. A week later, there was a rainstorm, and rain came through the broken window, ruining several of the tenant's books. The tenant angrily fixed the window himself for $400 and deducted $400 from the next month's rental payment. The landlord sued, arguing that the tenant owed her $400 for the window. The jurisdiction adheres to the rules of common law. **Select one.**

Do you tell the tenant that he owes the landlord $400?

(A) Yes, because the tenant repaired the window before the landlord could do so.
(B) Yes, because the lease did not require the landlord to make apartment repairs.
(C) No, because the broken window breached the implied warranty of habitability.
(D) No, because the landlord intentionally failed to repair the broken window before the tenant's personal property was damaged.

3. Your clients, the children of a deceased doctor, want to know what rights they have in land owned by their late father. Years ago, the neighboring farmer asked the doctor if he could use some of the doctor's large estate to start growing Christmas trees. The doctor was a big fan of Christmas and enjoyed the idea of having Christmas trees near his property. Consequently, the doctor conveyed the eastern corner of his property to his neighbor for "so long as the property continues to be used as a Christmas tree farm." Twenty years later, the doctor died, and the doctor's children inherited the doctor's estate. Three years after that, the farmer died without a will. The farmer's son received all of the farmer's land through intestacy, including the Christmas tree farm. After 12 years of running the Christmas tree farm, the farmer's son closed the Christmas tree farm and sold all of the land to a real estate developer who planned to build condominiums. The farmer's son did not tell the doctor's children before selling the land. The doctor's children opposed the building of the new condominiums. The statutory period for adverse possession in the state was ten years.

The doctor's children ask you whether they could successfully sue to get back the land that was used as a Christmas tree farm? **Select one.**

(A) Yes, because the doctor's children did not receive notice of the son's intention to sell the land.
(B) Yes, because the doctor's children inherited the doctor's property upon his death.
(C) No, because the farmer's son gained title to the land through adverse possession.
(D) No, because the farmer's son was not a party to the original agreement.

4. A man rented a house in a large city. When he arrived at the house on the scheduled day for the man to move in, he was shocked to discover a squatter on the property. The man called the landlord and told him that he was not paying rent until the landlord got the squatter out. The jurisdiction follows the minority rule for delivery of the premises.

The landlord comes to your office and asks if he could successfully sue the man to get the rent owed? **Select one.**

(A) Yes, because the English rule only requires that the landlord deliver legal possession of the premises.
(B) Yes, because the American rule only requires that the landlord deliver legal possession of the premises.
(C) No, because the English rule requires that the landlord deliver both legal and actual possession of the premises.
(D) No, because the American rule requires that the landlord deliver both legal and actual possession of the premises.

5. A landowner granted her property "To my son for life, then six months after my son's death, to my daughter." The daughter comes to your office for advice regarding the land grant.

Which of the following property interests are created by the landowner's grant? **Select two.**

(A) The son has a life estate *pur autre vie*.
(B) The son has a fee simple determinable.
(C) The daughter has a springing executory interest.
(D) The daughter has a shifting executory interest.
(E) The landowner has a possibility of reverter.
(F) The landowner has a reversion.

6. A landlord rented a warehouse to a brewery according to a three-year commercial lease agreement. To save money, the brewer moved into the warehouse and resided there for two years. Although the brewer did not formally notify the landlord that he was living on the property, the landlord was aware that the brewer had moved a bed and furniture into the warehouse. During the third year, the warehouse was struck by a thunderstorm that severely damaged the roof, resulting in several leaks and ruining the personal possessions the brewer had stored in the warehouse when he decided to start living there. The day after the storm, the brewer called the landlord and informed her of the damage. When the landlord failed to respond after a week, the brewer called and informed the landlord that he would be bringing suit against her for breaching the implied warranty of habitability.

The landlord comes to your office for advice and asks whether the brewer's threatened lawsuit is likely to be successful. **Select one.**

(A) Yes, because the landlord knew that the brewer lived on the premises.
(B) Yes, because the brewer gave the landlord proper notice regarding the warehouse's need for repair.
(C) No, because there was no indication that the brewer agreed to be responsible for repairs caused by wind and rain.
(D) No, because the brewer rented the warehouse according to a three-year commercial lease.

7. One night while drinking at a local bar, a landowner asked his neighbor if he could have an easement to build a road across his neighbor's land to get to a public lake. The neighbor said that he had no problem with an easement, so long as the landowner kept the road nice and neat. The landowner hired a construction crew, who came and built a paved asphalt road lined with river stones. Six months later, the neighbor ran into the landowner at the same bar. The landowner was wearing a shirt celebrating another state's football team. The neighbor said, "I hate those guys! I revoke my permission for your stupid road!" The landowner did not take the neighbor seriously until he was served with an action for trespass the following week. The landowner was very upset and came to your office for advice.

What rights does the landowner likely have to the road? **Select one.**

(A) A revocable license
(B) An irrevocable license
(C) An irrevocable easement
(D) None

8. A professor leased an apartment to a student under a written agreement. The agreement was to last for four years, with a monthly rent of $500 due at the beginning of each month. The lease was silent regarding subleases or assignments. The student lived in the apartment and paid rent for two years. In her third year, the student participated in a study abroad program and sublet the apartment to her friend for a year. The friend lived in the apartment for four months, but never paid any rent. The friend then abandoned the apartment. Eight months later, the student returned from abroad and stayed in the apartment for the final year of the lease. The student made rent payments again from the time she moved back in until the original lease term ended. At that point, the student entered a graduate program in another city. The professor, who was a very bad bookkeeper, realized that he was missing a year's worth of rent, or $6,000. The professor came to your office and hired you to file a lawsuit against the student and the friend for the missing rent.

If the professor's lawsuit is successful, which of the following statements are correct? **Select two.**

(A) The student will be individually liable for $6,000.
(B) The student will be individually liable for $4,000.
(C) The student will not be individually liable for any of the unpaid rent.
(D) The friend will be individually liable for $6,000.
(E) The friend will be individually liable for $2,000.
(F) The friend will not be individually liable for any of the unpaid rent.

9. A man entered an oral agreement to lease an apartment from a landlord for six months. The rent was $1,000 per month, due on the first of the month. When the six months were over, the man was unsure whether he wanted to move to a new place. Without providing the landlord with any additional notice, the man sent $1,000 to the landlord on the first of the month. The landlord deposited the $1,000 into his bank account. A week later, the landlord met another potential tenant who was willing to pay $1,200 in rent. The landlord came to you for advice regarding his ability to rent the property to a new tenant.

Which statement is most correct regarding the relationship between the man and the landlord? **Select one.**

(A) Because the landlord accepted the $1,000, the man and the landlord have a periodic tenancy.
(B) Because the original lease term is over, the man is a tenant at sufferance.
(C) Because the original lease failed to meet the requirements of the statute of frauds, the man has an at-will tenancy.
(D) Because the landlord accepted the $1,000, the man has an at-will tenancy.

10. A man bought a piece of real property to build a restaurant. A bank gave the man a $3 million loan and recorded a lien against the property. The loan specified that installment payments would begin on the first of the following year. A few weeks later, the man obtained a loan of $500,000 from a restaurant supplier. The supplier then filed a lien against the property. After some construction delays, the man requested that the bank reschedule his installment payments. The bank agreed to do so and modified its lien to reflect the new installment agreement. The bank then came to your office for advice regarding the current state of its mortgage in relation to the supplier's mortgage.

Which of the following statements is correct? **Select one.**

(A) The supplier's mortgage takes precedence over the bank's because the bank modified the bank loan's repayment terms.
(B) The supplier's mortgage takes precedence over the bank's because the bank modified the loan's terms in a lien theory jurisdiction.
(C) The bank's mortgage retains its status as a senior mortgage because the rescheduling of the loan's installment payments does not materially prejudice the supplier.
(D) The bank's mortgage retains its status as a senior mortgage because the supplier did not object to the change in the bank loan's installment payments.

11. Your client owned a 200-acre piece of property in the country that she used for hunting, fishing, and recreation. She lived in another state but went to the property three or four times a year with her business colleagues and family. The property had a large guest house that sat on a quarter acre on the southwest corner next to a public highway, but the rest of the property was undeveloped except for a small shed for canoes next to the property's lake, several dirt roads and trails, and three deer blinds scattered in the northwest corner. One day, one of your client's employees was hiking alone and went to the northeast corner, where your client never went. In that corner, the employee discovered a small, recently built cabin. No one was there, and the cabin was locked. A car-sized trail had been cut from another public highway to the cabin, and it appeared to have been used quite a bit, possibly for several years. Your client called you in alarm and asked what she should do about the cabin.

What legal topics would be most useful for you to research before you call her back? **Select two.**

(A) Conversion
(B) Easements
(C) Adverse possession
(D) Estoppel
(E) Takings
(F) Trespass

12. You represent a man who built a small hunting cabin in the woods. Now the owner of the property where the cabin sits has told the man that he needs to remove the cabin. The man would like to keep the cabin.

Which of the following questions would be most helpful to ask your client? **Select two.**

- **(A)** Did you live in the cabin?
- **(B)** Did the landowner permit you to build the cabin?
- **(C)** Did you know you did not own the land you built the cabin on?
- **(D)** How long ago did you build the cabin?
- **(E)** Did you take out a mortgage on the cabin?
- **(F)** Have you filed your interest in the cabin in the county records?

13. During the summer, a tenant came to you for advice about his apartment situation. He told you that he had been fighting with his landlord on and off about his apartment's electricity bill. The electricity bill was paid by the landlord according to the rental agreement. Under state law, the air conditioner in a rental unit had to be able to maintain a temperature of 72 degrees or below during the summer. However, the landlord was constantly complaining about the electricity bill, arguing that the tenant's use of the air conditioner was driving up the cost. A month ago, the tenant came home to find the air conditioner not on. Since that time, the tenant had been unable to get the air conditioner to work. His rent was due, and he wanted to know what his rights were regarding the apartment.

Which of the following facts would be most useful for you to know from your client? **Select two.**

- **(A)** Whether the tenant remained in the apartment since the air conditioner stopped working.
- **(B)** The current temperature of the apartment.
- **(C)** Whether the common law governed the rental agreement.
- **(D)** The temperature the tenant set the air conditioner.
- **(E)** The reasonableness of the extra electricity cost caused by the air conditioner.
- **(F)** Whether the landlord turned off the air conditioner intentionally.

14. Your client owned a large beachfront property consisting of a house, a dock, and a small private beach. After working for 50 years, your client decided to retire and move to the mountains. Consequently, he wanted to give his property to his only child, a daughter. Your client's daughter was recently married and has just learned she is pregnant; your client would like to give the property to her as a surprise baby shower gift. The client records a video of himself orally giving the property to his daughter so she can play it at the baby shower and be surprised. The client sent the video to you and requested your advice on whether the gift would be valid and what parts might need to be modified.

Which of the following parts of the planned gift might be most likely to make the property transfer invalid? **Select two.**

- **(A)** The client describes the property as being "From the Old Southern Rock Jetty, 60 yards south along the coastline to the Stand of 200-year Live Oak Trees, then 75 yards west to the public highway, then along the public highway 60 yards north until reaching the Old Southern Rock Jetty again."
- **(B)** The client states, "This property is being given without any consideration."
- **(C)** The client states, "To my daughter, I know you don't want this property because you think I am being too generous, but you are a wonderful daughter, and you deserve everything in the world."
- **(D)** The client states, "This video overrules any prior will or grant made by me and is intended as the final legal record regarding the property."

(E) The client states, "I intend that you, my daughter, get to enjoy the property as yours for your lifetime and maybe you'll think about giving it to my grandchildren or great-grandchildren someday."

(F) The client states, "I ask you to keep the property as close to what it is now as possible, simply because I care, and I think you do, about the effect of any construction, etc., on the local environment."

15. A client comes to you asking whether she should buy a piece of property that has been offered to her by a seller. After doing some research on the property, you discover that there are no deeds or other records recorded to show who owned the property from 1970-1985.

What should you do to best protect your client? **Select one.**

(A) Tell your client not to buy the property because there is a significant break in the chain of title.

(B) File a quitclaim deed on behalf of your client stating that she acknowledges the gap in title.

(C) File an affidavit on behalf of your client stating that she has made all reasonable efforts to discover the identity of the property's owner from 1970-1985.

(D) Bring a quiet title action in court.

16. A property seller came to you for advice on selling his property. According to the seller, the buyer would only buy the property if the seller provided him with a general warranty deed. The seller asked you what he would be promising if he agreed to provide the buyer with a general warranty deed.

Which of the following things would the seller *not* be promising if he sells the property to the buyer with a general warranty deed? **Select two.**

(A) The seller is the sole owner of the land.

(B) The land valuation in the purchase price is reasonable.

(C) The seller will do whatever is needed to remove title defects.

(D) The transfer of funds between the buyer and seller will occur at the time of sale.

(E) The buyer has the right to use the property without interference from others.

(F) The seller has a good and marketable title.

17. You represent a woman who wants to stay in her apartment in a large apartment building. She has rented the apartment from a landlord corporation for the last five years on a month-to-month, year-long lease. Her current lease is up for renewal next month, and the landlord has inserted a new clause in the lease that states pets are not allowed. However, two years ago, the woman got a therapy dog to help her with a seizure disorder. She called the landlord, but the landlord is refusing to allow the dog to stay in the apartment, telling her that they will not renew the lease if she wants to keep the dog. Several of the current tenants have cats, but the landlord informs the woman that those individuals will be required to give up their pets when it is time to renew their leases.

What would be your best argument to keep the tenant in the apartment? **Select one.**

(A) Not allowing the woman to keep the dog in the apartment is a violation of the Fair Housing Act.

(B) Not allowing the woman to keep the dog in the apartment is a violation of the woman's Equal Protection rights.

(C) The landlord has impliedly consented to the dog staying in the apartment because the dog has already lived there for two years.

(D) By allowing the dog to stay for two years, the tenant can now force the landlord to allow her to keep the dog through promissory estoppel.

18. Your client wants to buy a new house. The house is located in a residentially zoned neighborhood. There is a small apartment on top of the house's detached garage, which the current homeowner rents to college students to help pay the mortgage on the house. The current homeowner still owes $250,000 on the mortgage. According to local building codes, residential homes must have wooden windows and concrete driveways. The house's windows are made of plastic, and the driveway is composed of gravel. Due to a 20-year-old measuring error, the neighbor's fence extended over the house's property line in the corner behind the garage, which was not visible from the main house. The current homeowner has not trimmed the trees in many years, and several branches hang over the neighbor's house.

Which of the following will the current homeowner need to address before he can deliver a marketable title to your client? **Select two.**

(A) The detached apartment
(B) The neighbor's fence
(C) The plastic windows
(D) The gravel driveway
(E) The outstanding mortgage on the property
(F) The tree limbs hanging over the neighbor's house

19. You represent a client who has recently bought a new home in another state. He would like to keep his old home and rent it out on the Internet to vacationers. His old home, which is over 100 years old, is located in a residential neighborhood near the city center. Due to its age, the home lacks wheelchair ramps and other accessibility features. However, he says he is happy to rent to anyone and make any reasonable accommodations they need. He asks you whether there are likely to be problems with renting the property.

Which of the following topics should you research regarding the potential rental of the home? **Select two.**

(A) The home's compliance with the Fair Housing Act
(B) The local zoning laws
(C) Whether there are equitable servitudes on the property
(D) Whether there is an affirmative covenant on the property
(E) The marketability of the property's title
(F) Whether there is a lien on the property

20. A man contacted your office with questions regarding a piece of property he held with another person. He had read in an online forum that sometimes people hold property with another person in a joint tenancy, and that a joint tenancy had special rules regarding transfer and inheritance.

Which of the following would *not* need to be true for the man to have a joint tenancy? **Select two.**

(A) The man and the other person are married.
(B) The man and the other person received the property at the same time.
(C) The man and the other person have equal rights to use the property.
(D) The property was granted to the man, and another person was granted the property with "the right of survivorship."
(E) The man and the other person received the property through a devise.
(F) The man and the other person received their interests through the same document.

ANSWERS

1. The correct answer is (B). Here, because the landlord intentionally locked the tenant out of the shared basement, the landlord is acting like an "ass" and has actually evicted the tenant. In that case, the majority rule penalizes the landlord by allowing the tenant to stay in the rental without paying rent. (A) is incorrect because the landlord intentionally locked out the tenant, making this an actual eviction. (C) is incorrect because a tenant does not have to move out of a property for an actual eviction to occur. (D) is incorrect because the fact that the landlord is paying more for the shared property is irrelevant.

2. The correct answer is (B). Under the common law, the tenant has the responsibility of keeping out "wind, rain, and raccoons." Here, because the lease did not state that the tenant was responsible for fixing the window, which was a minor repair intended to keep out the elements, the tenant had the duty to make the repair and could not deduct $400 from his rental payment. (A) is incorrect because the fact that the tenant fixed the window does not change the analysis. (C) and (D) are incorrect because the tenant had the duty to fix the window under the common law.

3. The correct answer is (B). The doctor's conveyance of the property "so long as the property continues to be used as a Christmas tree farm" was a fee simple determinable. In such a conveyance, the doctor was left with a possibility of reverter if the property was no longer used as a Christmas tree farm. A possibility of reverter is alienable, devisable, and descendible. The doctor's will devised all of his property to his children, including the possibility of reverter on the Christmas tree farm. When the property ceased to be used as a Christmas tree farm, it automatically reverted to the doctor's children as the holders of the possibility of reverter. (A) is incorrect because the conveyance creates no notice requirement. (C) is incorrect because the property had been conveyed to the farmer as a fee simple determinable, which is descendible through intestacy, so the farmer's son was not adversely possessing the property. (D) is incorrect because there is no requirement that the son be a party to the original agreement.

4. The correct answer is (B). The minority rule is the American rule, which states that the landlord only has to deliver legal possession of the leased premises. Consequently, the man has to pay rent and deal with the squatter. (A) is a misstatement of the English rule, which is the majority rule. (C) is a correct statement of the English rule, but that is the majority rule, and the question says that this is a minority jurisdiction. (D) is incorrect because it misstates the American rule.

5. The correct answers are (C) and (F). (A) and (B) are incorrect because the son has a life estate, not a life estate *pur autre vie* or a fee simple determinable. (D) is incorrect because the daughter's interest is a springing executory interest because it springs into life after the property reverts to the landowner as grantor for six months. (E) is incorrect because a possibility of reverter is dependent upon a stated event happening. Here, the property automatically reverts to the landowner for six months upon the son's death.

6. The correct answer is (D). In the majority of jurisdictions, commercial leases do not include an implied warranty of habitability. Consequently, the brewer cannot sue the landlord for breaching the implied warranty of habitability. If a question does not ask you to take the minority view, always choose the answer that conforms with the majority. (A) is incorrect because the landlord's knowledge of the brewer's living arrangement would not change the analysis. (B) is incorrect because there is no implied warranty of habitability in a commercial lease, and the question specifically states that the brewer is suing for violation of this warranty. (C) is incorrect because this is a commercial lease. This answer choice is designed to catch test-takers who are considering the common law rule regarding "wind, rain, and raccoons."

7. The correct answer is (B). Here, because the agreement was oral, the road could only be considered an easement, not a license. While licenses are usually revocable, this one became irrevocable because the landowner relied to his detriment on the neighbor's statement by spending money to build the road. Thus, (A) and (D) are incorrect. (C) is incorrect because there was no written agreement creating an easement.

8. The correct answers are (A) and (F). The student sublet the apartment to her friend because she gave the friend less than the full amount of time left on the lease. In that case, the professor could not recover any damages from the friend because the friend was a subletter, and the student is entirely liable for the year of missing rent. Consequently, the other answer choices are incorrect.

9. The correct answer is (A). Here, by accepting another month's rent, the landlord has created a month-to-month tenancy by implication. Consequently, the landlord would need to provide proper notice before evicting the man. It does not matter that the man did not give the landlord actual notice that he intended to continue renting the apartment. (B) is incorrect because a tenant at sufferance means that the tenant has stayed past the end of the rental period. Here, the man created a new rental period by having the landlord accept another month's rent payment. (C) is incorrect because the statute of frauds only applies to leases with terms of a year or more. Here, the lease was only for six months. (D) is incorrect because an at-will tenancy lasts only as long as the tenant and landlord desire, and this tenancy lasted in periods of at least one month.

10. The correct answer is (C). Unless a senior mortgage modification materially prejudices a junior mortgage, the senior mortgage retains its senior status. Generally, courts do not look at changes in installment payments as modifications that materially prejudice junior mortgages. (A) is incorrect because a senior mortgage only loses its status if a modification materially prejudices a junior mortgage. (B) is incorrect because the fact that this is a lien theory jurisdiction does not change the analysis. (D) is incorrect because there is no requirement that a junior interest object to changes in a senior interest.

11. The correct answers are (C) and (F). (C) would be useful because the cabin owner may have gained title to the land if they fulfilled the jurisdiction's requirements for adverse possession. (F) would be useful because they entered the property without permission, so it was likely a trespass. (A) would not be useful because conversion deals with chattel or personal property, not land. (B) would not be useful because easements deal with another person's right to cross over a person's property, and here, the cabin is a permanent addition. (D) is incorrect because there is no potential agreement between your client and the cabin owner that could be enforced through estoppel. (E) is incorrect because "takings" are done by the government, and there is no indication that the government is connected to the cabin in any way.

12. The correct answers are (B) and (D). Here, it is important to determine whether your client might have acquired title to the land through adverse possession. First, (B) is correct because if the landowner gave the client permission to build the cabin, the client could not claim the cabin through adverse possession. Second, (D) is correct because whether the client acquired title through adverse possession would be dependent upon how long the cabin was there. (A) would be incorrect because the client's use of the cabin would not make a significant difference. (C) is incorrect because whether the client knew he did not own the land would not change his chance of getting the property through adverse possession. (E) and (F) are incorrect because they would also not change whether the client could obtain the land through adverse possession. (B) and (D) are the two questions that are most relevant to determining whether the real landowner can evict the client from the land.

13. The correct answers are (A) and (F). If the air conditioner stopped working accidentally, this constituted a constructive eviction, and the tenant could only stop paying rent if they vacated the apartment. If the tenant had stayed in the apartment, he would have been liable for the past rent (because, clearly, the problem with the air conditioner was not severe). Consequently, (A) is correct. (F) is correct because if the landlord turned off the air conditioner intentionally, this would be an actual eviction, and in such a case, the tenant can remain in the apartment without paying rent until the landlord fixes the situation. (B) is incorrect because it is irrelevant to the effectiveness of the air conditioner, which is not on. (C) is incorrect because, under the common law, the tenant would be responsible for repairs to keep out wind and rain. The air conditioner has nothing to do with either of them. (D) is incorrect because, again, this is irrelevant to the operation of the air conditioner. (E) is incorrect because it is also irrelevant to the operation of the air conditioner.

14. The correct answers are (C) and (D). The transfer of property requires a proper deed. (C) is correct because the grantee of a deed needs to accept it for the transfer to be valid. If the daughter is planning not to accept the deed, this could be a problem. (D) is correct because a deed must comply with the statute of frauds. As such, it needs to be in writing, and if the client intends to do this video and nothing else, the statute of frauds is violated. (A) is incorrect because a metes and bounds description in a deed is valid. (B) is incorrect because the transfer of property by deed does not require consideration. (E) and (F) are incorrect because these statements do nothing to affect the deed adversely. A deed does not require any particular words of transfer, except for words showing a general intent to transfer the property. These statements show an intent to transfer the property to the daughter.

15. The correct answer is (D). A break in the chain of title for a piece of property is a serious title defect. However, this can be remedied by a suit to quiet title, where a judge examines the records to determine the true owner of the property. (A) is incorrect because the client can still buy the property if you file suit to quit title. (B) is incorrect because a quitclaim deed is filed when a person relinquishes any claim they might have to a piece of property. Here, the client is actually trying to get the title to the property. (C) is incorrect because an affidavit like this would not do anything to protect your client.

16. The correct answers are (B) and (D). A general warranty deed does not cover any matters related to the actual sales contract. However, the holder of a general warranty deed guarantees that they hold all six covenants of title: the covenant of seisin; the covenant of the right to convey; the covenant against encumbrances; and the covenant of quiet enjoyment, warranty, and further assurances. Seisin states that the seller is the sole owner of the land. The right to convey states that the seller has the right to convey the land. The holder also promises that there are no encumbrances affecting the use of the land, the seller has a good and marketable title, the buyer has the right to use the property without interference from others, and the seller will take all necessary steps to remove any title defects. Consequently, (A), (C), (E), and (F) are incorrect.

17. The correct answer is (A). If the landlord does not allow the therapy dog to stay, they might be violating the Fair Housing Act, which provides protections for disabled tenants in large apartment complexes. (B) is incorrect because the landlord is a private company, not the government. (C) is incorrect because the landlord has not impliedly consented to anything. (D) is incorrect because the landlord has not made any promises regarding the dog, so promissory estoppel cannot apply.

18. The correct answers are (A) and (B). (A) is correct because the rental apartment likely violates the house's residential zoning, and the title is made unmarketable by a zoning violation. (B) is correct because the title can also be made unmarketable if there is an encroachment on the property, which the neighbor's fence is doing because of the mistake. Importantly, it is unclear whether the neighbor could have acquired part of the property through adverse possession. (C) and (D) are incorrect because mere violations of building codes are insufficient to render the title unmarketable. (E) is incorrect because the outstanding mortgage will likely be paid off with the proceeds from the property sale. (F) is incorrect because the fact that the trees hang over the neighbor's house is irrelevant to the property title.

19. The correct answers are (B) and (C). (B) is correct because if the local zoning laws do not allow rentals of residential property, the client may not be able to rent their property. (C) is correct because if there is an equitable servitude on the property stating that it will not be used as a rental, then the client cannot rent their property. Although the Fair Housing Act applies to vacation rentals, the act is likely to be less of an issue so long as the client is willing to make any reasonable accommodations requested by disabled guests and does not refuse to rent to people based on their disability. Since he is happy to rent to anyone and make reasonable accommodations for them, this should not be an issue. (D) is incorrect because an affirmative covenant requires the property owner to do something, like pay a housing association fee. It does not stop a property owner from doing something. (E) is incorrect because the client is not selling the property, so the marketability of the property's title is irrelevant. (F) is incorrect because a lien on the property would not affect its ability to be rented to others.

20. The correct answers are (A) and (E). In a joint tenancy, two or more people own the property with a right of survivorship. When one tenant dies, the other tenants split up the dead tenant's interest and add it to their own. In addition to the right of survivorship, the joint tenancy requires four more unities to be valid: (1) Possession—equal right to use and possess property; (2) Interest—each interest must be equal to the other interests; (3) Time—interests created at the same time; and (4) Title—interests created by same document. (A) and (E) are correct because the man and the other person do not need to be married for a joint tenancy, nor do they have to receive the property through a devise.

Torts

7

Topics with asterisks (*) require you to know the black letter law cold; topics without an * require you to recognize the topic as part of the fact scenario or require you to analyze and apply legal resources provided for the topic efficiently.

MAIN POINT OF TORTS—PROVIDE A REMEDY IF SOMEONE IS HURT BY SOMEONE ELSE'S FAULT

OUTLINE

I. INTENTIONAL TORTS

A. Harms to the Person

1. Intent

a. **The Defendant's Act**—The defendant must act voluntarily—meaning spasms and hypnotism do not count.

b. **Knowledge to a Substantial Certainty**—The defendant must act to cause the consequences or with substantial certainty of causing the consequences. A classic example is moving a chair knowing that a person intending to sit on it will fall.

c. **Transferred Intent**—If a defendant intends a tort against one person but causes the consequences to another, or if the defendant intends one kind of tort but actually accomplishes another. For example, throwing a stick at one kid and hitting another.

d. **Distinction Between Intent and Motive**—Intent means that a person voluntarily did something; motive is the reason why they did it.

e. **Who Can Form Intent (Minor Children)**—Children as young as two can form intent. Additionally, those who have a mental illness can form intent.

f. **Causation**—The act must result in the harm or offense caused.

g. **Harm/Damages**—Under the "eggshell plaintiff" rule, a defendant is liable for all damages caused by their tort. Remember this with Humpty Dumpty—if you punch him and he explodes into shell and yolk, that is on you.

2. **Assault***—A plaintiff's reasonable apprehension of threatened imminent harmful or offensive bodily contact. While mere words are not usually an assault, words coupled with an action count. For example, "I'm going to punch you!" while waving a fist. Look out for situations where the defendant is calling on the phone from somewhere else—in that case, the threat cannot be imminent.

3. **Battery***—A harmful or offensive touching of another person. That touching can be with something closely associated with a person, like knocking a plate from their hands. The touching may also be simply offensive to dignity, like blowing smoke in someone's face. Generally, offensiveness is based on a person of ordinary sensibilities, but a defendant may be liable if they know the plaintiff is hypersensitive. Think about little kids poking each other simply because one of them is hypersensitive to being touched and says not to do so. I have spent many car trips like this. You might have too.

4. **False Imprisonment***—Confining another person within certain boundaries. An area is not bounded if there is a reasonable means of escape. The plaintiff must know that they are being confined and may be confined by either force or threats.

5. **Intentional Infliction of Emotional Distress***—acting with extreme or outrageous conduct that causes the plaintiff severe emotional distress, for example, falsely telling someone their family is dead

B. **Interference With Property Interests**

1. **Trespass to Land***—Physical invasion of someone else's land. The defendant does not need to know they are trespassing to be liable.

2. **Trespass to Chattels***—intentionally taking or using someone else's tangible personal property, for example, stealing a car and driving it around town

3. **Conversion***—a more serious trespass to chattels that completely deprives the plaintiff of their tangible personal property, for example, stealing a car and intending to keep it

C. **Defenses to Intentional Torts**

1. **Consent***

a. **Actual**—The plaintiff expressly consents to the conduct by words or deeds.

b. **Implied**—The plaintiff says nothing but acts in such a way that consent may be implied. For example, a person implicitly consents to some touching by getting on a crowded elevator or playing pickup basketball.

c. **Scope**—The scope of the consent may either be express or implied by the situation. For example, playing pickup basketball probably means you have consented to some pushing and possible eye-poking if you contest a rebound, but not to being punched straight in the teeth. A common question is when consent is required for one type of operation, and the doctor decides to perform a second procedure while they are already in the patient's body. The patient did not consent to the second operation, no matter how minor or unintrusive.

d. **Validity**—consent must be intelligent and voluntary to be valid, so consent given by the very young, intoxicated, incompetent, or people under duress does not count.

e. **Unnecessary (Life-Saving Surgery on Unconscious Person)**—In an emergency, the consent of an unconscious person is implied.

2. **Other Defenses to Intentional Torts**

a. **Self-Defense**—A person may use reasonable force to defend themselves.

b. **Defense of Others**—A person may use reasonable force to defend another if they have a reasonable belief the other person could use such force in self-defense.

c. **Defense of Property**—Use of reasonable, nondeadly force may be used to defend property.

d. **Recapture of Chattels**—A person may use reasonable force to retake personal property that was wrongly taken.

i. **Shopkeeper's Privilege**—A shopkeeper may reasonably detain a suspected shoplifter.

e. **Necessity**

i. **Public**—Private property may be entered or destroyed if necessary to protect the public. For example, knocking down a house to stop a fire from spreading to the city.

ii. **Private**—A person may enter land if necessary to prevent an injury from nature or something else not connected to the plaintiff. The plaintiff may recover actual damages. For example, a storm forces a boat to land on the plaintiff's dock to avoid being sunk.

f. **Parental Discipline**—A parent may use reasonable force or reasonable confinement to discipline their child.

g. **Privilege of Arrest**—A police officer or a private citizen must be reasonable in making an arrest.

II. NEGLIGENCE

A. Duty of Care to Foreseeable and Unforeseeable Plaintiffs

1. **Duty to Control Third Persons***—A person who has the actual ability to control a third person might have a duty to do so. For example, a parent controlling a child.

2. **Duty to Act When Previous Actions Exacerbate a Risk of Harm***—A person has no duty to act to help another unless they put that other in danger in the first place. For example, a suicidal person owes a duty to a person coming to their rescue.

3. **Duty of Owners and Occupiers of Land**

a. **Entrants**

i. **Traditional Approach**—dependent on whether the person is an invitee, licensee, or trespasser

[a] **Invitee**—"I Need You"—People on the land for a commercial purpose—duty to inspect and protect the invitee from dangerous conditions. The duty of protection is nondelegable, so if a business hires a commercial contractor to fix something, the business can still be liable.

[b] **Licensee**—"I like you"—someone on the land for social reasons—duty to warn of known concealed dangers

[c] **Trespasser**—There is no duty to undiscovered trespassers, but the landowner owes a duty to warn discovered trespassers of concealed and dangerous artificial conditions.

ii. **Modern Approach**—reasonable care to prevent harm from artificial conditions, but generally no duty for natural conditions. These courts do not distinguish between licensees and invitees.

b. **Passersby**

i. A landowner generally owes no duty to people not on the land harmed by natural conditions on the land but has a duty to protect passersby from artificial conditions reasonably.

4. **Duty to Avoid Unreasonable Risk of Causing Emotional Distress**

a. **Zone of Danger**—If a plaintiff was placed in fear of a threatened physical impact. For example, the defendant lost control of a truck and almost struck the plaintiff.

b. **Bystander Cases**—A bystander can recover if they are closely related to the person injured, were present at the scene of the injury, and saw the injury.

c. **Physical Symptoms of Distress**—The plaintiff must suffer from a physical symptom, like ulcers or nightmares.

d. **Special Relationships Between the Parties**—If the defendant and the plaintiff have a special relationship, the defendant may be liable for negligent infliction of emotional distress. For example, if a doctor negligently tells her patient that they are dying.

e. **Negligent Reporting of a Family Member's Death**—A defendant may be liable for negligently telling the plaintiff that a family member has died.

B. Standard of Care

1. **Reasonably Prudent Person***—objective standard of what a reasonable person would do under the circumstances

a. **Children**—What a reasonable child of similar age, experience, and intelligence would do under the circumstances. However, if a child is engaged in an adult activity, such as driving a car, the child will be held to the same standard of care as an adult.

b. **Physically and Mentally Impaired Individuals**—Physical characteristics are considered (such as blindness), but mental and emotional impairments are not.

c. **Professionals**—held to the standard of care of other reasonable professionals in that field

d. **Persons Acting in Emergency Situations**—What a reasonable person would do in the same emergency. This lightened duty only occurs when the defendant did not cause the emergency.

2. **Rules of Conduct Derived from Statutes; Relevance of Custom***

a. **Negligence Per Se**—The majority rule is that violation of a statute establishes negligence if the statute is intended to protect against the type of harm that occurred.

3. **How It Affects Plaintiff's Case**—If the situation fits negligence per se, negligence is established as a matter of law. If a plaintiff violates a statute, it might be contributory negligence per se.

4. **How Statute Affects Defendant's Case**—Generally, compliance with a statute does not prove the absence of negligence.
5. **Use of Statute to Defend**—Compliance with certain federal regulatory schemes may be a defense to negligence.
   a. **Custom in Establishing Standard of Care**—Evidence of a community or industry custom is admissible but not conclusive to establish a standard of care, mainly because everyone in that community or industry might be behaving negligently.
   b. **Weight Given to Statutes and Customs**—Generally, statutes and customs are evidence establishing a standard of care, but they are not dispositive.
   c. **Use of Rebuttal Evidence by Opposing Party**—The opposing party may use statutes and customs as rebuttal evidence.

C. **The Use of Direct and Circumstantial Evidence to Prove Fault***

1. **Direct Evidence**—can use eyewitness testimony, video, physical objects, confessions, etc., to prove fault
2. **Circumstantial Evidence**—Can prove fault through evidence that allows a court to reasonably infer that a defendant caused an injury. For example, evidence that the defendant was at the scene of the accident.
3. ***Res Ipsa Loquitur***—If an accident does not usually occur without some negligence and the agent or instrumentality of the injury is within the exclusive control of the defendant, a plaintiff may use the doctrine of *res ipsa* to prove fault even without direct evidence. However, be on the lookout for things that are not in the complete control of the defendant. For example, if someone is hit by a chair falling from a hotel window, *res ipsa* will not work against the hotel because a guest could have launched the chair.

D. **Actual Causation***

1. **But-For Test**—The plaintiff's injury would not have occurred but for the defendant's negligence.
2. **Substantial Factor Test**—If the defendant's act was a substantial factor in the plaintiff's injury. In the case of multiple defendants causing an indivisible injury, each defendant is jointly and separately liable for the damages.
3. **Multiple Necessary Causes**—When two or more things act together to cause the injury. For example, two kids throw baseballs at each other, the balls hit each other and bounce apart, and one ball hits a person standing off to the side.
4. **Multiple Sufficient Causes**—When two or more causes of an injury are all sufficient to cause the injury on their own. For example, a professor accidentally pours poison into a student's water bottle, and then a custodian accidentally pours poison into the student's water bottle, and then the student drinks it.

E. **Proximate Causation***

1. **Scope of the Risk Test**—That the harm was foreseeable and not too remote in time from the defendant's conduct.
2. **Intervening Cause**—A foreseeable intervening cause will not cut off liability, even if it happened in an unforeseeable manner. For example, a doctor negligently operated on the plaintiff after the defendant caused the injury.
3. **Superseding Cause**—An unforeseeable intervening cause will cut off liability. For example, acts of God or a third party's criminal act.

F. Liability for the Acts of Others

1. **Parental Responsibility**—A parent has a duty to reasonably control their child.
2. **Nondelegable Duties**—Duties established by law, such as a storeowner's duty to invitees. For example, if a store owner hires someone to fix something, and that person does it negligently and hurts an invitee, the store owner may still be liable.

G. Pure and Modified Comparative Negligence*

1. **Pure Comparative Negligence**—A plaintiff's recovery is reduced by the amount of their negligence.
2. **Modified Comparative Negligence**—If the plaintiff is more at fault than the defendant, the plaintiff may not recover. Otherwise, it acts like pure comparative negligence.

H. Express Assumption of Risk—Generally, parties may contract to waive a negligence claim when doing a risky activity, but waivers will not be enforced if there is a gross difference in bargaining power, the negligence was reckless or wanton, or it is against public policy.

III. COMMON-LAW STRICT LIABILITY FOR ABNORMALLY DANGEROUS ACTIVITIES AND DEFENSES TO SUCH CLAIMS

A. Abnormally Dangerous Activities—A defendant engaged in an abnormally dangerous activity is strictly liable for any damages caused. An abnormally dangerous activity is an uncommon activity that creates a foreseeable and highly significant risk of harm, even when the defendant exercises reasonable care—for example, using explosives or disposing of hazardous wastes.

B. Who May Sue—Superseding events can cut off liability.

C. Comparative Negligence as a Defense—Because the abnormally dangerous activity only takes away the plaintiff's duty to prove negligence, the defendant may still defend themselves with comparative negligence.

D. Harm Must Arise from Risk That Made It Abnormally Dangerous—For example, accidentally knocking over a plaintiff with a barrel of toxic waste would be regular negligence because toxic waste is not abnormally dangerous due to the possibility that one might get run over by a barrel containing it.

IV. PRODUCTS LIABILITY BASED ON THE DESIGN, MANUFACTURE, AND DISTRIBUTION OF PRODUCTS AND DEFENSES TO SUCH CLAIMS

A. Different Theories of Liability—An injured plaintiff may generally sue under negligence, strict products liability, or manufacturing defect.

B. Different Types of Defects

1. **Manufacturing Defect**—whether the injury-causing product conforms to the manufacturer's own quality conditions
2. **Design Defect**—Does the product contain a condition that the ordinary consumer would not know was unreasonably dangerous, or do inherent risks in the product outweigh its utility?
3. **Failure to Warn**—when the manufacturer fails to include an adequate warning on the product

C. **Who May Sue**—anyone foreseeably injured by the defective product, not just purchasers

D. **Who May be Sued**—The product's manufacturer, distributor, and retail seller may be sued for the defect. Casual sellers and auctioneers may not be sued.

E. **Defenses**

1. **Alteration**—If a product is changed dramatically between the time it leaves the manufacturer and gets to the consumer, it may be a superseding cause that cuts off liability.

2. **Misuse**—Unforeseeable misuse of the product by the consumer generally negates liability.

3. **Foreseeable Misuse**—Foreseeable misuse of a product does not generally preclude a plaintiff's recovery.

V. NUISANCE AND DEFENSES TO SUCH CLAIMS

A. Private Nuisance*

1. **Private Nuisance**—An activity or thing that substantially and unreasonably interferes with someone else's use and enjoyment of their land. Remember that the fact the plaintiff moved to the nuisance is not a defense. So, if someone moves next to your pig farm, they can still sue you for nuisance.

2. **Locality Rule**—What constitutes a nuisance is dependent on the locality of the property. For example, a house in a predominantly industrial area would be expected to tolerate more noise.

3. **Distinction Between Trespass, Public Nuisance, and Private Nuisance**—A trespass requires physical invasion of another's land; a nuisance does not. Additionally, a trespass does not need to be continuous, whereas a nuisance typically does.

B. **Public Nuisance**—An activity or thing that substantially and unreasonably interferes with a right common to the public. A private person can claim a public nuisance if they suffer in a manner different from that of members of the general public. For example, a business pollutes a public lake adjacent to a restaurant. The restaurant could bring a private claim for public nuisance, while a general member of the public could not.

VI. MISREPRESENTATION AND DEFENSES TO SUCH CLAIMS

A. **Fraudulent Misrepresentation**—Typically arising in contract law and occurs when a defendant makes an intentional or reckless factual misrepresentation that causes the plaintiff to act. Typical negligence defenses cannot be used in defense.

B. **Negligent Misrepresentation**—Like fraudulent misrepresentation, but the defendant merely makes the statement without using reasonable care to ensure its accuracy. Typical negligence defenses can be used in defense.

VII. DAMAGES

A. Apportionment of Responsibility Among Multiple Tortfeasors

1. **Joint and Several Liability**—If multiple tortfeasors cause an injury and cannot be split into each tortfeasor's specific acts, the tortfeasors are jointly and severally liable for any damages.

2. **Apportionment**—If the damages are divisible, they can be divided so that each party only pays the damages they are responsible for.

B. Categories of Damages Recoverable in Tort Actions

1. **General**—noneconomic damages such as pain and suffering
2. **Special**—economic damages such as medical bills, lost wages, and property damage
3. **Punitive**—damages intended to punish a party for their actions and used when the actions were wanton or done with malice
4. **Nominal**—Even if no damage occurred, a plaintiff might be entitled to nominal damages for the defendant's commission of an intentional tort because the tort was an insult to the plaintiff's dignity.
5. **"Egg-Shell Plaintiff"**—Even if a plaintiff is particularly susceptible to injury, the defendant is responsible for all injury caused by the tort, even if it is more than would occur to an average person.
6. **Failure to Mitigate**—A plaintiff has a duty to take reasonable steps to mitigate damages. For example, if a battery causes a gaping head wound, the plaintiff is expected to seek medical attention to prevent infection from setting in. The plaintiff cannot simply let it go and then sue the defendant for the infection as well.
7. **Attorney's Fees**—Attorney's fees and interest are not recoverable in negligence actions.
8. **Statutory Limitations on Recovery**—Local laws can sometimes put limitations on recovery in tort.

PRACTICE MULTIPLE-CHOICE QUESTIONS

1. A man was walking through a grocery store that was undergoing repairs to its freezers in the frozen food aisle. As he walked down the frozen food aisle, he saw a frozen dinner that he wanted in one of the freezers. Across the front of the freezer was a line of yellow tape that said "CAUTION" and a typed sign that said, "Freezer Under Repair." As the man reached into the freezer to get the frozen dinner, he slipped on a piece of ice that had fallen from one of the freezers and cracked his head open. The man comes to you, asking your advice on suing the grocery store for his injuries.
   Which of the following questions are most relevant to the store's potential liability? **Select two.**

   (A) Was the person repairing the freezers an independent contractor?
   (B) Had the piece of ice been on the floor for a long time?
   (C) Had the store put the sign and caution tape up?
   (D) Did the man notice the sign and caution tape before reaching into the freezer?
   (E) Could a store employee have seen the piece of ice?
   (F) Was the fallen piece of ice caused by a manufacturing defect?

2. A woman was late to work and pulled into a drive-through coffee line. In front of her was a police officer in his car. While waiting for his coffee, the officer was checking the safety on his handgun. The woman got frustrated after waiting one minute and leaned hard on her car horn. The officer was startled by the car horn blast and accidentally pulled the trigger, shooting the barista in the arm as she passed him his coffee. The barista hired you to sue the woman for her injury.
   Is a court likely to rule in the barista's favor? **Select one.**

(A) Yes, because the woman was unreasonable in blowing her car horn.
(B) Yes, because the woman's blowing of the car horn caused the officer to pull the trigger.
(C) No, because the woman could not have guessed that the barista would have been shot.
(D) No, because the police officer's mishandling of his gun was a superseding cause of the accident.

3. According to state law, all childcare facilities have to have childproof locks on all interior doors. A childcare facility has a rule that if a child is left in the facility after 5 P.M., the child's family must pay a $100 fine. A parent was running late to pick up her child due to a car wreck on the highway that backed up traffic for miles. Even if the car wreck had not occurred, the parent would not have had enough time to get to the childcare without driving over the speed limit. The parent got to the childcare with a minute to spare, ran inside, and accidentally tripped and fell against a door leading to the childcare's basement. Because the door did not have a lock, the parent fell through the door and down the stairs, breaking both her legs. The childcare had recently been cited by the local building inspector, who had ordered it to put locks on the interior doors as required by law within 30 days. The parent's accident occurred on the 31st day. The parent sued the childcare facility for her injuries, arguing that she was entitled to judgment under the doctrine of negligence per se. The childcare facility hired you as its defense attorney.

What would be the childcare facility's best defense against the parent's claim? **Select one.**

(A) The woman was contributorily negligent because she did not leave herself enough time to get to the childcare facility without speeding.
(B) The childproof lock law was intended to protect children in childcare facilities from injury.
(C) It was unforeseeable that the parent would run inside the childcare to pick up her child, trip, and fall down the stairs.
(D) It was unforeseeable that a car wreck would cause a traffic jam that would make the parent late.

4. A man was walking on the street next to a hotel when a falling object hit him. Evidence indicated that the falling object originated from the hotel. The man wants to sue the hotel for the injuries he sustained. Because there are no witnesses to what occurred, the man sued under the doctrine of *res ipsa loquitur*. The hotel hired you as its defense attorney.

In planning your defense against the man's claim, what are likely the most important questions you need to ask? **Select two.**

(A) How many people were staying at the hotel?
(B) What object fell from the hotel?
(C) How many employees were on duty at the hotel when the man was injured?
(D) Was the man walking on the street or the sidewalk?
(E) Did the man see the object falling toward him?
(F) Did the man have the last clear chance to avoid the object?

5. A woman was walking down the street when she saw a man selling computer gaming systems from the back of his van. Because she needed a birthday present and thought an expensive gaming system would be impressive, she asked the man how much he was selling the systems for. The man said that he would sell her one for $50. The woman knew that the systems usually sold for more than $600. She gave the man $50 and put the system in her bag. At that moment, a police officer arrived and seized all the systems, including the one in the woman's bag. It turned out that the systems had been stolen from a local computer store. The store sued the woman for conversion. The woman hired you to defend her.

Does the store have a strong claim against the woman? **Select one.**

(A) Yes, because the woman intended to make the system her own.
(B) Yes, because the woman knew that $50 was much too low a price for the system.
(C) No, because the woman did not know the system was stolen.
(D) No, because the woman paid $50 for the system.

6. A chemical company operated a factory that produced noxious odors along with its chemicals. Due to the odors, the company constructed the factory in an unincorporated area far from any homes or businesses. It paid neighboring landowners a yearly stipend to use their land for purposes that would not be affected by the odors. The factory operated for over 50 years until one of the neighboring landowners passed away, and his grandson inherited the land. The grandson decided to build a small farm on the land to breed and raise a rare type of chinchilla for the fur industry. After a year of operating the farm, the grandson realized that the chinchillas were becoming sick and refusing to breed due to the odors from the factory. The grandson brought suit against the chemical company for private nuisance. The chemical company hired you as its defense attorney.

   Which of the following would be the chemical company's best argument in defense? **Select one.**

   (A) The factory had operated for 50 years.
   (B) The grandfather's knowledge of the odors could be imputed to the grandson.
   (C) The factory had taken reasonable precautions to protect others from the odors.
   (D) The chinchilla farm was an unusually sensitive use of the grandson's land.

7. A man invited a woman on a date. The man picked the woman up at her home in his car. It started to rain, and the roads became very slick and dangerous. The man had been late to pick up the woman and was speeding to make their reservation at the fanciest restaurant in town. As they were driving, a loose dog ran across the road, and the man had to slam on the brakes. The man's brakes had been malfunctioning for weeks, but he had declined to take them in for repair because of the cost. A truck driver was following too closely behind the man's car and could not stop in time. The truck driver's truck crashed into the back of the man's car. Although neither the man nor the truck driver was hurt, the woman broke her arm because she had not put on her seatbelt as required by state law. The jurisdiction had a modified comparative negligence statute.

   The woman hired you to sue the truck driver for her injuries. At trial, the jury found that the man was 60 percent negligent for speeding and failing to fix his brakes, and the truck driver was 40 percent negligent for following too closely. The woman suffered $200,000 in damages.

   Based on the jury's findings, what amount should be entered in the woman's favor? **Select one.**

   (A) $200,000
   (B) $120,000
   (C) $80,000
   (D) $0

8. A man was walking along the beach when a fisherman negligently cast his line and hooked the man, injuring his eye and mouth. The man went to an eye doctor, who treated the man's eye but negligently caused an infection in the man's nose. The man then went to a mouth surgeon recommended by the eye doctor, who negligently treated the man's mouth and created an abscess in the man's gums. The man hired you to sue the eye doctor for his injuries. The jurisdiction followed a pure comparative negligence scheme.

   Which injuries would a court likely hold the eye doctor liable for? **Select one.**

(A) The man's nose infection.
(B) The man's nose infection and gum abscess.
(C) The man's injuries to his eye, mouth, nose, and gums.
(D) None of the man's injuries.

9. A professional rodeo horse rider was riding his horse along the side of a road when the reins snapped, and the horse sprinted into traffic. A car driving on the road swerved to miss the horse and crashed into a tree. The driver of the car hired you to sue the rider for his injuries.
What would be the driver's most effective argument in support of his claim? **Select one.**

(A) The rider is strictly liable for engaging in a hazardous activity.
(B) The rider is a professional rodeo horse rider.
(C) It was unreasonable to ride a horse along the side of the road.
(D) The rider is strictly liable for the horse's actions.

10. A woman was training in a gym with a boxing ring. A man, who was a professional boxer, invited her to put on some boxing gloves and spar a little with him. The woman put on a pair of gloves, and the two threw a few punches back and forth. One of the woman's punches hit the man in the stomach and knocked the wind out of him. In retaliation, the man punched the woman hard in the face and broke her nose. The woman sued the man for battery. The man hired you to defend him.
What would be the man's best argument in defense? **Select one.**

(A) The woman assumed the risk of getting hit by sparring with him.
(B) The woman impliedly consented to getting hit by sparring with him.
(C) The woman expressly consented to getting hit by sparring with him.
(D) It was unreasonable for the woman to get into the ring with a professional boxer.

11. A man was walking out of a store with a new glass lamp. He accidentally knocked into a woman walking on the sidewalk. It turned out that the woman owned the coffee shop next to the store and was tired of the store's foot traffic interfering with her business. In a fury, the woman grabbed the lamp and tossed it into the street, smashing it to pieces. The man came to your office to discuss potential claims against the woman.
Which of the following claims should you bring on the client's behalf? **Select two.**

(A) Trespass to chattels
(B) Intentional infliction of emotional distress
(C) Conversion
(D) Battery
(E) Assault
(F) Negligence

12. Your client owned a large speedboat. While sailing around on a lake, your client had a sudden pain in his chest. His 12-year-old son grabbed the steering wheel and turned the boat back to shore to get help. Because the son was in a panic and was not looking at where he was going, the client's speedboat banged into a nearby boat, which sank to the bottom of the lake. A woman on that boat fell into the water. The woman screamed because she could not swim. The client's boat got to shore while the woman was still thrashing around in the water, yelling for help. Eventually, another boat rescued the woman from the water. The woman sued your client.
Which of the following legal issues are likely to be most important to the woman's claim? **Select two.**

(A) Battery
(B) Intentional infliction of emotional distress
(C) Conversion
(D) Standard of care
(E) Assault
(F) Negligence

13. You worked as a government attorney. A low-level government employee signed a contract on behalf of the government to drill oil near a farm. The drilling company was well regarded. However, when installing the drill equipment, the drilling company was careless in designing the drill pipe. The well itself was mainly controlled remotely by computer software. One evening, the software failed, and the drill pipe ruptured, spewing oil onto the neighboring farm. The farmer sued the government for negligence, which was allowed under the Federal Tort Claims Act.

Which of the following facts would be most useful in crafting the government's defense? **Select two.**

(A) The government contract was negotiated by a low-level employee.
(B) The drilling company was well regarded.
(C) The drilling company was careless in designing the drill pipe.
(D) The drilling rig was entirely within the drilling company's control.
(E) The government could not have anticipated the well failure.
(F) The failure of the software was the proximate cause of the accident.

14. A local coffee shop had a notice board where community members could post advertisements for their events. A band posted a sign stating that they were conducting a video shoot at a private pool in the area. The band encouraged everyone to arrive at the pool at midnight, "ready to party." The band had not secured the pool operator's permission, and the pool operator knew nothing about the planned video shoot. On the night of the video shoot, the pool operator drained the pool and left the gate unlocked because workers were scheduled to arrive the next morning to retile the deep end. At midnight, several hundred kids from the area arrived at the pool. A kid who had learned about the video shoot from the sign at the coffee shop immediately jumped off the pool's high dive without seeing if there was water in the pool and broke both of his legs. The kid sued the coffee shop for negligence in allowing the band to post its sign on the coffee shop's notice board. The coffee shop hired you as its defense attorney.

Which of the following arguments would be most useful in crafting the coffee shop's defense? **Select two.**

(A) The coffee shop had no duty to protect others from intentional misuse of the notice board.
(B) The band members were not employees of the coffee shop.
(C) The pool operator failed to lock the pool gate on the night the accident occurred.
(D) The pool operator drained the pool without placing warning signs around the pool.
(E) The notice board was only a platform for others in the community to advertise their events.
(F) The kid should have looked into the pool before jumping off the high dive.

15. For 25 years, a bar had a band play on Saturday nights. The bar was situated in a city neighborhood, but no neighbor was ever disturbed by the sound. A woman, who frequented the bar, bought a house in the neighborhood a year ago. The woman was abnormally sensitive to sound and told the bar that she could hear the band's sound system on Saturdays, and it was keeping her awake at night. The bar responded that the sound level complied with city requirements. The woman brought a nuisance claim against the bar for the noise coming from the bar on band nights. The bar hired you as its defense attorney.

Which of the following arguments would be most useful in crafting the bar's defense? **Select two.**

- **(A)** The bar had bands play for over 25 years.
- **(B)** The woman moved to the neighborhood a year ago.
- **(C)** No other neighbor was disturbed by the noise.
- **(D)** The noise levels from the bar complied with city requirements.
- **(E)** The bar only had bands on Saturday nights.
- **(F)** The woman knew about the bar when she moved to the neighborhood.

16. A woman hired you to represent her in her claim against a dog kennel. The kennel was situated in the middle of a large residential neighborhood, caring for dogs while their owners were away. One day, while the woman was walking down the street where the kennel was, a large pack of family dogs came running off the kennel property and knocked the woman to the ground. The woman suffered a fractured hip. The jurisdiction followed comparative negligence principles.

Which of the following arguments would be most useful for the woman's claim? **Select two.**

- **(A)** The dogs were abnormally dangerous.
- **(B)** The kennel owner assumed the risk of having a dog kennel in a residential neighborhood.
- **(C)** The woman was not negligent in walking down the street with the kennel on it.
- **(D)** The dogs would not ordinarily escape the kennel without some negligence.
- **(E)** The kennel owner should be held strictly liable for escaped animals.
- **(F)** The kennel was in exclusive control of the kennel owner.

17. A man and his neighbor continued to argue verbally over the fact that the man had parked his car on the public street. One day, the man came home and found that the neighbor had written on his car, "We all wish you would die!" The man was shocked and struggled to breathe. The man then touched the writing on the car and found that it came off easily because it was written with chalk. The man hired you to sue the neighbor over the incident.

Which of the following claims should you bring on the man's behalf? **Select two.**

- **(A)** Trespass to chattels
- **(B)** Conversion
- **(C)** Assault
- **(D)** Intentional infliction of emotional distress
- **(E)** Battery
- **(F)** Trespass to land

18. A woman was working in her garden shed when her neighbor suddenly appeared and blocked the doorway. The neighbor said, "I know you have my cat! If you don't give me my cat back now, you're going to get it!" The neighbor waved a baseball bat that he was carrying. The woman pointed behind the neighbor and asked, "Is that your cat?" The neighbor looked behind him and saw that it was indeed his cat and apologized before taking the cat home. The woman was seriously shaken and came to your office to ask about suing the neighbor for scaring her.

Which of the following claims should you bring on the woman's behalf? **Select two.**

- **(A)** Trespass to chattels
- **(B)** Trespass to land
- **(C)** False imprisonment
- **(D)** Intentional infliction of emotional distress
- **(E)** Battery
- **(F)** Assault

19. A man hired you to represent him in a personal injury claim. He was walking in a public park that had a sign stating, "No vehicles allowed." The man was knocked over by a child riding a tricycle. The man fell in a bizarre way and ended up impaling his hand on a metal knife that had been dropped by someone else walking through the park the day before. The child's parents picked the man up and apologized to him. The man then went to an emergency care walk-in clinic, where the on-site doctor had very little training. The doctor negligently used the wrong kind of stitches when stitching up the man's hand, causing a big infection. The man wanted to sue the parents of the child who knocked him over.

Which of the following two legal terms would be most useful for you to research for the man's claim? **Select two.**

- **(A)** Battery
- **(B)** Intervening cause
- **(C)** Zone of danger
- **(D)** Persons acting in an emergency
- **(E)** Negligence per se
- **(F)** Superseding cause

20. A woman went to a doctor for surgery to repair a hernia. While the doctor was repairing the hernia, he saw that the woman's appendix looked like it was about to burst. Because a burst appendix can be life-threatening, the doctor removed it. A month later, the woman suffered an infection that seemed to have been caused by the appendix removal. The woman came to your office for advice on a possible lawsuit against the doctor.

Which of the following two legal terms would be most useful for you to research for the woman's claim? **Select two.**

- **(A)** Superseding cause
- **(B)** Intervening cause
- **(C)** Battery
- **(D)** Consent
- **(E)** Negligence per se
- **(F)** *Res ipsa loquitur*

ANSWERS

1. The correct answers are (B) and (E). The landowner's duty to an invitee, a person on the land for a commercial purpose, is to inspect and protect the invitee from dangerous conditions. The duty of protection is nondelegable, so if a business hires a commercial contractor to fix something, the business can still be liable. Consequently, the most relevant questions concern whether a store employee could have seen the ice before the man was hurt. Thus, (B) and (E) are correct. Because the duty of care is nondelegable, (A) and (F) are irrelevant. Finally, (C) and (D) are incorrect because even if the store put up the warnings and the man ignored them, the store could still be found to violate the duty of care owed to invitees. For example, perhaps the store did an unreasonable job of protecting against injury and should have shut down the entire frozen food aisle.

2. The correct answer is (C). For a person to be liable in a tort, the consequence of their action must be foreseeable. Here, it was unforeseeable that blowing on a car horn in frustration in a drive-through line would cause a police officer to shoot the barista. (A) is incorrect because even if the woman was being unreasonable, the result of her actions was still unforeseeable. (B) is incorrect because although the woman's blowing of the horn was the actual cause of the barista being shot, it was not the proximate cause. (D) is incorrect because the issue is foreseeability. For a superseding cause to be at issue, the result must have been foreseeable but cut off by something completely unforeseeable in the middle.

3. The correct answer is (B). For negligence per se to apply, the accident that occurred because of the violation of the law must have been of the type of law that was meant to protect against. Here, the childcare facility's best defense against the parent's negligence per se claim is to argue that the childproof lock law was meant to protect children from injury, not to protect others who might fall through an unlocked door. (A), (C), and (D) are incorrect because they would not be valid defenses against a negligence per se claim.

4. The correct answers are (A) and (B). If an accident does not normally occur without some negligence, and the agent or instrumentality of the injury is within the exclusive control of the defendant, a plaintiff may use the doctrine of *res ipsa* to prove fault even without direct evidence. Here, (A) would be correct because if there were a lot of people staying at the hotel, it would be more likely that someone else might have tossed the object from the hotel. (B) would be correct because it would be important what object fell—if it were a chair, it could have been tossed out a window by a guest; if it were a gargoyle on the roof, it would likely be in the complete control of the hotel. (C) is incorrect because the number of employees on duty would not help the hotel in its defense, as the best defense would be to show that other people (guests or people off the street) could have thrown the object. (D), (E), and (F) would be defenses involving contributory negligence on behalf of the man, but these defenses would not help attack the *res ipsa* claim itself.

5. The correct answer is (A). Conversion is a more serious trespass to chattels that completely deprives the plaintiff of their tangible personal property. Importantly, the relevant intent is simply the intent to take the property of another and deprive the other person of its use. A purchaser of stolen goods is liable to the rightful owner. Here, (A) is correct because it states the correct intent requirement. (B) is incorrect because her knowledge of a reasonable price for the system is irrelevant to the requirements of the tort. (C) is incorrect because conversion does not require whether a person knows something was stolen. (D) is incorrect because her paying $50 has no relation to her intent to keep the property.

6. The correct answer is (D). A private nuisance is an activity or thing that substantially and unreasonably interferes with someone else's use and enjoyment of their land. Coming to the nuisance is not a defense. Importantly, what constitutes a nuisance is dependent on the locality of the property. Consequently, the company's best argument in defense would be that the grandson is engaging in an unusually sensitive use of the land by running his chinchilla farm. (A) is incorrect because the length of time the nuisance existed would not change the analysis. (B) is incorrect because the grandson's knowledge of the odors would not change the fact that the company is creating a nuisance with the factory's odors. (C) is incorrect because the fact that the company took reasonable precautions to protect others would not change the analysis.

7. The correct answer is (A). In a modified comparative negligence jurisdiction, if the plaintiff is more at fault than the defendant, the plaintiff may not recover. Here, however, there is no indication that the jury found the woman negligent at all, despite the fact that she was not wearing her seatbelt. Consequently, there is no reason that her recovery should be reduced, and the court should enter judgment in her favor for $200,000. Thus, (B), (C), and (D) are incorrect.

8. The correct answer is (A). For a person to be liable in negligence, their actions must be both the actual and proximate cause of the victim's injuries. Here, the only injury caused by the eye doctor was the man's nose infection. If the man were suing the fisherman, the fisherman could be held liable for all the man's injuries because the original tortfeasor may also be held liable for a doctor's negligence in treating the injury. However, because the question only inquires about the man suing the eye doctor, (B), (C), and (D) are incorrect.

9. The correct answer is (C). A person is liable in negligence if they fail to act reasonably. Thus, if it were unreasonable to ride a horse along the side of the road, the rider could be held liable. (A) is incorrect because riding a horse is not generally regarded as an ultrahazardous activity creating strict liability. (B) is incorrect because there was no indication that the rider broke the standard of care of a professional rodeo horse rider. (D) is incorrect because a horse is not generally considered a wild animal that creates strict liability in the owner.

10. The correct answer is (B). By getting into a boxing ring and sparring, the woman likely impliedly consented to battery and getting hit in the face. (A) is incorrect because the assumption of the risk is a defense to a party's negligence, and battery is an intentional tort (which makes consent a complete defense). (C) is incorrect because the situation is more correctly described as implied consent than express consent, in that the woman did not expressly say, "Hit me in the face!" (D) is incorrect because the woman's potential negligence would not be a defense to the intentional tort of battery.

11. The correct answers are (C) and (D). Here, (C) is correct because the woman could be liable for conversion of the lamp because she smashed it to pieces. (D) is correct because grabbing something closely associated with a person can constitute battery. (A) is incorrect because trespass to chattels is for situations where there is no lasting harm to the property, and here the lamp was smashed to bits. (B) is incorrect because the woman's actions seem to be closer to a moment of losing control than to an intentional assault on the man's emotions. (E) is incorrect because there was no indication that the man even knew the woman was going to touch him until he grabbed the lamp. (F) is incorrect because the woman's actions were intentional.

12. The correct answers are (D) and (F). (D) is correct because a significant issue will be that the son will be held to an adult standard of care, given that he was driving a speedboat, an adult activity. (F) is correct because the crash with the other boat was an accident, which would involve a negligence claim. (A), (B), (C), and (E) are incorrect because these torts require intent, and the son crashed into the other boat by mistake.

13. The correct answer is (B) and (E). The focus here is on the potential negligence of the government. The government's only action was to hire the drilling company, so if the company was well-regarded and the government could not have anticipated the well failure, the government could not be found liable for negligence. Thus, (B) and (E) are correct. (A) This is incorrect because the low-level employee still had the apparent ability to bind the government, as that employee was authorized to sign the contract. (C) is incorrect because this does not relate to the government's potential negligence. (D) is incorrect because the government could still be found liable if the government had allowed an incompetent drilling company to be in complete control of the drilling project. (F) is incorrect because the failure of the software is irrelevant to the government's potential negligence.

14. The correct answers are (A) and (E). Here, the only way the coffee shop could be found negligent is if it breached a duty it owed to the kid. Consequently, (A) is correct. (E) is correct because it highlights the coffee shop's lack of involvement in the band's video shoot. (B) is incorrect because there is no evidence that the band members were employees of the coffee shop, so there's no real point in arguing this one. (C) and (D) are incorrect because the pool operator's actions have nothing to do with the coffee shop's potential negligence. (F) is incorrect because while the kid's own negligence might lessen potential damages, (A) and (E) completely protect the coffee shop from a negligence claim.

15. The correct answers are (C) and (E). A person has a successful claim for nuisance if a potential nuisance causes significant, substantial, and unreasonable harm to an average member of the community. Here, (C) is correct because no one else has been bothered by the sound, and the woman is abnormally affected by it. (E) is correct because a once-a-week band concert on a weekend night is unlikely to be substantial and unreasonable. (A) and (B) are incorrect because even if the woman had just moved into the area, the bar's sound system could be a nuisance if it also disturbed others. (D) is incorrect because the bar's compliance with city regulations would not defend it against a nuisance claim. (F) is incorrect because the woman's knowledge of the bar would not change the analysis.

16. The correct answers are (D) and (F). If an accident does not normally occur without some negligence and the agent or instrumentality of the injury is within the exclusive control of the defendant, a plaintiff may use the doctrine of *res ipsa* to prove fault even without direct evidence. Here, if the woman can show (D) and (F), she has a good claim under *res ipsa*. (A) is incorrect because these are family dogs (plus, they only knocked the woman over—they did not bite her). (B) is incorrect because the kennel owner's assumption of any risk would not relate to the woman's claim. (C) is incorrect because the woman can still recover even if she was negligent, as this jurisdiction follows comparative negligence principles. (E) is incorrect because these were family dogs, which do not normally create strict liability.

17. The correct answers are (A) and (D). (A) is correct because the neighbor wrongfully wrote on the man's car with chalk, but that chalk was only a temporary mark on the car. (D) is correct because the neighbor's writing on the car was likely extreme and outrageous. (B) is incorrect because the damage to the car was only temporary. (C) is incorrect because the man was never put in fear of battery. (E) is incorrect because the man was never touched. (F) is incorrect because the man's car was parked on a public street.

18. The correct answers are (C) and (F). (C) is correct because the neighbor confined the woman inside her garden shed. (F) is correct because the neighbor threatened to hit the woman with the baseball bat. (A) and (B) are incorrect because the neighbor did not touch the woman's property. (D) is incorrect because the neighbor only threatened the woman to retrieve his cat, not to cause her emotional distress. (E) is incorrect because the neighbor never touched the woman.

19. The correct answers are (B) and (E). Here, the doctor's negligence would be an intervening cause, which the child's parents could also be liable for. Consequently, (B) is correct. Under negligence per se, a violation of a statute establishes negligence if the statute is intended to protect against the type of harm that occurred. Here, the park had a sign saying no vehicles were allowed, and a tricycle might fall under the definition of a vehicle. Consequently, (E) is correct. (A) is incorrect because there is no indication of intent on the child's part. (C) is incorrect because there was no indication that the man was ever placed in fear of anything. (D) is incorrect because this refers to the standard of care of a reasonable person in an emergency, which is not relevant here. (F) is incorrect because a superseding cause refers to an unforeseeable event, such as an act of God.

20. The correct answers are (C) and (D). Here, if the doctor's removal of the appendix was harmful or offensive, the removal could be a battery. Consequently, (C) is correct. (D) is correct because a major issue in the claim would be whether consent to the hernia surgery included consent to the appendix removal. (A) and (B) are incorrect because the doctor's actions are the only cause of the potential tort. (E) is incorrect because there is no issue here of following a law or statute. (F) is incorrect because the tortfeasor, the doctor, is known.

Business Associations and Relationships

8

Topics with asterisks (*) require you to know the black letter law cold; topics without an * require you to recognize the topic as part of the fact scenario or require you to analyze and apply legal resources provided for the topic efficiently.

MAIN POINT OF BUSINESS ASSOCIATIONS—DECIDING WHO IS LIABLE OR RESPONSIBLE WHEN PROBLEMS ARISE

OUTLINE

I. AGENCY AND AUTHORITY

A. Creation*

In general, a principal is bound by an agreement entered into by the agent on the principal's behalf. The agent's power to bind the principal can be expressed by oral or written agreement, implied by the principal's conduct, or because of a third party's misunderstanding that the agent had the necessary authority. Four elements create an agency relationship: (1) a principal assents to an agent, (2) the agent does something on the principal's behalf, (3) the principal controls the agent's actions, and (4) the principal shows consent to the agency.

B. Agent's Authority to Bind Principal

1. **Actual Authority***—When the principal specifically tells the agent to do something. Actual authority can also be found when the agent takes actions necessary or incidental to achieving the principal's objectives. For example, when an agent obtains the necessary permits for the principal's project.
2. **Apparent Authority***—When the principal acts in such a way as to cause a third party to reasonably believe the agent has authority. For example, a principal introduces the agent to a third party and says, "He's been my agent for years."

C. Agent's Fiduciary Duties to Principal

1. **Duty of Care***—An agent must act with the competence, care, and diligence of a reasonable agent in similar circumstances.
2. **Duty of Loyalty***—Because an agent is acting on the principal's behalf, there are several things that the agent cannot do: (1) treat the principal as an adverse party in an agreement, (2) get a material benefit from transactions done on the principal's behalf unless the principal agrees, (3) take a business opportunity away from the principal, (4) compete with the principal, (5) work for another principal without disclosure, or (6) disclose the principal's confidential information.

D. Termination*

Either the principal or the agent can terminate the agency by giving notice to the other party. The agency can also be terminated if circumstances change in such a way as to give the agent a reasonable belief that the agency ended. For example, if the agent receives notice that the principal has died.

II. VICARIOUS LIABILITY OF PRINCIPAL FOR ACTS OF AGENT*

A. *Respondeat Superior*

If the agent acts within the scope of their agency, the principal can be held legally responsible for any wrongful acts. For example, hitting another person's car while looking at potential business sites for the principal. *Respondeat superior* is based on an employment relationship, so it is a narrower situation than vicarious liability below.

B. Vicarious Liability

The principal is vicariously liable for any torts committed by the agent within the scope of their authority. For example, an agent tortiously interferes with another company while negotiating an agreement on behalf of the principal.

C. Joint Venture Liability

All participants in a joint business venture are jointly and severally liable for any of the venture's debts or obligations.

D. Distinctions Between Employees and Independent Contractors

1. **Employees**—Generally, under the control of the employer regarding tasks, performance, and work schedule—for example, the law school registrar
2. **Independent Contractors**—have control over their own work schedules—for example, a plumber hired to fix the law school bathroom

III. FORMATION, MANAGEMENT, AND CONTROL OF GENERAL PARTNERSHIPS

A. De Facto Treatment of Improperly Created Corporations and Limited Liability Companies as General Partnership—If an owner makes a good-faith effort to comply with incorporation requirements but fails in some way, the entity will be treated as a de facto corporation. In the past, the owner would still be protected from personal liability for entity obligations, but the Model Business Corporation Act abolished this doctrine.

B. The Authority of General Partners to Manage the Partnership—A partner has the authority to act on behalf of the business. For example, a partner could hire an employee for the business.

C. **Creation of a General Partnership**—All a partnership requires is the agreement of at least two persons to carry on a business for profit. *See* Revised Uniform Partnership Act 101(6). In addition, a person entering into a partnership can be a natural person or a legal entity, such as a corporation, trust, estate, limited liability company, governmental entity, or another partnership. *See* Revised Uniform Partnership Act 101(10). A person's subjective intent not to create a partnership does not prevent the formation of a partnership. *See* Revised Uniform Partnership Act 202(a). A person forming a partnership does need the capacity to contract. While a written partnership agreement must satisfy the Statute of Frauds, a partnership can be created through an oral agreement. Finally, a partnership is created by the sharing of profits, not gross returns.

IV. FORMATION OF CORPORATIONS AND LIMITED LIABILITY COMPANIES

A. Corporations

1. **Incorporation Documents**—Articles of incorporation must be filed with the state. They must include basic information, including the name of the corporation, the number of shares issued, the registered agent's name and address, and each incorporator's name and address. The corporate name must include the words "corporation," "company," "incorporated," or "limited," although these words can be abbreviated. For example, "The Bar Exam Stinks, Inc." is perfectly acceptable. Generally, the articles of incorporation control in the case of a conflict between the bylaws and the articles of incorporation.
2. **Bylaws**—The rules governing the corporation's day-to-day business. For example, when shareholder meetings are held, the number of people on the board of directors, the duties of each corporate officer, and other relevant matters. The corporation's board of directors adopts the initial bylaws.
3. **Amendments to Incorporation Documents and Bylaws**—Incorporation documents may be amended according to state law, while bylaws provide the rules regarding their own amendment. The board of directors or the shareholders can amend or repeal a bylaw, and the shareholders may amend the bylaws to limit the board of directors' power.

B. Limited Liability Companies

1. **Certificate of Organization**—the document filed with the state that creates the LLC
2. **Operating Agreement**—the rules governing the day-to-day operation of the LLC
3. **Amendments to Certificate of Organization and Operating Agreement**—Certificate may be amended according to state law, and the operating agreement may be amended according to its own rules.

V. CORPORATE PROMOTERS: PRE-ORGANIZATION CONTRACTS AND FIDUCIARY DUTIES

A promoter does things before the corporation's formation to create the corporation—for example, finding investors and entering into contracts. A promoter is personally liable for corporate liabilities before the corporation is formed, and jointly and severally liable after the corporation comes into existence unless a novation releases the promoter's liability. A promoter has a fiduciary duty to the corporation—for example, the promoter cannot make a secret profit on any preincorporation agreements.

VI. MANAGEMENT AND CONTROL OF CORPORATIONS AND LIMITED LIABILITY COMPANIES

A. Corporations

1. Powers and Rights of Shareholders

a. **Preferred**—Generally, a preferred stockholder has precedence over common stock when it comes to corporate distributions. Preferred stock might also have special voting rights.

b. **Common**—Standard stock that comes with general voting rights

2. Requirements for Annual Meetings

a. **Notice**—A corporation must have a general meeting every year. For special meetings, all shareholders entitled to vote must be given notice between 10 and 60 days before the meeting date, unless the shareholder has waived notice.

b. **Quorum**—For a shareholders' meeting to be valid, there must be a majority of shareholders entitled to vote on a particular matter in attendance.

3. Powers and Rights of Directors

a. **Requirement for Directors' Meetings**

i. **Notice**—A regular meeting may be held without notice, but special meetings require two days' notice.

ii. **Quorum**—Unless the articles of incorporation or bylaws state otherwise, a majority of the directors must be present at the meeting for a vote.

iii. **Action by Committee**—The board of directors may appoint committees to undertake corporate actions.

4. **Powers and Rights of Officers**—The board of directors may elect officers to run the business. Usually, the officers are the president, secretary, and treasurer. The corporate bylaws dictate their powers. Like other corporate employees, an officer is protected from some personal liability.

B. Powers and Rights of Members and Managers of Limited Liability Companies—"Members" of an LLC own the LLC, while "managers" run the business's day-to-day operations. A person can be both a member and a manager.

VII. FIDUCIARY DUTIES WITHIN BUSINESS ASSOCIATIONS

A. **Fiduciary Duties of General Partners***—General partners have both a duty of care and a duty of loyalty to the partnership (*see* above).

B. **Fiduciary Duties of Corporate Officers and Directors***—Officers and directors have both a duty of care and a duty of loyalty (*see* above).

C. **Fiduciary Duties of Limited Liability Company Members and Managers***—Members and managers have both a duty of care and a duty of loyalty (*see* above).

VIII. SHAREHOLDER AND MEMBER LITIGATION

A. Who Is Suing Whom in Direct and Derivative Litigation

1. **Direct**—Shareholder is suing either the corporation, officers, or directors for personal injury.

2. **Derivative**—Shareholder is suing the corporation's directors, officers, or third parties on behalf of the corporation.

IX. LIABILITY RULES RELATED TO BUSINESS ASSOCIATIONS

A. **Liability of General Partners Under the Revised Uniform Partnership Act (1997)*—**General partners are jointly and severally liable for the partnership's liabilities. Also, a person's subjective intent does not prevent the formation of a partnership.

B. **Liability of Corporate Officers and Directors Under the Model Business Corporation Act (2016)*—**Generally, officers have limited liability for corporate actions so long as they are acting in good faith. The act also provides that a corporate officer is entitled to mandatory indemnification when successfully defending against a legal action in which the officer is a party due to their role in the corporation.

   1. **Liability for Illegal Actions—**If an officer attends a meeting where the board votes to do something unlawful, the officer can protect himself or herself by promptly objecting at the meeting, ensuring the officers dissent was noted in the minutes of the meeting, or delivering notice of dissent to the presiding officer of the meeting before the meeting is adjourned or to the corporation immediately afterward.

C. **Liability of Limited Liability Company Members and Managers Under the Uniform Limited Liability Company Act (2013)*—**Members generally have limited liability for corporate actions.

D. **Piercing the Veil*—**If creditors can show that there is a lack of separation between members and an LLC, the creditors may hold the members personally liable for the LLC's liabilities. Essentially, the creditor can "pierce the veil" that separates the member from the LLC.

PRACTICE MULTIPLE-CHOICE QUESTIONS

1. A man wanted to start a wedding photography business with his brother. Before incorporating the business, the man visited a camera store to purchase an expensive camera and several specialized lenses. The man informed the store that he was purchasing the camera and lenses for a soon-to-be incorporated business, and that he could pay half the price upfront, with the balance due after the business was incorporated. The store owner agreed and asked the man to sign an agreement regarding the deal. The man signed on behalf of "Wedding Photos, Inc." as "agent to the corporation." A month later, the man received a letter from the store owner demanding immediate payment. The man comes to you for advice, stating that his brother has the camera and lenses and that they never incorporated because they had a big fight. He asks you if the store owner can hold him personally liable for the other half of the purchase price for the cameras and lenses.

   Which of the following topics would be most useful to research in determining the man's potential liability? **Select one.**

   (A) Promoters
   (B) Agents
   (C) Partners
   (D) Members

2. Your client is a woman who created an online program for tutoring college students. She asked a friend to help her start a business to expand the tutoring program to more markets.

Before incorporating the business, the friend used funds set aside for the business to lease marketing and design software. When the client found out, she confronted the friend, who said the leased software was the best in the business. Despite her reservations, the client went ahead and incorporated the business with her friend. The client then discovered that the friend owned the company that made the marketing and design software and that it was priced much higher than any other software on the market. The client is considering suing her friend.

Which of the following legal topics would be most helpful to research regarding the client's possible lawsuit? **Select two.**

(A) A partner's implied waiver of notice
(B) A promoter's duty of loyalty
(C) An agent's authority
(D) An agent's duty of care
(E) A promoter's duty of notice
(F) A partner's duty of care and supervision

3. Your client is a builder. The builder was playing pickleball with the president of a fast food corporation. While the two were playing, the president said, "Let's make this interesting—if you win, I'll sign a contract right now with you to build our next four restaurants." The builder agreed, won the game, and then the president wrote and signed an agreement saying the builder could build the restaurants. The agreement made no mention of the pickleball bet. The next day, a corporate board member called the builder and stated that the corporation did not support the president's gambling habit, as a result of which the president could not sign contracts on behalf of the corporation; therefore, the contract was invalid. The builder would like to bring suit against the corporation to enforce the contract.

Which of the following would be the best argument in support of the builder's claim? **Select one.**

(A) As the corporation president, the president had actual authority to sign the building contract.
(B) A corporation president has apparent authority to sign contracts on behalf of the corporation.
(C) There was no indication that the builder knew the president had a gambling problem.
(D) There was no mention of the pickleball bet in the signed agreement.

4. Your client wanted to create a hunting and fishing business with his two friends. One of the friends came to your office with the client, but the other one was overseas for the next two months. The other friend was unreachable until he returned. The client had found several investors for the business, but the investors demanded that the articles of incorporation be filed that week. The jurisdiction followed the Model Business Corporation Act.

What should you tell your client to do if he wants to file the articles of incorporation this week? **Select one.**

(A) The articles of incorporation may be filed with only the client's or a friend's signature.
(B) You may sign the articles of incorporation on behalf of the business if the client and friend give you the authority to do so in writing.
(C) The client and friend must both sign because the signatures of a quorum of incorporators are required to file articles of incorporation.
(D) The client and friend must wait until the other friend returns home before incorporating the business.

5. A farmer sold vegetables at the end of an isolated road. The farmer asked his neighbor, who lived closer to the highway, if the neighbor would display a sign in his yard advertising the vegetables. The neighbor agreed to allow the farmer to put up a sign in his yard if the farmer gave him a bushel of vegetables per month. The farmer agreed. Soon, the farmer's vegetables got really popular. Sometimes, if the neighbor was standing in the yard, he would talk up how good the vegetables were if people stopped and asked about the sign. After a year, the farmer was overrun with customers, so he removed his sign from the neighbor's yard because he no longer needed any advertising. The neighbor came to you for advice, asking if he had a partnership with the farmer for selling vegetables and if he could sue for a portion of the profits.

   Did the farmer and the neighbor have a partnership? **Select one.**

   (A) Yes, because the neighbor allowed the farmer's sign to be placed in his yard.
   (B) Yes, because the farmer paid the neighbor with the business's goods.
   (C) No, because the neighbor did nothing to further the business.
   (D) No, because the neighbor was not paid from the profits of the business.

6. Your client owns several commercial properties in the area. Your client rented a space to a small, limited liability corporation that sold women's clothing. The lease agreement stipulated that the corporation would lease the space for a period of five years. Two years into the lease, the corporation stopped paying rent due to an economic downturn. Six months later, it moved out of the space without informing your client. The client knew that several of the corporation's members were very wealthy, and he asked you for advice on whether he could recover the unpaid rent from one of the members personally.

   Which of the following facts, if true, would be most useful in supporting the client's claim? **Select two.**

   (A) The members were closely involved in the corporation's day-to-day operations.
   (B) A women's clothing store is generally classified as a risky business.
   (C) The members did not observe corporate formalities.
   (D) The corporation had insufficient capital to cover expenses.
   (E) Imposing personal liability would warn other potentially risky businesses in the area.
   (F) The members acted as promoters before incorporation.

7. Your client and a friend decided to run a business together building electric guitar effects pedals. Your client and his friend agreed to share in the business profits, but they divided up the business operations by having your client responsible for all the financial aspects of the business, while the friend was only responsible for building and designing pedals. Your client and his friend signed an agreement to memorialize their understanding of their roles. While your client was on vacation, the friend bought $50,000 worth of electronics for the business. Your client discovered the issue and called you in a panic. He told you that the business did not currently have $50,000 in its bank account, but that the friend thought the business would make over $100,000 next week when its new pedal was introduced at a major corporate exposition as the preferred pedal of a world-famous guitarist. Your client was scared that he could be held personally liable for the $50,000 if the friend's prediction regarding incoming profits proved incorrect.

   Can your client be held personally liable for the $50,000? **Select one.**

   (A) Yes, because your client was acting as chief financial officer of the business.
   (B) Yes, because your client was a partner in the business.
   (C) No, because your client did not authorize his friend's $50,000 purchase.
   (D) No, because the friend was not authorized to spend money for the business according to their signed agreement.

8. Your client is on a corporation's board of directors. At the last board meeting, the board voted for the corporation to engage in actions that your client thought might be illegal. She did not object and abstained from taking part in the vote. She comes to your office and asks if she could be held liable for the potentially illegal actions.

Can your client be held liable for the potentially illegal actions? **Select one.**

(A) Yes, because your client did not communicate her dissent to the board.
(B) Yes, because your client is a member of the board.
(C) No, because your client did not vote in favor of the potentially illegal actions.
(D) No, because only the corporation could be held liable for the potentially illegal actions.

9. You were hired by a small business that incorporated five years ago. The business asked you to review its articles of incorporation and bylaws. The articles of incorporation were filed before the bylaws were established. You discover that the business has been acting in accordance with the bylaws for several years, but those bylaws conflict with several statements in the articles of incorporation.

Which of the following statements is correct? **Select one.**

(A) The bylaws control because the company has been acting in accordance with them for several years.
(B) The bylaws control because they concern the day-to-day operations of the business.
(C) The articles of incorporation control because they were filed before the bylaws.
(D) The articles of incorporation control because they incorporated the business.

10. Your client worked as an editor for a small publishing company. Your client requested to be added to the company's insurance, but the company refused, stating that your client was an independent contractor and only company employees were eligible for the company's health insurance plan. Your client visited your office seeking advice on whether she was considered an employee or an independent contractor of the company.

Which of the following facts is most helpful in proving that your client is an employee? **Select one.**

(A) Your client is paid once per month.
(B) Your client works from home.
(C) The company tells your client which book projects she should work on.
(D) The company requires your client to track her hours.

11. Your client wanted to start a food truck specializing in lobster rolls. He asked a successful chef from a seafood restaurant to help him set up the business as a corporation. Before the corporation was formed, the chef used business funds to purchase a subscription service that provided plastic utensils, plates, and napkins. Your client had no idea that the chef was going to buy the subscription. The chef argued that they needed that stuff, and a subscription service was the easiest way to ensure that they would not run out once they started serving lobster rolls. The chef then completed the incorporation of the food truck. A short time later, your client discovered that the chef owned the subscription service. Your client feels that they have been taken advantage of and would like to sue the chef.

Which of the following legal terms would be most useful for you to research for the client's claim? **Select two.**

(A) *Respondeat superior*
(B) Independent contractors
(C) Employees
(D) A promoter's fiduciary duties
(E) De facto corporation
(F) An agent's authority

12. A subdivision developer built a new home in a residential neighborhood. The developer used a subcontractor, a builder, to build garages for his properties. The developer called the builder and left a message stating that the developer would be in Europe on business for two weeks and would be unable to answer calls. In the same message, the developer instructed the builder to construct a garage for the new home, 30 feet from the south and east property lines, by next Tuesday. This was necessary because a buyer was interested in the home, and it needed to pass a home inspection before the developer's return from Europe. The builder observed that local building codes mandated garages to be located within five feet of a property line. Consequently, the builder built the garage five feet from the south and east property lines to comply with the building codes. When the developer returned from Europe, he saw where the builder had put the garage and refused to pay him for his work. The builder has come to you for advice regarding a potential claim against the developer.

Which of the following facts are most useful in supporting the builder's claim? **Select two.**

- **(A)** The developer was required to ratify moving the garage back because of the building code.
- **(B)** The builder had actual authority to move the garage back.
- **(C)** The builder could not knowingly violate the building code.
- **(D)** The developer was primarily liable if the garage was not moved back.
- **(E)** The developer's objective made moving the garage back necessary.
- **(F)** The builder had apparent authority to move the garage back.

13. A company's compliance officer was not on the company's board of directors but was chosen to speak at a shareholder conference on behalf of the company. During the conference, the compliance officer made a speech where she mistakenly stated that the company's shares were worth more than double their true value. Her mistake was made in good faith, and she believed she was acting in the best interest of the company when she made the statement.

A shareholder who was at the conference sued the compliance officer for fraud. The compliance officer was found not liable.

The compliance officer visited your office and inquired whether the company would be required to indemnify her for her trial expenses. The jurisdiction followed the Model Business Corporation Act. The company's articles of incorporation said nothing about indemnification.

Which of the following facts are most important to the compliance officer's ability to recover her trial expenses? **Select two.**

- **(A)** The compliance officer believed she was acting in good faith while representing the company at the conference.
- **(B)** The compliance officer was a party to the lawsuit due to her company position.
- **(C)** The compliance officer believed she was acting in the best interest of the company while representing the company at the conference.
- **(D)** The compliance officer was found not liable for fraud.
- **(E)** The articles of incorporation do not provide for indemnification.
- **(F)** The board has discretion in deciding whether to indemnify its officers.

14. A man came to your office for legal advice. The man had recently been hired as an agent for a new corporation. The corporation purchased properties near a local university, refurbished them into apartment units, and then rented them to students. The man was tasked with scouting out suitable locations, and the corporation gave him the authority to sign lease agreements on its behalf. The man was concerned that the corporation's officers were engaging in possible illegal transactions, and he wanted to know what duties he owed to the corporation itself.

What duties does the man have as an agent of the corporation? **Select two.**

(A) Duty of care
(B) Duty to warn
(C) Duty to defend and settle
(D) Duty of loyalty
(E) Duty of compliance
(F) Duty of indemnification

15. You are an attorney working for a small corporation. The corporation has asked you to organize its annual shareholder meeting, during which it will elect new directors and vote on several pending issues. You have not yet looked at the company's bylaws.

Which of the following are the most important things you should do for the shareholder meeting to be lawful? **Select two.**

(A) Include the time, date, and place of the meeting in the notice sent to shareholders.
(B) Provide a sign-in so all shareholders who wish to speak are allowed to do so.
(C) Notify attending shareholders that every shareholder owes the corporation a duty of care and loyalty.
(D) Notify attending shareholders that a quorum is not necessary to conduct new business.
(E) Notify shareholders that failure to have a quorum at the meeting could adversely affect the corporation's business.
(F) Send out notice of the meeting to shareholders at least 10 days before the meeting date.

16. A small corporation asked you to review its corporate bylaws. The bylaws stated: "The shareholders of the corporation adopt these initial bylaws. These bylaws take precedence in cases of conflict with the corporation's articles of incorporation. Either the board of directors or the shareholders may amend or repeal any bylaw. These bylaws govern the management of the business by its officers and directors. If the shareholders so desire, these bylaws may be amended to limit the board of directors' power. The board of directors will consist of five members." The corporation asked you if any of the statements in the bylaws differed from what was usually stated in corporate bylaws.

Which of the following statements should you point out as differing from usual corporation bylaws? **Select two.**

(A) These initial bylaws are adopted by the shareholders of the corporation.
(B) These bylaws control in cases of a conflict with the corporation's articles of incorporation.
(C) Either the board of directors or the shareholders may amend or repeal any bylaw.
(D) These bylaws govern how the business will be managed by its officers and directors.
(E) If the shareholders so desire, these bylaws may be amended to limit the board of directors' power.
(F) The board of directors will consist of five members.

17. A group of doctors formed a limited liability company to provide professional services. A doctor, one of the company's members, visited your office to inquire about potential personal liability.

Which of the following events is MOST likely to expose the doctor to personal liability? **Select two.**

- **(A)** The doctor used a company check, which bounced, to pay for the company's nursing services.
- **(B)** The doctor failed to pay the bill for his company car.
- **(C)** The doctor left a bag of dog waste on the car of the dentist next door because the dentist kept parking in the doctor's space.
- **(D)** The doctor personally signed the lease for the company, which committed the company to leasing its current property for three years.
- **(E)** Unbeknownst to the other members, the doctor pledged to donate $2,000 to a local animal shelter on behalf of the company.
- **(F)** Due to a company error, the doctor acted in good faith but wrongfully removed a patient's appendix.

18. A woman ran a local sticker business that started growing nationally. The woman decided she needed a business partner and came to your office for advice on creating a partnership.

Which of the following statements are true regarding the creation of a partnership? **Select two.**

- **(A)** A corporation, trust, or governmental entity can be a partner.
- **(B)** The sharing of gross returns creates a partnership.
- **(C)** All partners must subjectively agree to create a partnership.
- **(D)** Partners do not need the capacity to contract.
- **(E)** The woman only needs one other person to create a partnership.
- **(F)** Any partnership agreement is subject to the Statute of Frauds.

19. A woman owned and operated a vintage clothing store. She hired a teenager to offer same-day delivery to local customers for online orders. She gave the teenager a store credit card and instructed him to visit the local sign shop to purchase custom magnetic signs to attach to his car while making deliveries. She told the teenager to spend no more than $200 on the signs, but when he went to buy them, the signs were actually $600. The teenager bought the signs. On the way back to the store from the sign shop, one of the signs came off the teenager's car and shattered the windshield of a pickup truck. The woman was furious, but the teenager was so upset that she told him everything was fine and that he still had a job at her store. The next day, the woman came to your office to inquire about her potential liability resulting from the teenager's actions.

Which of the following legal concepts would be most helpful to research in determining the woman's potential liability? **Select two.**

- **(A)** Actual authority
- **(B)** Apparent authority
- **(C)** Ratification
- **(D)** The Uniform Commercial Code
- **(E)** Joint venture liability
- **(F)** *Respondeat superior*

20. A farmer asked a man who worked for him to buy a thresher from the supply store on the farmer's behalf. The farmer gave the man a signed blank check for the purchase. The man went to the supply store, told the clerk that he was buying a thresher for the farmer, and bought a thresher that was then delivered to the farmer. The farmer told the man that he thought it was a good thresher and started using it immediately. When the supply store took the check to the bank, it discovered that the farmer had asked the bank to stop payment on it. The owner of the supply store has come to your office asking for legal advice regarding the farmer's potential liability for the thresher sale.

Which of the following facts are LEAST important to the question of whether an agency relationship existed between the farmer and the man? **Select two.**

(A) The farmer asked the man to buy the thresher.
(B) The agreement between the farmer and the man was not in writing.
(C) The farmer told the man to buy the thresher from the supply store.
(D) The man told the clerk he was buying the thresher for the farmer.
(E) The man bought the thresher on the farmer's behalf.
(F) The farmer accepted the thresher from the man.

ANSWERS

1. The correct answer is (A). The man would be best viewed as a promoter, making "promoters" the best answer. A promoter does things before the corporation's formation to create the corporation—for example, finding investors and entering into contracts. A promoter is personally liable for corporate liabilities before the corporation is formed, and jointly and severally liable after the corporation comes into existence unless a novation releases the promoter's liability. (B) is incorrect because an agent generally acts on behalf of a principal, and here the man is trying to establish his and his brother's planned corporation. Consequently, there's no principal here. (C) is incorrect because the facts do not suggest a partnership has been created. (D) is incorrect because an LLC has members, and nothing has been incorporated yet.

2. The correct answers are (B) and (C). Here, the friend was acting as a promoter when she acted on behalf of the business before it was incorporated. As a promoter, she owed a duty of loyalty to the business, which might be compromised by the fact that she purchased software from a company she owned at a price significantly higher than that of other companies. So (B) is correct. (C) is correct because there is also a question as to whether the friend had the authority to bind the business to a contract, as the client did not authorize what the friend was doing. (A) is incorrect because a "partner's implied waiver of notice" is a made-up term. (D) is incorrect because the big issue in this question is whether the friend signed an unfair contract that favored her personal interests, not that she might have acted negligently in carrying out her duties. "Duty of care" usually deals with negligence issues, making (B) and (C) better answers. (E) is another made-up duty. Finally, (F) is incorrect because there is no indication of a partnership at the time the questionable contract was signed.

3. The correct answer is (B). A corporation president has apparent authority to enter into contracts for a corporation even if they lack actual authority. Here, the builder's best argument is that the president created apparent authority to enter into an agreement for the restaurants when he made the bet. (A) is incorrect because there is no indication that the president had actual authority to sign the contract, and the board member's statement seems to confirm this. (C) is incorrect because the president's potential gambling problem is irrelevant as far as his authority to sign a contract goes. (D) is incorrect because it is irrelevant whether the pickleball bet was stated in the signed agreement.

4. The correct answer is (A). The Model Corporation Act §1.2 only requires the name and signature of one person to incorporate a business, even if more than one person is involved in running it. Because only one of the incorporators must sign the incorporation documents, (B), (C), and (D) are incorrect.

5. The correct answer is (C). Under the Revised Partnership Act 202, a partner generally must do something to support and further the business to be considered a partner. Here, the neighbor only allowed the farmer to pay him to put a sign in his yard and occasionally mentioned the vegetables. Ultimately, his passive involvement with the business would not be enough to make him a partner. (A) is incorrect because the farmer paid the neighbor to allow him to put an advertisement in his yard, which is not enough to create a partnership. (B) is incorrect because how the neighbor was paid is irrelevant. (D) is incorrect because how the neighbor was paid is irrelevant.

6. The correct answers are (C) and (D). Whether a creditor can pierce the corporate veil to hold LLC members personally liable depends on the totality of the circumstances. "Piercing the corporate veil" means the ability of a corporate creditor to receive payment from an LLC member despite protections provided by incorporation. This is an equitable remedy, and courts are generally reluctant to use it because of the specific purpose of incorporating a business (which is to protect potential members from personal liability if the business goes wrong). There is no bright-line rule regarding whether a court will allow a creditor to pierce the corporate veil; however, courts consider factors such as undercapitalization, disregard of corporate formalities, intermingling of corporate and personal assets, and potential fraud committed on a shareholder's behalf. Here, only choices (C) and (D) would lead a court to believe that the corporation was set up merely as a ruse to hide a business that was not actually a true corporation. Consequently, (A), (B), (E), and (F) are incorrect.

7. The correct answer is (B). Because the client and his friend agreed to run the business as coowners for profit, they created a general partnership. Under the Revised Uniform Partnership Act (1997), a partner in a general partnership is personally liable for the partnership's obligations. Consequently, the client can be held personally liable for the $50,000. (A) is incorrect because the client's liability is not based upon his role in the business. (C) and (D) are incorrect because the client is a partner in a general partnership, so he will be personally liable whether or not he authorized the friend to spend the $50,000.

8. The correct answer is (A). Under the Revised Model Business Corporation Act §8, the client can protect herself from liability either by promptly objecting to the holding of the meeting, ensuring that her dissent was noted in the minutes of the meeting, or delivering written notice of her dissent to the presiding officer of the meeting before the meeting is adjourned or to the corporation immediately afterward. Here, since she did none of these things, she could be held liable. (B) is incorrect because the client could have protected herself from liability by noting her dissent with the board. (C) is incorrect because the client must do more than not vote in favor of potentially illegal actions to protect herself from liability. (D) is incorrect because a director of the corporation could be found liable for the corporation's actions.

9. The correct answer is (D). Under the Revised Model Business Corporation Act §2, the articles of incorporation control if there is a conflict with the bylaws. (A) and (B) are incorrect because the articles of incorporation control in the event of a conflict with the bylaws. (C) is incorrect because the order of filing does not change the analysis.

10. The correct answer is (A). The difference between an employee and an independent contractor depends on how much control the company has over the independent contractor. Here, the fact that the client is paid regularly, once per month, shows the most control over the four possible answer choices. (B) is incorrect because working from home is more likely to be true of an independent contractor. (C) This is incorrect because the company would dictate to the client which projects to undertake, regardless of whether she was an independent contractor. (D) is incorrect because both employees and independent contractors are likely to have to track their hours worked.

11. The correct answers are (D) and (F). (D) is correct because the issue is whether the chef had the authority to act on behalf of the business. (F) is correct because the issue is whether the fact of the chef's ownership of the subscription company implicated the chef's duty of loyalty to the business. (A) and (B) are incorrect because there is no fact indicating that the chef engaged in tortious conduct on the business's behalf, so these concepts are irrelevant. (C) is incorrect because there is no indication that the business has any employees yet. (E) is incorrect because no one attempted to incorporate the business before the chef bought the subscription service.

12. The correct answers are (B) and (E). Here, (B) is correct because the builder had actual authority to build in compliance with local ordinances because the principal's goal was to pass the home inspection. Thus, (E) is correct as well. (A) is incorrect because ratification would not be needed in this situation. (C) and (D) are incorrect because these are irrelevant to whether the developer had to pay the builder. (F) is incorrect because apparent authority involves third parties, and there is no third party in question.

13. The correct answers are (B) and (D). Under the Model Business Corporation Act (2016), officers generally have limited liability for corporate actions so long as they are acting in good faith. The act also provides that a corporate officer is entitled to mandatory indemnification when successfully defending against a legal action in which the officer is a party due to their role in the corporation. Here, since the compliance officer was sued based on her position in the company and found not liable, she is entitled to indemnification. (A) and (C) are incorrect because the officer's subjective belief is not part of the test for indemnification. (E) is incorrect because the right to indemnification is statutory and not based on a company's articles of incorporation. (F) is incorrect because the right to indemnification is statutory and does not provide the board with discretion in deciding whether to indemnify its officers.

14. The correct answers are (A) and (D). The agent of a corporation has both duties of care and loyalty to the corporation. (B) is incorrect because this is a duty from tort law. (C) is incorrect because this is a duty from insurance law. (E) and (F) are incorrect because these are not legal duties of an agent.

15. The correct answers are (A) and (F). Here, you have not looked at the corporation's bylaws, which may have more information on meeting necessities, but (A) and (F) are the most likely necessities under the Revised Model Business Corporation Act. Generally, notice of a shareholder meeting must include the time, date, and location of the meeting and is typically sent between 10 and 60 days before the meeting. (B) is incorrect because a corporation usually has the right to dictate the details of meetings. (C) is incorrect because shareholders do not owe corporations a duty of care and loyalty. (D) is incorrect because a quorum is usually necessary for a valid vote. (E) is incorrect because the failure to hold a meeting would not adversely affect the corporation's existence.

16. The correct answers are (A) and (B). The bylaws govern the corporation's day-to-day business—for example, when shareholder meetings are held, the number of people on the board of directors, the duties of each corporate officer, etc. The corporation's board of directors adopts the initial bylaws. Bylaws provide the rules regarding their own amendment. Generally, the board of directors or the shareholders can amend or repeal a bylaw, and the shareholders may amend the bylaws to limit the board of directors' power. Consequently, (C), (D), (E), and (F) are incorrect.

17. The correct answers are (C) and (F). An LLC only protects its members from the debts and obligations of the business. Consequently, any member of the limited liability company would still be personally liable for any torts they committed. (C) is correct because the doctor may be liable for trespass to chattels or intentional infliction of emotional distress for leaving the bag of dog waste on the dentist's car. (F) is correct because even if the company made the mistake, the doctor could still be liable for battery. (A), (B), (D), and (E) are incorrect because these are all examples of a debt or obligation of the business.

18. The correct answers are (A) and (E). All a partnership requires is the agreement of at least two persons to carry on a business for profit. *See* Revised Uniform Partnership Act 101(6). In addition, a person entering into a partnership can be a natural person or a legal entity, such as a corporation, trust, estate, limited liability company, governmental entity, or another partnership. *See* Revised Uniform Partnership Act 101(10). A person's subjective intent not to create a partnership does not prevent the formation of a partnership. *See* Revised Uniform Partnership Act 202(a). A person forming a partnership does need the capacity to contract. While a written partnership agreement must satisfy the Statute of Frauds, a partnership can be created through an oral agreement. Finally, a partnership is created by the sharing of profits, not gross returns. Consequently, (B), (C), (D), and (F) are incorrect.

19. The correct answers are (B) and (F). Here, whether the woman is liable for the cost of the signs will depend upon the teenager's apparent authority. Additionally, since the teenager is an employee, the woman will likely be liable for the shattered windshield under the doctrine of *respondeat superior*. (A) This is incorrect because the teenager did not have actual authority to spend $600 on signs, as he was told not to spend more than $200. (C) is incorrect because the woman telling the teenager that things were fine was not a ratification of anything. (D) is incorrect because the Uniform Commercial Code governs the sign sale, but the actual sale itself is not a significant issue. (E) is incorrect because this is not an example of a joint venture.

20. The correct answers are (B) and (D). Four elements create an agency relationship: (1) a principal assents to an agent, (2) the agent does something on the principal's behalf, (3) the principal controls the agent's actions, and (4) the principal shows consent to the agency. (B) is correct because an agency agreement does not have to be in writing. (D) is correct because the question asks whether an agency relationship existed between the farmer and the man, and any statement to the clerk would not have anything to do with the formation of the agency relationship (although it could create an apparent authority issue, which is not what the question is asking for). Consequently, (A), (C), (E), and (F) are incorrect.

Practice Tests

II

Integrated Question Set 1

You are an associate in a criminal defense firm. One of the firm's clients was arrested on drug charges after police officers entered his hotel room without a warrant and found drug paraphernalia. The client has been charged with aggravated felony possession of cocaine. The police report and relevant criminal statutes are presented below.

POLICE REPORT

At approximately 3:26 P. M., a hotel manager called the police department to report gunshots on the first floor of a hotel. He told the 911 operator that, just before he heard the gunshots, he saw a white van pull up in front of the hotel and a woman with red hair wearing a light blue hoodie exit the van and walk to a first-floor hotel door that the manager could not see from his office. The manager said that there must have been a fight because he then heard "banging and yelling and then the gunshots." After the gunshots, he saw the red-haired woman run to the van and drive away. He then saw another man run to a different vehicle and also speed away. The manager went to the hotel room door and saw a knife with white paint chips on the ground. The manager said it looked like someone had tried to break into the room. The manager knocked on the door, but no one answered.

An officer was dispatched to the scene at approximately 3:55 P. M. The officer saw several drops of what appeared to be blood and a spent shell casing on the sidewalk in front of the hotel room door, along with the knife and paint chips. The manager told the officer he had rented the room to a man for the past week. "I didn't know it when I rented him the room, but people are always going in and out. I was scared to kick him out. I guess someone tried to shoot him." The officer banged on the hotel room door several times but received no answer. The officer then asked the manager if he could recognize the hotel room occupant's car, and the manager said, "Yes," and pointed out where it was parked in the parking lot. The officer called his sergeant and said he was worried someone in the hotel room might be injured. The officer then asked the manager to open the room, and the manager got a key from his office and opened the door for the officer. The officer quickly searched the room, but no one was inside. On the floor under a blanket were two scales, clear plastic bags filled with white powder (which turned out to be cocaine), and three pipe bombs (bombs made with a 5-inch length of steel pipe, gun powder, and a fuse). The officer waited at the hotel until late evening, when the renter of the hotel room returned from a party. The officer spoke with him for several minutes. According to the officer, the conversation was cordial and casual as he tried to determine if the renter was the man who had rented the room, and, if so, whether he was injured or in any danger. After a 20-minute conversation, the officer decided to place the renter under arrest.

STATE CRIMINAL STATUTES

Section 2030—Possession, Manufacture, and Trafficking of Methamphetamine and Cocaine Base

(A) A person possessing less than one gram of methamphetamine or cocaine base is guilty of a misdemeanor.

(B) A person who manufactures, distributes, dispenses, delivers, purchases, or otherwise aids, abets, attempts, or conspires to manufacture, distribute, dispense, deliver, or purchase, or possesses with intent to distribute, dispense, or deliver methamphetamine or cocaine base, is guilty of a felony. Possession of more than three grams of methamphetamine or cocaine is *prima facie* evidence of a violation of this section.

(C) A person who violates Section (B) while in possession of a firearm is guilty of an aggravated felony and will have any criminal sentence obtained upon conviction doubled. The term "firearm" means (1) a shotgun having a barrel or barrels of less than 18 inches in length; (2) a rifle having a barrel or barrels of less than 16 inches in length; (3) a weapon made from rifle if such weapon as modified has an overall length of less than 26 inches or a barrel or barrels of less than 16 inches in length; (5) a machinegun; (6) any silencer; and (7) a destructive device.

QUESTION 1

Your client wanted to challenge the officer's warrantless entry into his hotel room. Which of the following legal topics would be most useful to research for a potential challenge? **Select one.**

(A) Consent
(B) Exigent Circumstances
(C) Reasonable Suspicion
(D) Probable Cause

QUESTION 2

The client wanted to see if he can reduce the crime charged from aggravated felony possession of cocaine to misdemeanor possession of cocaine. What are three things you need to investigate to find out if the current charge can be reduced? List three.

QUESTION 3

The client felt strongly that he should testify on his own behalf. He told you that he was arrested for a few drug crimes "years ago" and once for a check fraud scheme. However, he had recently decided to become a minister. He says the drugs and scales were left by his former girlfriend, the girl with red hair who came to his apartment, whose name he refused to divulge. He had taken them away from her so she could go to rehab. He also wanted to tell the jury that the pipe bombs were not his, but that he took them away at the request of a friend, a mentally ill man, who was afraid he might use them because he was having hallucinations. The client also did not want to use the man's name because he promised to keep it a secret. Finally, the client wanted to talk about his young family with his ex-wife and the harm his imprisonment might cause to his children's lives, both of whom were severely disabled.

Please write a short answer as to whether you would encourage the client to testify on his own behalf, and why.

QUESTION 4

The client wanted to challenge the admission of the drug evidence and pipe bombs. In seeking the admission of this evidence, which of the following concepts is the state most likely to rely on? **Select one.**

(A) Plain View
(B) Search Incident to Arrest
(C) Inventory Search
(D) Protective Sweep

QUESTION 5

The client told you that while talking to the officer before his arrest, the officer asked, "What's going on?" and the client answered, "Drugs." The officer did not give the client *Miranda* warnings until after the client was taken to the police station. The client wanted to have that statement suppressed due to the lack of *Miranda* warnings. Please write a short answer (two to three sentences) outlining your challenge to admitting the statement.

QUESTION 6

After the client was arrested, the hotel manager wrote out a statement for the police. The statement said: "I work as the manager of the hotel. I called the police because I heard gunshots. Just before I heard the gunshots, I saw a white van pull up in front of the hotel and a woman with red hair wearing a light blue hoodie exit the van and walk to a first-floor hotel door that I couldn't see from my office. The defendant had rented that hotel room for a week. People were always going in and out, and I was scared to kick the guy out because I thought he was a drug dealer. I heard banging and yelling and then the gunshots. After the gunshots, I saw the red-haired woman run to the van and drive away. I saw another man run to a different vehicle and also speed away. When I went to the hotel room door, I saw a knife with white paint chips on the ground. It looked like someone had tried to break into the room. I knocked on the door, but no one answered. Eventually, I let the officer into the hotel room, and that's when he found the drugs." The client would like to suppress the statement, "I was scared to kick the guy out because I thought he was a drug dealer." The prosecution would like to use it to explain why the client was allowed to remain in the hotel room despite the manager's suspicions. Please write a short answer (two to three sentences) answering the question of whether the court is likely to suppress the statement, and why.

INTEGRATED QUESTION SET 1 ANSWERS

QUESTION 1 ANSWER

The correct answer is (B). The only way the prosecution is going to be able to show that the warrantless entry into the hotel room was valid is if the state can prove there were exigent circumstances allowing it. Under the exigent circumstances doctrine, an officer can enter a home or hotel room without a warrant if they reasonably believe that someone inside requires immediate aid or that evidence is being destroyed. Here, the prosecution will likely argue that the blood, paint chips, and gunfire, along with the fact that the client's car was still in the parking lot and no one was answering the hotel room door, are evidence for a reasonable belief that the client could be hurt inside. Thus, researching this topic is necessary to determine if other courts have found that this level of evidence is indicative of a valid search based on exigent circumstances. (A) is incorrect because the hotel manager could not consent to the officer's entry to the hotel room while the client was renting it. (C) is incorrect because merely having a reasonable suspicion that a crime is being committed is not enough to justify a warrantless entry. (D) is incorrect because mere probable cause will not make a warrantless entry lawful.

QUESTION 2 ANSWER

The three most important things to investigate would be the amount of cocaine found in the apartment; whether the client had the intent to distribute, dispense, or deliver cocaine; and whether a pipe bomb meets the definition of a destructive device.

QUESTION 3 ANSWER

The client should not testify because the prosecutor could impeach the client with his sizable criminal record for drug crimes and fraud. If the client does not testify, this criminal record is likely inadmissible. While he has some "reasons" for the things he has in his hotel room, they do not seem particularly plausible, and he will not give the names of any potential witnesses. Finally, the attempt to create sympathy with his family history is probably not enough to outweigh the danger of his criminal record being revealed.

QUESTION 4 ANSWER

The correct answer is (D). A protective sweep allows officers to search a room or building for potential assailants. Here, the state's best argument to admit the evidence is that the officer moved the blanket because he reasonably believed someone could be lying under the blanket. (A) is incorrect because the drug paraphernalia and pipe bombs were under a blanket and thus not in plain view of the officer when he entered the room. (B) is incorrect because the client was not arrested at the time the drug paraphernalia and pipe bombs were discovered. (C) is incorrect because an inventory search refers to the search of vehicles impounded by the police.

QUESTION 5 ANSWER

Miranda requires interrogation and custody. The client should argue that he was in custody because the officer was questioning him about his hotel room. He should also argue that "What's going on?" was an interrogation that the officer should have known was likely to elicit a damaging statement.

QUESTION 6 ANSWER

The statement is unlikely to be suppressed because it is being used to explain why the manager did not kick the client out of the hotel, not as evidence that the client is, in fact, a drug dealer. Hearsay is an out-of-court statement used to establish the truth of the matter asserted. Here, the "truth" of whether the client was a drug dealer does not matter because the statement is only explaining the manager's fear.

Integrated Question Set 2

You are working as an associate at a small law firm. Your supervising attorney has assigned a new client to you and sent you the following memorandum:

MEMORANDUM

To: [You]
From: [Supervising partner]
Re: Arbitration Clause for CosmicFlyer MiniMoto Bikes

I recently met with the Chief Operating Officer (COO) of CosmicFlyer Minimoto Bikes (CosmicFlyer). CosmicFlyer designs and manufactures mini-motorcycles that it markets to consumers for outdoor recreation. Recently, a user of one of the motorcycles sued CosmicFlyer for permanent disfigurement after being involved in an accident. The user claimed design and manufacturing defects. Discovery revealed that the user had been using the motorcycle to do tricks on a skateboard ramp, which conflicts with the safety instructions in the motorcycle owner's manual. The court ultimately decided in favor of the user, resulting in a $1.2 million judgment against CosmicFlyer.

The COO asked our firm to draft an arbitration clause to include in the motorcycle sales contract, so that any future accidents would be resolved through arbitration rather than trial. The arbitration clause and the arbitration itself should be governed by Franklin law. I've included a transcript of my meeting with the COO, our firm's standard arbitration agreement, and a case binding in Franklin that you should follow in drafting the arbitration clause. Please draft the clause and an explanation for your draft.

End of Memorandum

You review the following transcript of the supervising partner's meeting with the COO:

TRANSCRIPT OF MEETING WITH COO

[Supervising Partner]: So, what are your concerns with the arbitration agreement?

[COO]: Of course, I want to control costs and not be hit with another expensive judgment, but I also want to take care of the bad publicity. A national newspaper did a big piece on the last trial, and then the bloggers and TikTokers and all those Internet folks got hold of it and acted as if our motorcycles were death traps and said we hated our customers and would fight tooth and nail every claim. It was a mess. We lost a lot of sales, I think. CosmicFlyer is supposed to be synonymous with good times and outdoor fun and all that, and we really lost a lot of public goodwill.

[Supervising Partner]: Even though the plaintiff was misusing the motorcycle?

[COO]: That doesn't matter in these kinds of things. People look at our motorcycles and think, "What do you think people are going to do with it?" The man was trying to do a flip on a skateboard track. There was a video! It went viral! In the end, no one cared about that. And I can't say they're completely wrong. We sell mini-motorcycles—people are going to do all kinds of things with them.

[Supervising Partner]: What do you think the big issues are with potential lawsuits?

[COO]: I would think most people would sue, alleging we made a mistake somehow. That's what the last suit claimed—design and manufacturing defects. Basically, what happened is that a 300-pound man tried to flip a 40-pound mini-motorcycle—he might as well have jumped off a four-story building onto it. That's why it went viral—the bike was crushed and its tires shot off in either direction like rockets. The man's attorney argued that we should have built stronger bikes, and the court believed him. Next thing you know, someone will try to drive one through a volcano and say we didn't make them fireproof.

[Supervising Partner]: So, are your goals just to protect yourself from lawsuits?

[COO]: Yes. But no one has an issue with being fair. We're willing to share costs of arbitration if we need to.

End of Transcript

You review the firm's standard arbitration agreement:

THE FIRM'S STANDARD ARBITRATION AGREEMENT

Arbitration shall be the only method of settling any claim or controversy arising out of or relating to this contract or the breach thereof. The costs of arbitration shall be 100 percent paid by any plaintiff, unless the arbitrator makes a special finding otherwise regarding costs.

End of agreement

You review the following judicial opinion, which is binding in your jurisdiction:

EGAN V. INDUSTRIAL COOKIE FACTORY, INC.

FRANKLIN COURT OF APPEAL (2023)

Anne Egan serviced and cleaned Industrial Cookie Factory, Inc.'s (Industrial) main cookie ovens under a service contract drafted by Industrial. The contract included a provision that required arbitration for "any controversy or claim arising from or relating to this service agreement."

Because of the delicate nature of the ovens, Industrial supplied Egan with the only cleaner that she could use to clean the ovens. One day, some of this cleaner got in Egan's eyes and made her blind. Egan sued Industrial, alleging that Industrial failed to warn her of the danger caused by the oven cleaner. Industrial moved to compel arbitration as required under the service contract. Ultimately, the district court found that Egan's claims arose out of the service contract because her claims were for personal injuries that Egan suffered while performing the contract. The district court thus granted Industrial's motion.

Egan appeals, arguing that tort claims for personal injury were not "any controversy or claim arising or relating to this service agreement."

The law generally favors arbitration. *Turner v. Lehman* (Fr. Ct. App. 2000). An arbitration clause should encourage plaintiffs to pursue any valid claim with the understanding that the plaintiff and defendant should work together to resolve issues in a fair and equitable manner. *The MF Company,*

LLC v. Kennedy (Fr. Ct. App. 2018). However, arbitration clauses will not be enforced when the plaintiff is placed at an unfair disadvantage by the party seeking to enforce arbitration. For example, onerous arbitration costs that dissuade plaintiffs from pursuing valid claims should be avoided. *Jones v. Shainwald* (Fr. Ct. App. 1998) (arbitration clause included three times arbitration costs penalty for unsuccessful claims). Additionally, the plaintiff must be given a reasonable opportunity to read and understand the arbitration agreement and also be encouraged to seek additional counsel if necessary. *Amason v. Harmon* (Fr. Ct. App. 2004). The arbitration clause should be signed separately along with any other signature required by the contract, and that signature must be made voluntarily and without any form of duress. *Chevaliers Motors, Inc. v. Burgundy* (Fr. Ct. App. 1998) (signatory duress found when defendant kept telling the plaintiff, "This deal isn't going to last long—just sign and read it later.").

For a plaintiff, an important part of understanding an arbitration claim is understanding which legal claims are covered by arbitration and which are not. As the plaintiff here points out, the arbitration clause under consideration in this case does not specify what types of legal claims may be affected by the clause. All the clause says is "any." "Any" could mean negligence claims—but it could also mean contract claims, especially when viewed as part of a contract. "Any" could mean intentional torts claims brought by the plaintiff. This seems to be something the average plaintiff would not expect or understand. For example, if Industrial decided it didn't like Egan's work and intentionally went around defaming her so that she wouldn't get any more jobs, it would seem grossly unfair to force Egan's claim into arbitration. What if Industrial's agents started a campaign of harassment against Egan, intending to inflict emotional distress upon her? The harassment campaign would clearly be connected to her work under the services agreement, because why else would Industrial choose to torture her? The average plaintiff signing a contract with an arbitration agreement like this could not expect to lose his or her day in court if the company does something intentional to harm the plaintiff! In fact, if intentional actions were covered under this arbitration clause, one would necessarily think of an intentional breach of contract, which would make one even less inclined to believe that this arbitration clause covers any torts.

While arbitration should be encouraged, it should not be wielded as a weapon by those who best understand it. Ultimately, because the arbitration clause at issue stated it covered "any" potential claim, it was too vague to be enforced against a tort claim for injuries such as the one brought by Egan.

Reversed and remanded.

End of Opinion

INTEGRATED QUESTION SET 2, QUESTION 1 OF 1

Following the instructions in the memorandum from your supervising attorney, draft an arbitration clause for CosmicFlyers' sales contract and an explanation of your draft.

SUGGESTED ANSWER

ARBITRATION CLAUSE

Arbitration shall be the sole method of settling any claim or controversy arising under this sales contract, including claims for damages based on CosmicFlyers' negligence, design defects, failure to warn, manufacturing defects, or other torts. The costs of arbitration shall be shared 50/50 by CosmicFlyer and the plaintiff. This arbitration clause shall be governed by Franklin Law. The signer of this clause agrees that they have had a reasonable opportunity to read and understand this clause, and their signature was made voluntarily and without any form of duress. Finally, the signer of this clause has been encouraged to seek additional counsel to help understand this clause if necessary.

Signed: ____________________

Answer Explanation: The above clause specifically notes that negligence and other tort claims are covered by arbitration, which is one of the main concerns of the COO and is also necessary under the case law. The clause also encompasses all the express requirements stated in case law. Finally, because CosmicFlyer is most interested in compelling arbitration and fairness, the clause divides the arbitration costs 50/50 to ensure the clause does not indicate that it could dissuade a plaintiff from pursuing a valid claim.

Performance Task 1

After reviewing the file and the resources in the library, please answer the following questions and complete the writing assignment.

PERFORMANCE TASK ASSIGNMENT—MEMORANDUM FROM SUPERVISING ATTORNEY

To: [You]
From: [Supervising attorney]
Date: [Today]
Re: Moorwood's Potential Liability for Cyberbullying

Moorwood Private School has retained us to determine whether Moorwood is potentially liable for cyberbullying done by one of its students on a school-issued laptop computer.

I have attached the relevant material from the file, which includes an excerpted transcript of a conversation I had with Moorwood's chief technology officer, as well as other supporting documents.

Additionally, I have included the following four sources for your consideration:

1. Excerpts from the Franklin Cyberbullying Act of 2023;
2. *Jones v. Dartmouth Education Center* (Franklin S. Ct. 2024);
3. *Shainwald v. Trinity Church* (Franklin Ct. App. 2025); and
4. *Cathcart v. Les Merry Chevaliers School* (Columbia S. Ct. 2025).

Assume that any claim filed by the victim's parents against Moorwood will be filed in the Franklin District Court.

EXCERPT OF TRANSCRIPT OF INTERVIEW WITH MOORWOOD CHIEF TECHNOLOGY OFFICER (CTO)

[Supervising attorney]: Can you tell me what the Moorwood student did with the computer that resulted in your concerns?

[CTO]: At Moorwood, we give each of the students a laptop computer with which to do their work, study, research, whatever. All students are required to submit their work on their computers and use them during exams. Teachers and the school also communicate with the students through email.

We put some pretty serious firewalls and blocks on the computers so the students can't access adult websites or play video games or buy things, but they clearly can research the web and use email. One of our students used her computer and found out that the victim's mom, a doctor, had been fired years ago for using drugs on the job. That student then started harassing the victim, who goes to another school and dates a boy she likes or something. For some reason, there's beef there.

[Supervising attorney]: What exactly did the student do to the victim?

[CTO]: She sent emails over and over saying that the mom had been fired for using drugs while operating on people. She sent the emails to other people, too. She also posted about it on the victim's social media.

[Supervising attorney]: How did the victim react?

[CTO]: Well, our student did this for months. Then the boy broke up with the victim, maybe because of the mom thing. The victim told our student that she was really sad and to stop bothering her, but our student kept popping up on the victim's social media, repeating the drug story. Finally, the victim took a handful of pills. She wasn't hurt, but it really scared everyone. The victim's mother found out about the emails and bullying, and now she's threatening to sue Moorwood because of what the student did.

[Supervising attorney]: Did you know the bullying was happening?

[CTO]: No. But we do have access to student emails and browser history. If we'd known something was wrong, we could have found it fairly quickly and easily. After I heard about the threatened lawsuit, I went into the student's email and history and copied everything, so there's a record. I also confiscated that laptop and gave her a new one.

[Supervising attorney]: How old is the student and the victim?

[CTO]: Our student is a senior in high school, and I think the victim is a junior in high school.

[Supervising attorney]: How did the student find out about the mother's drug use and firing?

[CTO]: It's a public record because the mom, as a doctor, was publicly reprimanded. A simple search on the Internet will find it if you look hard enough.

[Supervising attorney]: So, the allegations against the mother and the firing are true?

[CTO]: Yes, it's all on Franklin court records.

EXCERPTS FROM THE FRANKLIN CYBERBULLYING ACT OF 2023

Section 101. Definitions and Rules of Construction

. . .

(a) The term "cyberbullying" means intentionally using a computer or other digital device to bully another person.

. . .

(q) "Use" of a computer or digital device means sending, posting, sharing, producing, or creating digital representations, writings, or pictures through the computer or digital device.

Section 301. Tort Liability for Cyberbullying

(a) A person may be found liable in tort for cyberbullying. Such liability may include compensatory, economic, non-economic, and punitive damages. However, the amount of potential liability is capped at $50,000 unless a special order of the court finds extreme and outrageous conduct on behalf of the tortfeasor.

JONES v. DARTMOUTH EDUCATION CENTER

FRANKLIN SUPREME COURT (2024)

The plaintiff, Juliet Jones (Jones), is the Chief Executive Officer of the Soda Village Museum of History and Culture. One October afternoon, Dartmouth Education Center (Dartmouth), an early-learning center for students from kindergarten to fifth grade, brought its students to tour the museum. As part of Dartmouth's general month-long Halloween celebration, the children were dressed as "witches and warlocks," and each had a wooden wand supplied to them by Dartmouth.

Dartmouth advertised its education principles as being completely based on "student-led and student-centered learning, no matter what the age." Consequently, during the course of the museum trip, the students were encouraged to explore the museum on their own while the Dartmouth chaperones sat in the museum coffee shop.

At some point, one of the students knocked over a vase with his wand. When no one appeared in response, the students started to hit all of the museum's pieces with their wands. Several vases, taxidermized animals, dioramas, and paintings were destroyed by the students. Eventually, one of the students told the chaperones, who then told all of the students to stop and took the students back to the school. Dartmouth apologized but offered no restitution to the museum.

Jones sued for damages on behalf of the museum, stating that the students had caused over $500,000 worth of damage. The trial court found that Dartmouth was liable for the actions of its students. The Franklin Court of Appeals reversed. Jones then appealed to the Franklin Supreme Court, arguing that Dartmouth should be liable for the students' actions because the Dartmouth chaperones and Dartmouth itself were negligent in failing to supervise the students' use of the wooden wands.

It is well-settled that parents may be held liable for the negligent acts of their children. *McIntyre v. Ariathurai* (Franklin Ct. App. 1988). Additionally, schools are generally considered to act in loco parentis in relation to their students. *Escobedo v. Coughlin* (Franklin S. Ct. 2001). Students, who, in most cases, are children, are oftentimes less able to control either their accidents or their intentional acts. While it may seem too obvious to mention, these students often do not have their own financial resources, and any legal claim against them personally is likely to be fruitless. However, schools are run by adults who supervise the students. A school likely has more resources to pay any judgment.

While Dartmouth's educational philosophy sounds noble on its face, it is frankly incredible that Dartmouth chaperones would give their students "wands," basically large wooden sticks, and then allow them to run wild through a museum. It would be obvious to anyone who has ever been near a young child, and all of these children were in fifth grade or below, that allowing a child to run unsupervised through a building full of fragile items is negligent to the highest degree. And giving the students a school-provided object with which to cause destruction adds to the negligence. If you give a child a stick, the child is likely to hit something with it. Consequently, the relevant issue here is that Dartmouth should have supervised the students, not that the students' actions were intentional. The damage here is caused by the failure of the supervising school, not because the students chose to damage the property. Notably, the students would be unlikely to commit any intentional harmful act if Dartmouth had been keeping an eye on them and had not armed them with sticks.

We hold that Dartmouth was negligent in failing to supervise its students' use of the school-provided wands during the museum trip. As such, Dartmouth was liable for damages caused by its unsupervised students.

Ultimately, while Dartmouth Education Center may not be responsible for the intentional acts of its students, it was responsible for its own failure to supervise its students, giving them weapons, and allowing them to engage in wanton damage and destruction.

Reversed and remanded.

SHAINWALD v. TRINITY CHURCH

FRANKLIN COURT OF APPEALS (2025)

Defendant Trinity Church (Trinity) appeals the lower court's decision holding Trinity liable for a battery committed by one of its students against the plaintiff, Anna Shainwald (Shainwald). The trial court found that Trinity could be held liable for the student's battery of Shainwald.

Trinity ran a small music school that met five times a week for voice and music lessons. According to students, the school was very intense and competitive, which the school actively encouraged with weekly singing and sight-reading contests. During one of these contests, a Trinity student, "M," became so upset that she punched Shainwald in the face. Shainwald sued Trinity for damages, claiming it was responsible for the battery committed by "M."

Battery is defined as an intentional touching of another person that is harmful or offensive. *Garrick v. Donovan* (Franklin S. Ct. 1967). Generally, others are not held vicariously liable for the intentional torts of others. *Hughes v. Storm* (Franklin Ct. App. 1988). For example, a bar was not held liable for the intentional actions of its waiter, who was found liable for intentional infliction of emotional distress for hiding a small lizard in a patron's hamburger. *Id.* In that case, the court found that an employer's liability was cut off at the moment the employee decided to commit a tort, because choosing to commit a tort would clearly not be in service of the employer. *Id.* However, schools act in loco parentis in relation to their students. *Escobedo v. Coughlin* (Franklin S. Ct. 2001). As such, schools are often held responsible for their students in the same way as parents may be held responsible for their children. See *Harmon v. Lehman Industrial Solvents* (Franklin Ct. App. 2024). "Students, who, in most cases, are children, are oftentimes less able to control either their accidents or their intentional acts. While it may seem too obvious to mention, these students often do not have their own financial resources, and any legal claim against them personally is likely to be fruitless. However, schools are run by adults who supervise the students. A school likely has more resources to pay any judgment." *Jones v. Dartmouth Education Center* (Franklin S. Ct. 2024). Additionally, a school, by its very nature, creates the "room" or space where a student's actions creating potential liability normally occur, namely the classroom or school building. *Portele Independent School District v. Dooner* (Franklin Ct. App. 2018).

The question here, a matter of first impression in Franklin, is whether a school can be held liable for the intentional torts of its students. We find that a school can be held liable in circumstances where the school has created the opportunity or causation for the student's intentional tort. In this case, the school actively encouraged students to participate in high-pressure music contests, which created the forum for the battery to occur in. Conceptually, the school created the "room" where the intentional tort took place by requiring the students to take place in the competitions.

We therefore conclude that, under the circumstances, Trinity is liable for the battery against Shainwald. The trial court's decision is AFFIRMED.

CATHCART v. LES MERRY CHEVALIERS SCHOOL

COLUMBIA SUPREME COURT (2025)

The parents of Maia Cathcart (Cathcart) sued Les Merry Chevaliers School (Chevaliers) on their child's behalf for damages Cathcart suffered at the hands of Cece Fern (Fern) during the 2022-2023 school year. The trial court ruled in Chevaliers's favor. Cathcart appealed to the Columbia Court of Appeals, which also found in favor of Chevaliers. Cathcart appealed to the Columbia Supreme Court, arguing that Fern's actions amounted to legally recognizable "bullying" under Columbia law.

Fern and Cathcart were both second graders at Chevaliers. Chevaliers had a daily recess where the children were allowed to play outside on the playground for 30 minutes. During these recesses, Fern and Cathcart were rivals for who got to use the "best" swing on the playground. Every day, Fern would push Cathcart to the ground and take over use of the swing. Neither party challenged the allegation that Cathcart suffered emotional and physical damage from being pushed by Fern.

However, children under the age of 10 cannot be held liable for a battery under Columbia law. *James-Wesley v. Queso McCheesy Restaurants, Inc.* (Columbia S. Ct. 2004). But the Columbia Anti-Bullying Act has no such age limitation. Consequently, for Cathcart's claim to be actionable, she must show that Fern's actions fell under the definition of "bullying" under the Act.

"Bullying" is not defined in the Act, so Columbia courts have been somewhat inconsistent in the Act's enforcement. However, looking at the relevant case law and legislative history, we hold that "bullying" occurs when a person intentionally and repeatedly harms another person physically or emotionally or damages another person's property, or intentionally and repeatedly places another person in reasonable fear of personal harm or property damage.

As such, since Fern's actions against Cathcart were intentional, repeated, and caused physical and emotional harm, Fern could be held liable for bullying under the Act.

REVERSED and REMANDED.

LEGAL RESEARCH QUESTION 1

Which of the following statements are true regarding the Franklin Cyberbullying Act of 2023? **Select two.**

(A) It contains a statement of the common law.
(B) It is primary authority.
(C) It is secondary authority.
(D) It contains an ambiguity that requires looking at additional resources.
(E) The act ranks lower than *Jones v. Dartmouth Education Center* (Franklin S. Ct., 2024).
(F) The act supersedes *Shainwald v. Trinity Church* (Franklin Ct. App., 2025).

LEGAL RESEARCH QUESTION 2

Which of the following statements are true regarding *Cathcart v. Les Merry Chevaliers School* (Columbia S. Ct. 2025)? **Select two.**

(A) It overrules *Shainwald v. Trinity Church* (Franklin Ct. App. 2025).
(B) In order of authority, it ranks higher than *Shainwald v. Trinity Church* (Franklin Ct. App. 2025).
(C) It contains a common law rule statement.
(D) It is mandatory authority for Moorwood's legal question.
(E) It is persuasive authority for Moorwood's legal question.
(F) It distinguishes *Jones v. Dartmouth Education Center* (Franklin S. Ct. 2024).

LEGAL RESEARCH QUESTION 3

Which of the following statements most accurately represents the court's decision in *Jones v. Dartmouth Education Center* (Franklin S. Ct. 2024)? **Select one.**

(A) Dartmouth Education Center was negligent in failing to supervise its students' use of wands.
(B) Parents may be held liable for the negligent acts of their children.
(C) Dartmouth Education Center acted in loco parentis in relation to its students.
(D) The lower court's decision was reversed and remanded.

LEGAL RESEARCH QUESTION 4

Review *Cathcart v. Les Merry Chevaliers School* (Columbia S. Ct. 2025). List two specific facts from Moorwood's situation that are distinguishable from the facts in the *Cathcart* case. The length of each answer should be about one sentence.

LEGAL RESEARCH QUESTION 5

For which of the following research questions is your library of four sources most in need of supplemental research? **Select one.**

(A) What is "extreme and outrageous" conduct in the context of bullying?
(B) Do the Moorwood student's actions fit under the definition of "use" of a computer?
(C) Can a school be found liable for its own actions in connection with student bullying?
(D) Does bullying require intent on the behalf of the tortfeasor?

WRITING ASSIGNMENT

Your research failed to produce any other information relevant to the potential claim against Moorwood. Using the sources provided here, write an email to your supervising attorney thoroughly analyzing whether Moorwood might be held liable for the student's cyberbullying of the victim.

Do not include a separate statement of facts, but be sure to refer to relevant facts when preparing your analysis. Do not include any greeting, closing, or any other writing that is not a part of the legal analysis needed to answer the question. However, do include the necessary citation when referencing a case or the act.

Performance Task 1 Answers

1. The correct answers are (B) and (D). (B) is correct because a statute is primary authority. (D) is correct because "bullying" is not defined in the statute. (A) is incorrect because common law rules come from judicial opinions, not statutory law. (C) is incorrect because a statutory act is primary authority. (E) is incorrect because statutes generally rank higher than case law. (F) is incorrect because there is no indication that the case conflicts with the act.

2. The correct answers are (C) and (E). (C) is correct because *Cathcart* contains the statement, "We hold that 'bullying' occurs when a person intentionally and repeatedly harms another person physically or emotionally or damages another person's property, or intentionally and repeatedly places another person in reasonable fear of personal harm or property damage." (E) is correct because *Cathcart* is a Columbia Court Case, making it persuasive authority in the jurisdiction of Franklin. (A) and (B) are incorrect because *Cathcart* is a Columbia case. (D) is incorrect because it would be persuasive, not mandatory authority. (F) is incorrect because it is a Columbia case.

3. The correct answer is (A). (A) is correct because the court was clear that its decision turned on the issue of Dartmouth Education Center's failure to supervise the students when they were using the wands to damage works of art. (B) is incorrect because parental negligence was not part of the case's decision. (C) is incorrect because this was a statement of the general rule regarding schools and students. (D) is incorrect because the decision of the case was not that it was "reversed and remanded."

4. Representative correct answers are: (1) Moorwood student's alleged bullying was done through a computer. (2) *Cathcart's* alleged student bullying was done in person. (3) The school in *Cathcart* did not provide the means of alleged bullying. (4) The students involved in *Cathcart* were much younger. (4) The alleged bullying in Moorwood was psychological and emotional, not physical.

5. The correct answer is (A). Under the Act, a defendant can be liable for more than $50,000 in damages if the tortfeasor's conduct is extreme and outrageous. Consequently, it is essential to determine what courts have deemed to be "extreme and outrageous" conduct in the context of bullying. (B), (C), and (D) are incorrect because these questions are answered by the materials provided.

WRITING ASSIGNMENT SAMPLE ANSWER OUTLINE

RULES

1. Under the Franklin Cyberbullying Act of 2023, "cyberbullying" means intentionally using a computer or other digital device to bully another person. "Use" of a computer

or digital device means sending, posting, sharing, producing, or creating digital representations, writings, or pictures through the computer or digital device.

2. The act's liability may include compensatory, economic, noneconomic, and punitive damages. However, the amount of potential liability is capped at $1 million, unless a special order of the court finds that the conduct of the tortfeasor was extreme and outrageous.
3. Dartmouth was negligent in failing to supervise its students' use of the school-provided wands during the museum trip. As such, Dartmouth was liable for damages caused by its unsupervised students. *Jones v. Dartmouth Education Center* (Franklin S. Ct., 2024).
4. A school can be held liable in circumstances where the school has created the opportunity or causation for the student's intentional tort. *Shainwald v. Trinity Church* (Franklin Ct. App., 2025).
5. "Bullying" occurs when a person intentionally and repeatedly harms another person physically or emotionally or damages another person's property, or intentionally and repeatedly places another person in reasonable fear of personal harm or property damage. *Cathcart v. Les Merry Chevaliers School* (Columbia S. Ct., 2025).

APPLICATION

1. The Moorwood student used a school-provided computer to bully the victim by continually emailing and posting about the fact that the student's mother was fired from her job as a doctor for drug use on the job.
2. Moorwood could have easily discovered the bullying but failed to supervise students' use of their computers.
3. While "bullying" is not defined under the act or Franklin law, Columbia law defines bullying as when a person intentionally and repeatedly harms another person physically or emotionally or damages another person's property, or intentionally and repeatedly places another person in reasonable fear of personal harm or property damage. Here, the Moorwood student's actions fit under this definition of "bullying."

CONCLUSION

1. Moorwood could be found liable both for negligent supervision and for providing the computer that allowed the student to commit the cyberbullying.
2. Damages are likely to be under $50,000 unless the bullying was "extreme and outrageous." However, there is no information regarding the definition of "extreme and outrageous" conduct.

Performance Task 2

Charles, Alexander, Palmer & Daniel

Attorneys at Law
120 Bellaire Road
Oceanview, Franklin 33447

MEMORANDUM

To: [You]
From: [Supervising attorney]
Date: January 17, 2025
Re: *Mary Frances Star Entertainment, Inc. v. Alena Brolly Pub. Group, Inc.*

We represent Mary Frances Star Entertainment, Inc. in a potential suit against Alena Brolly Pub. Group, Inc. for copyright infringement. Mary Frances is the producer and copyright owner of each episode of the *Queso and Fromage* animated television series. *Queso and Fromage* is very popular with children. The series revolves around the adventures of two dogs, one a "high pedigree" golden retriever, and the other a rescue mutt that is mostly "dingo." The stories are classic tales of mismatched friends that seek to entertain and instruct children on the importance of being kind, trustworthy, and happy.

Alena Brolly Pub. Group, Inc. is the publisher of *Quazy Questions with Queso and Fromage*, a trivia game based on the series. Alena produced, marketed, and sold the game without any permission from Mary Frances.

I have attached the relevant material from Mary Frances's file. I will meet with Mary Frances's CEO later this week in anticipation of filing a complaint.

Please draft a short memo that I may use for my meeting with the CEO. In the memo, explain whether a claim for copyright infringement against Alena Brolly Pub. Group is likely to be successful. Do not write a separate statement of facts, but be sure to incorporate the law and the relevant facts and reach a reasoned conclusion.

End of memorandum

EXCERPT OF INTERVIEW TRANSCRIPT

Excerpt of Interview Transcript with Mary Frances Star Entertainment, Inc., CEO
January 13, 2025

[Supervising attorney]: When did you first become aware of the *Quazy Questions with Queso and Fromage* game?

[CEO of Mary Frances]: Surprisingly, my daughter played it at a sleepover and asked why we didn't have one.

[Supervising attorney]: So, no one at Mary Frances gave Alena Brolly Publishing permission to make the game?

[CEO]: Absolutely not. We really admire those children's shows that manage to avoid being turned into all kinds of junk, like books, bedsheets, t-shirts, and stickers. It's more pure that way, I guess. We monetize other shows. We are a company after all. But this show is special to us. We'd like to keep it special for the children who watch it. So, we strictly keep an eye on our copyright on this one, and we don't let anyone do anything with Queso or Fromage. I mean, there's stupid bootleg t-shirts with Queso or Fromage drinking beer or chasing girls or whatever, but that tends to be low-volume college student nonsense. Nothing that would take away from the show itself.

[Supervising attorney]: Really? Your company doesn't want to make as much money as possible from the show?

[CEO]: Of course, we do. But that doesn't mean we have to have spin-off products and what-have-you. Every so often, we release a record of music from the show. We have a wonderful jazz trio that watches the cartoon and plays live to it, and we record that. Children deserve complicated music in their lives. Too much children's entertainment is saccharine and watered-down. I come from an art background, as do the creators of the show. You may think it's silly to consider a show about cartoon dogs art, but we do. Very strongly.

[Supervising attorney]: So, you're interested in a potential suit against Alena Brolly?

[CEO]: Absolutely. If we can protect the copyright of our show and stop people from making products based on it, we'd be very, very happy.

End of excerpt

EXCERPT OF INTERVIEW TRANSCRIPT

Excerpt of Telephone Interview Transcript with Alena Brolly Pub. Group CEO
January 14, 2025

[Supervising attorney]: I'm calling to let you know that Mary Frances Star Entertainment, Inc. is considering a lawsuit against you for copyright infringement.

[Alena Brolly Pub. Group CEO]: Yea? For what?

[Supervising attorney]: The *Quazy Questions with Queso and Fromage* game.

[CEO]: Good luck with that.

[Supervising attorney]: What makes you say that?

[CEO]: We talked to our lawyers, and what we did is absolutely protected by fair use. You can't sue us. One of our writers just watched the show and made up questions for it. All original. We copied nothing. We didn't even use pictures from the show. There's nothing you can do to us.

[Supervising attorney]: Did you ask Mary Frances Star for permission?

[CEO]: We did. They said no. We asked if they were going to make a game. They said no to that, too. It's just an example of a market failure that we filled.

[Supervising attorney]: What do you mean by that?

[CEO]: We've sold a lot of the game. There was a market for it. Kids like it. It makes them happy, and I like happy kids. Especially, if they have $20 for the game.

[Supervising attorney]: So, you don't think you did anything wrong.

[CEO]: The law and the Constitution said I didn't. I have nothing to apologize for. In fact, viewership for the show went way up after we made the game. Those folks over at Mary Frances just don't want to make money. And we made money for them anyway!

[Supervising attorney]: But didn't you just take something from someone else and profit from it?

[CEO]: Take a look at the copyright laws. First, the fact that we are testing knowledge of a kid's show doesn't make it any less fair use than making a book testing a student's knowledge of *Hamlet* or the Bible. All that stuff is fine under fair use. Learning is learning, even if you're doing it for fun. The law doesn't say *why* you have to be doing it. Second, the game restructures the show by decoding the obsession and mystery of the show. We put the questions in levels of mastery, "newbie" to "Queso," that connect to how well kids know the adventures of their heroes, Queso and Fromage. And, by extension, how good people they will grow up to be and what values the show has because that's the message of the show. There are 700 questions. The show never tests the kids on whether they're paying attention and learning anything. Ever.

End of transcript

EXCERPT OF COPYRIGHT LAW OF THE UNITED STATES (TITLE 17)

107. Limitations on exclusive rights: Fair use

Notwithstanding the provisions of sections 106 and 106A, the fair use of a copyrighted work, including such use by reproduction in copies or phonorecords or by any other means specified by that section, for purposes such as criticism, comment, news reporting, teaching (including multiple copies for classroom use), scholarship, or research, is not an infringement of copyright. In determining whether the use made of a work in any particular case is a fair use the factors to be considered shall include—

(1) the purpose and character of the use, including whether such use is of a commercial nature or is for nonprofit educational purposes;
(2) the nature of the copyrighted work;
(3) the amount and substantiality of the portion used in relation to the copyrighted work as a whole; and
(4) the effect of the use upon the potential market for or value of the copyrighted work.

The fact that a work is unpublished shall not itself bar a finding of fair use if such finding is made upon consideration of all the above factors.

End of excerpt

EXCERPT OF THE U.S. CONSTITUTION

Article I, Section 8, Clause 8:

[The Congress shall have Power . . .] To promote the Progress of Science and useful Arts, by securing for limited Times to Authors and Inventors the exclusive Right to their respective Writings and Discoveries.

End of excerpt

EXAMPLE TRIVIA CARDS FROM THE *QUAZY QUESTIONS WITH QUESO AND FROMAGE* GAME

NEWBIE LEVEL

1. What is Queso's favorite toy?
   - **(A)** A hose
   - **(B)** A ball
   - **(C)** A doll
   - **(D)** A skateboard

FROMAGE LEVEL

1. To catch the Squishy Skink, what did Queso do?
   - **(A)** Made a trap with cheese.
   - **(B)** Made a net out of spaghetti noodles.
   - **(C)** Made Fromage put on a pretty dress.
   - **(D)** Covered the floor in cooking oil.

QUESO LEVEL

1. When Fromage had to go to the dentist, who was in the dentist's lobby waiting to have their teeth cleaned?
   - **(A)** Allan Anole
   - **(B)** Roland Racoon
   - **(C)** Belvedere Bat
   - **(D)** Owen Ocelot

End of trivia card examples

LIAM PARKER V. LOESCHMAN JOHNSON PUBLISHING

FRANKLIN COURT OF APPEAL (2006)

This is an appeal from a judgment against Loeschman Johnson Publishing (Loeschman) in favor of Liam Parker (Parker). The trial court ruled that Parker was protected by the fair use doctrine from liability for copyright infringement. The trial court found that Parker's use of characters copyrighted by Loeschman was sufficiently transformative because his book, *Handsome Werewolves That Smell Good,* was a satire and parody of Loeschman's copyrighted book, *Wherewolves.*

In determining fair use in copyright, the first factor under Section 107 is "1) the purpose and character of the use, including whether such use is of a commercial nature or is for nonprofit educational purposes." Although whether the use is commercial or educational is important, the more critical inquiry under the first factor is generally whether the allegedly infringing work merely supersedes the original work or "is transformative by adding something new, with a further or different character, that alters the first with new meaning or messages." *Froman v. Berg* (Franklin S. Ct. 2019). In short, the goal of copyright, to promote science and the arts, is generally furthered by the creation of new transformative works.

Here, Parker's book is a direct satire, comedy, and parody of Loeschman's very popular book. Parker produced ample evidence that, among fantasy and horror readers, *Wherewolves* is a hated book because there is nothing horrific about being a werewolf, in contradiction to commonly followed tropes, legends, and stories about werewolves, who are men or women who are cursed and unwillingly change into horrible wolves under the light of the full moon. In *Wherewolves*, being a werewolf is actually fun and all of the werewolves are young people who are incredibly good-looking, can change from wolf to human and back again at will, and mainly seem to have romantic troubles with each other. Parker's book makes direct fun of *Wherewolves* by changing the names of the main characters and making all of the romantic tribulations so prevalent and over-the-top that it makes the Loeschman book seem ridiculous. As an illustrative example, the main character in the Loeschman book is a werewolf named "Henry" who "has eyes that fall into the universe, deep sad pools, that burst with blue around the edges like a burgeoning sunrise." In Parker's book, the main werewolf character is named "Hunky" who "has eyes that fall backward into his skull sockets and make you want to eat cheese—blue cheese."

The second factor under Section 107's fair use test asks the nature of the copyrighted work, namely whether the copyrighted work is fictional or nonfiction. Fictional works are generally given greater protections. *James v. Peterson* (Franklin Ct. App. 1995). Here, while *Wherewolves* is fictional, Parker's book is clearly transformative, as stated above, which weighs in favor of fair use.

The third factor under Section 107's test is "the amount and substantiality of the portion used in relation to the copyrighted work as a whole." Here, Parker's book used nothing directly taken from *Wherewolves.*

The fourth factor under Section 107's test is "the effect of the use upon the potential market for or value of the copyrighted work." Here, Parker's book is unlikely to have any effect at all on a potential market for *Wherewolves*.

Parody, satire, and comedy are some of the oldest creative expressions of man. Many great fictional works transformed older fictional works by making light of their plots and characters. As part of this long tradition, Parker's book is clearly transformative. Thus, Parker's book is protected by the goals of the Constitution and the law of fair use.

AFFIRMED

End of opinion

BIG JIM DOLLS, INC. v. AUGUST TOY GROUP, LLC

FRANKLIN COURT OF APPEAL (1999)

August Toy Group, LLC (August) appeals an order granting summary judgement in favor of Big Jim Dolls, Inc. (Big Jim). The trial court found that August violated the doctrine of fair use by harming a potential market for ancillary products that Big Jim planned to develop itself. We agree with the trial court and affirm its decision that August violated the doctrine of fair use.

Big Jim manufactured, sold, and held the copyright for "Big Jim" dolls. The dolls were very popular with children. August, without permission from Big Jim, began manufacturing and selling clothes for Big Jim dolls. Generally, Big Jim dolls came with only one outfit, that of a lumberjack, but that outfit could be removed. August took advantage of this fact and made many different outfits that children could put on their Big Jim dolls, such as an astronaut suit, an army uniform, a business suit, an "explorer" outfit, and a baseball uniform. Because of Big Jim's unique size and dimensions, these outfits only fit Big Jim dolls and were expressly marketed and sold as outfits for Big Jim. Big Jim sued August, arguing that it had been planning to make Big Jim outfits, and that August violated copyright laws by making its own outfits for the doll.

Under Section 107, one of the factors the doctrine of fair use considers is "the effect of the use upon the potential market for or value of the copyrighted work." In evaluating this factor, our concern is not whether a secondary use suppresses or even destroys the market for the original work or its potential derivatives, but whether the secondary use usurps or substitutes for a market of the original work.

Here, the clothes for the dolls that August made filled a market niche that Big Jim would in general develop. In fact, Big Jim specifically stated that it planned to develop a market of alternative clothes and outfits for their dolls. Because August is meant exclusively for Big Jim dolls and not for any other doll or child's toy, August fills an exclusive market that Big Jim would be likely to profit from.

Ultimately, we find that copyright law's objective "[t]o promote the Progress of Science and useful Arts" would be undermined by permitting August to market clothes made exclusively for the Big Jim doll without Big Jim's permission. We therefore reject August's fair use argument.

AFFIRMED.

End of opinion

WRITING ASSIGNMENT

Please draft a short memo as requested by your supervising attorney.

Performance Task 2 Sample Answer Outline

I. RULES FOR COPYRIGHT

A. [The Congress shall have Power . . .] To promote the Progress of Science and useful Arts, by securing for limited Times to Authors and Inventors the exclusive Right to their respective Writings and Discoveries.

B. Factors for Fair Use

1. the purpose and character of the use, including whether such use is of a commercial nature or is for nonprofit educational purposes;
2. the nature of the copyrighted work;
3. the amount and substantiality of the portion used in relation to the copyrighted work as a whole; and
4. the effect of the use upon the potential market for or value of the copyrighted work.

II. FACTORS FOR FAIR USE

A. Purpose and Character

1. The more critical inquiry under the first factor is generally whether the allegedly infringing work merely supersedes the original work or "is transformative by adding something new, with a further or different character, that alters the first with new meaning or messages." *Froman v. Berg* (Franklin S. Ct. 2019).
2. For example, a satire or parody of a work. *Parker v. Loeschman Johnson Publishing* (Franklin Ct. App. 2006).

   a. Alena's game is a commercial work.
      i. No indication of education, despite Alena CEO's statement.

   b. Alena's game is not transformative.
      i. Alena's game just asks questions regarding what exactly happens in the episodes.
      ii. Despite the question-ranking system, nothing transformative at all.

   c. This factor weighs against fair use.

B. Nature of copyrighted work

1. The second factor under §107's fair use test asks about the nature of the copyrighted work, namely, whether the copyrighted work is fictional or nonfiction. Fictional works are generally given greater protection. *James v. Peterson* (Franklin Ct. App. 1995).

   a. *Queso and Fromage* is a fictional work, which gives it greater protection. *James v. Peterson* (Franklin Ct. App. 1995).

   b. This factor weighs against fair use.

C. The amount and substantiality of the portion used in relation to the copyrighted work as a whole.

1. Courts look at the amount taken from the copyrighted work. *Parker v. Loeschman Johnson Publishing* (Franklin Ct. App. 2006).

   a. Alena's game used characters and scenarios taken directly from Mary Frances's television show.

   b. The game is 700 questions made up entirely of things from the show.

   c. This factor weighs against fair use.

D. The effect of the use upon the potential market for or value of the copyrighted work.

1. In evaluating this factor, the concern is not whether a secondary use suppresses or even destroys the market for the original work or its potential derivatives, but whether the secondary use usurps or substitutes for a market of the original work. *Big Jim Dolls, Inc. v. August Toy Group, LLC* (Franklin Ct. App. 1999).

   a. In *Big Jim Dolls*, the court found a maker of doll clothes had usurped the copyright holder's potential market for clothes for its doll.

   b. In *Big Jim Dolls*, the copyright holder planned to market clothes for its Big Jim doll.

   c. Mary Frances has no plans to ever market spinoff materials for *Queso and Fromage*.

   d. There is a large market for a *Queso and Fromage* trivia game.

   e. The question does not seem to be whether Mary Frances would market a game, but that it is a market niche they would "in general" develop. *Big Jim Dolls*.

   f. This factor weighs against fair use.

III. CONCLUSION

A. A court would be unlikely to find that Alena's game is protected by fair use.

B. A copyright claim against Alena is likely to be successful.